Southern Music/American Music

W9-AGT-381

SOUTHERN MUSIC/AMERICAN MUSIC

REVISED EDITION

BILL C. MALONE AND DAVID STRICKLIN

THE UNIVERSITY PRESS OF KENTUCKY

Publication of this volume was made possible in part by a grant
from the National Endowment for the Humanities.

Scholarly publisher for the Commonwealth,
serving Bellarmine University, Berea College, Centre
College of Kentucky, Eastern Kentucky University,
The Filson Historical Society, Georgetown College,
Kentucky Historical Society, Kentucky State University,
Morehead State University, Murray State University,
Northern Kentucky University, Transylvania University,
University of Kentucky, University of Louisville,
and Western Kentucky University.

Editorial and Sales Offices: The University Press of Kentucky
663 South Limestone Street, Lexington, Kentucky 40508–4008

07 06 05 04 03   5 4 3 2 1

Library of Congress Cataloging-in-Publication Data

Malone, Bill C
    Southern music / American music.
    Bibliography: p.
    Includes index.
    ISBN 0-8131-9055-X (pbk.: alk. paper)
    1. Folk music, American–Southern States–History
and criticism. I. Title. II. Series.
ML3551.M27   781.7'75   79–4005

This book is printed on acid-free recycled paper meeting
the requirements of the American National Standard
for Permanence in Paper for Printed Library Materials.

Manufactured in the United States of America.

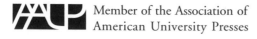 Member of the Association of
American University Presses

Bill C. Malone wishes to dedicate this book to his wife Bobbie and to the memory of his parents, Cleburne and Maude Malone. David Stricklin wishes to dedicate it to his daughters, Annie Bowyer Stricklin and Sarah Browder Stricklin.

Contents

Illustrations follow page 116

PREFACE TO THE REVISED EDITION

Southern Music/American Music first appeared over twenty years ago. In preparing this revision I have been joined by David Stricklin, who brings to the task an expertise in U.S. cultural history, southern vernacular culture, and the personal experience of having grown up as the son of Al Stricklin, piano player for Bob Wills during the "glory years" of the famous Texas Playboys. Abundant and enduring evidence reaffirms for us the relevance of our subject and the truth of its central thesis. We remain convinced that the South and southerners have shaped American music and its reception in significant ways. As this new edition is being prepared, the dramatic success enjoyed by a popular movie set in the South, *O Brother, Where Art Thou?*, once again demonstrates the fascination that music of presumed southern origin holds for countless listeners. A CD of the movie's soundtrack has passed the six-million mark in sales and has earned five Grammy awards, and one song from the collection, "I Am a Man of Constant Sorrow," has won awards from the National Academy of Recorded Arts and Sciences (NARAS), the International Bluegrass Music Association (IBMA), and the Country Music Association (CMA). Reviews of this Coen Brothers' movie, and of another popular film, *Songcatcher,* speak of a rediscovery of "Appalachian music," and of country music's periodic returns to its "mountain roots."

The *O Brother* phenomenon, however, more accurately reminds us that the *idea* of the South is generally more attractive than its reality, and that old symbols, images, and stereotypes still shape the ways in which the region's music is viewed. For all of its strengths, *O Brother* profited from the long-held perception of the South as an exotic region inhabited by an intellectually-retarded and culturally-degenerate people who nevertheless sure can make good music! Most significantly, the movie is not about Appalachia at all; it is set during the Great Depression in another time-honored mythic locale, the rural Mississippi Delta. The movie in fact makes use of one of the central myths of black musical folklore, the visit made by the blues singer to the mysterious crossroads where he sold his soul to the Devil in exchange for the gift of extraordinary talent. Most of the music heard on the soundtrack, however, has little identification with any specific locality or time period but is instead generically rural and southern. Apparently, the fact that the music sounds old and is played on acoustic instruments was enough to suggest to some reviewers a romantic Appalachian identity.

Appalachia, on the other hand, *did* speak to listeners through the lonesome voice of Ralph Stanley, a haunting sound that seemed to echo the stark and timeless roots from which much of our modern music grew. Stanley's singing was, incongruously, lip-synched by a character playing the role of a Ku Klux Klan wizard who "sang" the widely known southern ballad, "Conversation with Death." Stanley's voice clearly lent to the movie soundtrack an unmistakable southern presence, as did that of Norman Blake, who grew up in Rising Fawn, Georgia, and who actually made "You Are My Sunshine" sound poignant and sweet. Other singers, who clearly profited from Stanley's influence, illustrated the ways in which the southern sound, style, and repertoire have insinuated themselves into the performances of people who came from beyond the Mason-Dixon line. The Vermont-born Dan Tyminski, for example, won the IBMA's award for the best male vocalist of 2001 on the strength of his compelling performance of the movie's centerpiece song, "Man of Constant Sorrow," performed in an arrangement borrowed from Ralph Stanley. Alison Krauss and Gillian Welch, from Illinois and California respectively, acted as co-producers, along with Texan T-Bone Burnett, for the movie's music and earned awards for their duet rendition of "I'll Fly Away" and for a trio performance with Emmylou Harris of "Didn't Leave Nobody But the Baby." The movie, in short, provides all the evidence we need to realize that "southern music" still profits from the romantic associations that cling to the South, and that both insiders and outsiders have made vital contributions to its popularization.

Revising *Southern Music/American Music* is a response in part to the explosion of scholarly and popular writing that has occurred since the book's original release in 1979, much of it greatly insightful, some of it given to the romantic notions we have sought to dispel. Writing on blues and jazz has particularly benefited from the long-overdue intensification of attention to African-American culture and the many ways it has shaped the culture of the United States at large and that of much of the western world. We have felt the need to show how southern white music drew and benefited from southern black music, often in ways that surprised those who wanted and needed to view southern white musical culture as independent and "pure." In all these matters, we have tried to be sensitive to how scholarly writing owes a debt of responsibility to the people whose stories it reflects. We have also tried to place the music in the broader context of national events in which it arose, to give at least brief consideration to the social, economic, and political influences on these cultural phenomena that say so much about who the people of the United States have been and are.

Finally, while we have tried to be aware of the role played by fantasy and romance in the making of southern musical styles, we have striven above all to present the reality that undergirds the romance—the fact that the South has been America's most fertile domain for creative music making. Our central focus, then, is on the region's singers, musicians, and songwriters. This book is a tribute to them.

Bill C. Malone

The authors wish to acknowledge the assistance of Kenton Adler, Ramiro Burr, Charles Chamberlain, Gene Hyde, Ben Sandmel, Peggy Weaver, Sally Browder and Bobbie Malone.

INTRODUCTION

Few regions have been more cloaked in mythology than the American South. George B. Tindall speaks of "the infinite variety of Southern mythology," but suggests that most southern myths have become casualties of historians' endless speculations about the region or of the region's own flirtations with progress and social change.[1] The lazy South bows to the booster South; the genteel South wars with the violent South; the rural South recedes before the urban-industrial South; the solid Democratic South gives way to the Republican South. The focus alters with every interpretation, but one romantic notion persists—that of the South as a land of music. Conjure up almost any image of the South, whether of Mississippi Delta cotton fields and toiling slaves, East Texas pine barrens and poor whites, Birmingham factories and industrial laborers, or Atlanta office buildings and aggressive executives, and music will be an essential accompaniment. Hoedown fiddlers, Cajun accordionists, gospel and soul singers, barrelhouse piano players, blues guitarists, honky-tonk balladeers, hillbilly string bands, jazz groups, and Conjunto and rock bands populate the southern landscape of the imagination.

Although romance and fantasy have affected the perception, acceptance, and performance of southern styles, the idea of the musical South is more than myth. Music has been one of the great natural resources of the South and one of its most valuable exports. The South has exerted a powerful influence on American music in two important ways: as a source of images and symbols, both positive and negative, which have fueled the imaginations of musicians and songwriters, and as an incubus of entertainers and styles that have shaped the entire realm of American popular music. At least since the 1830s, when blackface minstrels began their exploitation of southern musical forms and images, and increasingly after the 1870s, when Nashville's Fisk Jubilee Singers became the first of a long and continuous line of southerners to take their music north, the world has grown ever more aware of the South's musical wealth.

The "southern music" that reached the ears of most Americans in the nineteenth century, however, was largely a caricature of the South and southerners, and was created and performed mostly by non-southerners. Southern plain folk, both black and white, made music at home, in church, at dances, or at work, but few "outsiders" heard them perform. The South had almost no real popular culture of its own or commercial venues through which music could be merchandised or distributed. A few tunesmiths and enterprising publishers—mostly in Virginia's Shenandoah Valley—had been producing religious songbooks since the early nineteenth century, but except for a handful of concerns such as Werlein's and Blackmer's in New Orleans, almost no one in the region issued secular forms of music. Even during the cataclysmic Civil War, when southerners put forward a body of music they hoped would support their bid for independence, especially through songbooks with names such as *Robert E. Lee Songster,* their songs tended to be reprints or pale imitations of those produced in New York, London, and elsewhere. With rare exceptions, the most popular songs in the Confederacy were such northern-produced tunes as "Listen to the Mockingbird" and "Lorena."

Southern reliance on the North for much of its musical culture in the nineteenth century is seen nowhere more strongly, nor more surprisingly, than in the realm of religious music. Although southerners convinced themselves in the years after the Civil War that theirs had been a holy cause, and that their institutions were morally superior to those of the North, they nevertheless borrowed many of their most beloved songs from Yankee composers. Southerners still sing songs such as "Shall We Gather at the River," "There's a Land that Is Fairer" (popularly known as "Sweet By and By"), "On a Hill Far Away" ("The Old Rugged Cross"), and others that came from the pens of northern-born writers such as Ira Sankey, P.P. Bliss, George F. Root, and Fanny Crosby.

If southern-produced musical material was rarely heard in American popular culture, North or South, prior to the twentieth century, then prominent southern-born entertainers seem to have been even more rare. Most of the blackface minstrels were northern-born, with a few exceptions such as the famous Dan Emmett, whose parents came from Virginia, and Joel Walker Sweeney, the alleged inventor of the five-string banjo, from Appomattox, Virginia. The one songwriter of the late nineteenth century who might be identified as "southern," Will S. Hays of Louisville, was highly derivative in style and sentiment. His songs bear the Victorian flair and ethos that colored the works of most songwriters who came after Stephen Foster, until the writers of the New York songwriting district that came to be known as Tin Pan Alley introduced new traits and techniques to the trade. After 1865, African Americans began to form their own minstrel units and did so increasingly for the rest of the nineteenth century. These secular minstrel entertainers, along with the Fisk Jubilee Singers and other purveyors of spirituals who began to thrive after 1867, were certainly born in the South. They reaffirmed the long-held

belief that blacks were inherently a "highly musical people," and they contributed to what had been a vague perception that the South was a land of music.
Not until the ragtime "revolution" of the last years of the nineteenth century
and early years of the twentieth, however, did southern-born musicians and
styles enter U.S. popular culture in great profusion. By the time the ragtime
style was co-opted and absorbed by non-southern musicians and by the
tunesmiths and publishers of Tin Pan Alley, southerners had found permanent places in the musical life of the nation.

Since the days of Charleston's Saint Cecilia Society in the eighteenth
century, the fine arts have had their champions in the South, and the fruits of
their endeavors have borne witness in the performances of the region's own
artists such as Leontyne Price, Van Cliburn, and Wynton Marsalis, and in the
emergence of fine symphonies and opera houses in most southern cities. Southern-born "classical" musicians, however, are not the subjects of this book, nor
are the multitude of southern-born singers and musicians—such as Johnny
Mercer, Kate Smith, Mary Martin, Tex Beneke, and Dinah Shore—who did
not simply adapt to, but often shaped, the mainstream popular music of the
nation in the twentieth century. Our chief focus is on the folk music of the
South and the popular commercial forms that emerged from it.

Early southerners, of course, were not unique in their indebtedness to
folk traditions. All American folk music grew from European and African
roots, but, as David Potter has argued, "the culture of the folk survived in the
South long after it succumbed to the onslaught of urban-industrial culture
elsewhere."[2] In the South it assumed a rich and varied texture, in part because
here more than anywhere else in the United States a long and vital interrelationship linked the country's two greatest folk music traditions, the British
and the African. Southern folk music also acquired a special character because
it arose in a society long defined by its limitations: a social context of poverty,
slavery, suffering, deprivation, religious extremism, and cultural isolation.
Southerners turned naturally toward music because it was an integral part of
their cultural inheritance and because it provided a means of release and a
form of self-expression that required neither power, status, nor affluence. The
result was the creation of a body of songs, dances, instrumental pieces, and
musical styles—joyous, somber, and tragic—that simultaneously entertained,
enriched, and enshrined the musicians and the folk culture out of which they
emerged. Southern musicians thus transformed the limitations of their region
into a bounty of worldwide dimensions. This musical transformation reflected
and paralleled the South's rise in national prominence, a process in which the
region became more like the country and the country became more like the
South. Our premise in this book is simple: that the South, where great Ameri-

can folk music traditions met and fused, was the land that gave rise to virtually every form of American popular music. The premise is simple, but the story is as complex as the multilayered relationships between the South and the rest of the United States. To begin to understand it better, we shall first turn to the folk roots of the music.

Chapter 1

FOLK ORIGINS OF SOUTHERN MUSIC

The folk music reservoir of the South was formed principally by the confluence of two mighty cultural streams, the British-Celtic and the African. But if one looks for purity in the music of the South, one searches in vain. Southerners are often thought of as highly traditional people, and southern music has deep roots in the past. However, to ignore the adaptability of southern music is to miss one of its greatest realities. British and African styles did not leave their home continents in undiluted forms; constant population movements and economic transformations warred against the kind of stability that would have promoted musical isolation or stasis. In this country, they did not simply overlap and interact; they also borrowed from and influenced the musical folkways of other subcultures in the South—the Germans of the Southern Piedmont and Central Texas, the Cajuns of Southwest Louisiana, and the Mexicans of South Texas. Music from Spanish sources, already admixed with African idioms, also came in from the Caribbean via New Orleans and the Gulf South or across the Mexican border into Texas. Ferdinand "Jelly Roll" Morton spoke of the "Spanish tinge" as an essential ingredient of early New Orleans jazz, but the influence was also felt in the rhythms of other styles as well. Furthermore, the songs and styles of English, Irish, Scotch-Irish, Scottish, and Welsh settlers intermingled so rapidly and frequently on the southern frontier that they defy the efforts of folklorists and ethnomusicologists to distinguish conclusively among them or to determine their exact origins. Alan Lomax is probably correct when, recalling the composite quality of this music, he describes it as "more British than anything one can find in Great Britain,"[1] but these styles reached across cultural boundaries and were influenced by the music of people who were not British at all.

Slaves built and occupied a community that white people could observe, and sometimes appreciate, but never wholly understand. In many ways, as Lawrence Levine has argued, their music "remained closer to the musical styles and performances of West Africa and the Afro-American music of the West Indies and South America than to the musical style of Western Europe."[2]

Intimately linked to work and worship, and marked by improvisation, an "overriding antiphony," and expressive bodily movement, African-American music spoke to the deepest needs of its creators with idioms that seemed both irresistible and alien to white listeners. Nevertheless, black and white southerners also shared a musical sphere. Acculturation of enslaved Africans to the ways of Europeans began early, from the first moments they encountered one another, particularly on board the slave ships. No one can date precisely the exact moment when black and white southerners began to exchange musical ideas, but the process probably began about the middle of the seventeenth century, when slaves and indentured servants mingled on the farms and plantations of colonial Virginia, Maryland, and the Carolinas.[3] Racial prejudice, then and since, did not deter cultural borrowing: slaves absorbed much of the white people's music while also retaining as much of their African inheritance as they could, or dared. White musicians, of course, ran up a huge, and continuing, debt to black sources. Levine notes that this "relatively free trade of musical ideas and forms" continued long after the imposition of segregation at the end of the nineteenth century.[4]

Musical interchange existed from such an early date in the South's history that it is not only difficult to calculate the degree of borrowing on either side, but also nearly impossible to determine the "racial" origin of many southern folk songs and styles. In fact, one can posit the existence of a folk pool shared by many blacks and whites, a common body of songs known in one form or another by poor people, regardless of race, that defied the ugly facts of racial bigotry and exclusion. Poor whites and blacks did not simply share a milieu that was rural, agricultural, and southern; they also had common experiences with poverty, isolation, and exploitation. The oppression of slavery, and the cruel system of racism on which it rested, set African Americans apart from poor whites in many crucial ways, but the two groups nevertheless fashioned an overlapping reservoir of culture and music that largely defined the rural South. Much that came to be termed "soul," for example, was not so much the product of a peculiar racial experience as it was of a more general rural southern inheritance. A taste for cornbread, black-eyed peas, and collard greens is not the exclusive province of any one race; it once was a class preference, and something of a necessity, that cut across racial lines. Common song preferences similarly reflected such a shared culture, permitting outlets for emotion, distractions from the cares of the day, occasions for communion with friends, and encouragement in the face of adversity.

That inclinations in music were not rigidly segregated, even during slavery, can be seen in the ballad tradition of the South, in the singing of the "songsters"—African-American singers who built diverse repertories aimed at both blacks and whites—and in much of the religious music that prevailed in the two communities. Black singers sometimes sang their own versions of the venerable British ballads, often regarded as the most durable manifestations of British culture in North America. Nineteenth- and early twentieth-century African-American songsters fashioned repertories that went far beyond what is now described as the blues, providing music for all sorts of social occasions, white and black, in the years before phonograph recordings appeared. Songster expectations were very high, and they prided themselves, says Paul Oliver, "on their range, versatility, and capacity to pick up a tune," a skill that came in handy particularly in their work singing and playing for dances. According to Oliver, they used "social songs, comic songs, the blues and ballads, minstrel tunes and popular ditties" to set the tempo for a variety of dancing requirements, "for spirited lindy-hopping or for low-down, slow-dragging across a puncheon floor."[5] Even well into the twentieth century, such songsters as Henry Thomas, John Hurt, Mance Lipscomb, and Huddie Ledbetter clung to a repertory that was older and more diverse than those of most blues artists, singing ballads, love songs, and pop tunes as well as blues numbers.

Religious music of southern blacks and whites also drew from common sources. The degree to which the Christian message replaced the religious world view of the Africans has been a much debated question,[6] but slaves received religious instruction from their masters by the mid-seventeenth century and the Church of England had begun its missionary work in the American mainland colonies as early as 1701. Along with the teachings of Christ came the English tradition of hymnody, a body of music that evolved from psalmody, the singing of the Psalms with a faithfulness to the English text, and with a minimum of melodic variation. White people, of course, had the greatest access to such music, but slaves learned songs from the English hymnbooks at least as early as the 1750s. Many blacks long cherished the old, stately long-meter hymns, which they often called "Dr. Watts's hymns" because of their similarity to the compositions of Isaac Watts, the eighteenth-century English composer who made the first significant departure from psalmody by creating new songs with less literal reliance on Scripture and greater melodic diversity. Black choirs still sing these old songs, revering a song such as "Amazing Grace" as strongly as white singers do and performing it in varying styles that appeal to both white and black audiences.

Although slaves received formal instruction in the Christian religion at an early date and worshipped often in segregated sections of white churches, their first major exposure to the religious music of the poorer whites came in the camp meetings of the Second Great Awakening in the early years of the nineteenth century. This revival movement had dramatic manifestations both in the North and in the South. It became especially noted, however, because of the use on the southern frontier of an evangelistic method called the "protracted" meeting, a revival event lasting several days, held in a rural setting in which participants camped, heard preaching, and sang, often having just learned the songs at the meeting. The camp meetings were giant outdoor arenas in which poor black and white southerners learned both songs and styles from each other. In these emotional, ecumenical gatherings, streams of Presbyterian, Methodist, and Baptist evangelists thundered their diverse yet remarkably compatible messages of foreboding tempered with hope. Along with the preaching, songs floated freely through the forest clearings and brush arbors from one group to another. Some old hymns were supplemented by the addition of choruses—possibly a black innovation that broadened a song's appeal by guaranteeing the sort of regular repetition that oral cultures frequently employ in memorized material, a feature of benefit to poorly educated southern whites as well as to African Americans. Other old hymns were replaced by new, spirited songs specifically designed for quick comprehension and mass performance.[7] Many of the songs were soon forgotten, but others appeared in printed hymnals or were absorbed into the folk culture where they became the common property of southern blacks and whites.

Many of the camp meeting songs, along with other types of religious song material, circulated in the South, and northward, accompanied by a form of musical notation long cherished by rural southerners. The shape-note method, introduced in New England around 1800 and first made available in 1802 in *The Easy Instructor,* published in Philadelphia, was a simplified form of musical instruction in which four musical syllables, "fa-sol-la-mi," were designated by geometric shapes to denote their pitch, with three shapes repeated to make a complete scale. The itinerant singing-school teachers of the early nineteenth century took their shape-note method from New England into Pennsylvania and then into the Shenandoah Valley where the first great concentration of southern shape-note activity occurred, proving of great benefit to earnest would-be singers with limited education and little or no formal musical training. Shape-note composers and songbook compilers adjusted readily to a new seven-note "do-re-mi" system, introduced in 1827 and widely popularized after the Civil War, but the most popular of all the southern-produced books, and one long revered in many southern homes as second only to the Bible, was Benjamin F. White's *Sacred Harp* (1844), a book that adhered to the four-note style and still serves as the principal instruction manual for many southern singers. White and other shape-note teachers and writers ministered largely to the needs of white people, but the method, and the hymnals that conveyed it, also moved into the homes of some African Americans.

George Pullen Jackson referred to black shape-note singers in 1933, and Joe Dan Boyd noted remnants of the tradition in the 1970s.[8] The paperback gospel songbooks of the twentieth century, which contained both the oldest hymns of Protestantism and the newest compositions, were color-blind. Songbooks with compositions by both blacks and whites, such as those published by R.E. Winsett in Dayton, Tennessee, could be found in great profusion in homes and rural churches throughout the South. Through such material, and through radio transmission after 1920, the gospel composers circulated their songs, on the whole oblivious to racial considerations. As a result, songs such as "I'll Fly Away" and "Turn Your Radio On," both by Albert Brumley, the popular Oklahoma-born white composer, became fixtures in the repertories of black singers. White gospel singers, on the other hand, might have been surprised to learn that such familiar songs as "Precious Lord" and "Peace in the Valley" were written by the black composer Thomas Dorsey, or that such standards as "Stand by Me" and "Take Your Burdens to the Lord (Leave It There)" came from the pen of a Philadelphia African Methodist Episcopal minister, Charles H. Tindley.

In response to the musical needs of southern religious folk, there arose in the nineteenth century a set of enterprising purveyors of tunebooks for singing schools and songsters for camp meetings whose love of music and the gospel was matched by their business sense and marketing expertise. They combined evangelistic and entrepreneurial instincts for the purpose of making religious music accessible to southerners of modest means but also inadvertently contributed to creating one of the few ways southern-produced music made its way into the North before the Civil War. The Shenandoah Valley became the seedbed of southern religious music, especially due to the efforts of a Mennonite named Joseph Funk, a resident of the little community of Singer's Glen, near Harrisonburg, Virginia. He printed, in German, his first songbook, *Choral-Music,* in 1816 and began educating students and siring offspring who contributed greatly to the circulation of the shape-note method throughout the southern backcountry and as far west as East Texas. The songbooks, usually paperback in the twentieth century but normally oblong hardbacks known as "long boys" in the nineteenth, were sold throughout the South and into the North by a network of companies mostly descended from the Ruebush-Kieffer Company, founded by J.H. Ruebush and Aldine Kieffer, two descendants of Joseph Funk. It was the parent organization, directly or indirectly, of virtually all of the southern religious music publishing houses that appeared in the late nineteenth and early twentieth centuries and of many of the singing schools and teachers that flourished throughout the South. Ruebush-Kieffer and its descendants and the R.E. Winsett Company helped blacks and whites, North and South, shape a body of religious music that came to be one of the most powerful forces in vernacular music in the country.

In addition to the often-intertwined religious music traditions of southern blacks and whites, a string-band tradition also encompassed musicians of both races, although African Americans tended to excel and innovate in the use of stringed instruments earlier than their white counterparts. Many slaves brought with them to the Americas a facility with stringed instruments that was deeply rooted in Africa. Several West African cultures possessed a wide array of stringed instruments, one-stringed or more, which were both plucked and bowed, descendants of which can still be found occasionally in the Deep South. African Americans mastered the guitar in the late nineteenth century, long before southern white musicians. In the most inaccessible regions of the South, the guitar appears to have been a somewhat late acquisition among white folk musicians, coming to the Appalachians after the 1880s and to the Cajun bayou country of Louisiana even later. Black musicians may have inspired one of the most distinctive of all styles of guitar playing, the so-called Hawaiian guitar technique of fretting with a steel bar, usually with the instrument lying flat across the musician's lap. Folklorist David Evans suggests that African-American sailors may have prompted this style when they introduced their bottleneck style of guitar playing into the Hawaiian Islands at the end of the nineteenth century.[9] At about that time, guitarists of both racial groups benefited from the arrival of widespread marketing of guitars by Orville Gibson. C.F. Martin had built guitars as early as 1833, but the instruments were not widely available until after 1894 when Gibson made his innovations. Both companies further strengthened the instrument's importance among southern folk musicians with the introduction of steel strings in 1900, an innovation of great benefit to musicians who often struggled to make themselves heard in noisy dance settings.

Long recognized as an instrument of African origin, the banjo has been associated with black Americans as early as 1749. The addition of the fifth, or drone, string is often attributed to a white southerner, Joel Walker Sweeney, a popular minstrel entertainer from Appomattox, Virginia, although there is little proof for this assumption and some evidence that slaves had added a fifth string long before Sweeney's time. Scholars also disagree about the means by which the instrument moved into the hands of southern white folk.[10] Did they learn directly from black people, as Sweeney probably did in the 1830s? Did the "frailing" and "clawhammer" styles of banjo picking—later popularly identified with white Appalachian musicians—come to the mountains with black musicians who arrived as slaves or as industrial laborers? Or did southern white rural musicians adopt the banjo and its performance styles from touring white song-and-dance artists, who came to the South as blackface minstrels or as members of circuses or medicine and tent shows? The answer to each question is probably "yes." Confederate soldiers, in many cases, were already playing banjos when they marched off to war, and they and other white rural musicians had ample opportunities to see and hear the instrument played by slaves and free blacks and by itinerant professional musicians. After the war, in fact, many of those traveling musicians were African Americans who had begun to professionalize their art through performances in blackface troupes. Regardless of its origins and stylistic sources, by the middle of the 1920s the five-string banjo was presumed to be the exclusive property of white musicians, first popular with stage entertainers, then with such southern folk or hillbilly performers as Uncle Dave Macon.

No instrument has been more readily identified with southern whites than the fiddle. Small enough to fit in a saddlebag, the fiddle moved westward with the southern frontier. Fiddlers could be heard practically anywhere a crowd gathered: at county court days, political rallies, militia musters, race days, country fairs, holidays, house-raisings and similar work/social functions, and of course at fiddle contests, which have been held in the South since at least 1736, when fiddlers competed for prizes in a contest in Hanover County, Virginia. The fiddle tunes constituted America's largest and most important body of folk music preserved and transmitted without benefit of written scores, and many of the tunes are still performed by country musicians, although in styles that their European or African forebears would scarcely recognize. Included among them were old British dance tunes such as "Soldier's Joy," indigenous tunes of anonymous origin such as "Hell among the Yearlings," songs commemorating historical events such as the Battle of New Orleans in "The Eighth of January," and songs learned from the popular stage or from sheet music such as "Arkansas Traveler" or "Over the Waves."

Aside from public gatherings, the country dance was the natural setting that showcased the fiddle's versatility. The country dance was the most important social diversion among rural southerners, and it continued to be so through the 1920s, although the tradition dates from the earliest stages of British colonization of the South. Southern colonists often described dances as "frolics," borrowing a British expression, by which they meant essentially any social or community event centered around dancing but usually accompanying weddings, holiday celebrations or some other occasion such as the conclusion of a barn raising or other communal work project. Although some dances convened in public settings such as taverns or dance halls, most typically they took place in private farm homes. Such dances were so closely associated with people's homes that they were commonly called "house parties" in the late nineteenth and early twentieth centuries. After a family sent out the word that a dance was scheduled for a particular evening, farm folk came by horse and wagon from all over the countryside and gathered in a room that had been stripped bare of furniture, usually moved outside the house. In some cases, two rooms were prepared for the dancers, and a fiddler sat or stood in the doorway between the two rooms. Because of the central importance of fiddlers to the house dance tradition, they were among the most prized members of a community. Quite often they played alone for the long duration of the dance, keeping the dancers happy with a variety of numbers, often featuring numerous choruses to guarantee everyone ample opportunity to dance to a particular favorite tune. It was exhausting, if rewarding, work. Occasionally, though, a fiddler worked with an accompanist playing a parlor organ, piano, French harp, banjo, or guitar. As late as the 1920s, in some parts of the Appalachian South, a fiddle and banjo duo was considered to be a band. Elsewhere, a fiddle and guitar formed the most popular combination, and it was this unit that anticipated and often formed the nucleus of the larger and more diverse country music bands of the future.

Fiddling has been so important in white country music for such a long time that it is easy to forget how popular it once was among blacks. Newspapers, travel accounts, memoirs, plantation records, runaway slave narratives, and WPA interviews with ex-slaves abound with references to slave fiddlers. Black fiddlers often played simply for the enjoyment of their fellow quarters-dwellers, but they were also in demand for the social festivities sponsored by the planters. Plantation balls and barbecues and town functions featured both individual fiddlers and entire orchestras composed of slaves. To what extent modern country fiddling is indebted to the techniques or styles of slave musicians, or to the tunes played by slaves, is unknown, but the degree of mutual borrowing between blacks and whites may have been very large. In the twentieth century, black fiddlers such as Clarence "Gatemouth" Brown, "Papa" John Creech, and Butch Cage performed publicly, but their numbers were dwarfed by the hordes of white country fiddlers.

No definitive explanation exists for the decline of the black fiddling tradition. Its demise, along with the virtual disappearance of the string-band and ballad traditions among African Americans, coincided with their transition from slavery to freedom and the emergence of widespread racial segregation. Emancipation brought African Americans new forms of discrimination and oppression, but it also permitted a self-expression that was not possible under slavery. Post–Civil War black musicians eagerly sought forms of artistic assertion that were uniquely their own, and they experimented with all types of instruments. African Americans' musical inclinations were shaped particularly by their contacts with cities. As their immersion in the urban experience deepened, ties to their rural past weakened. Younger black musicians generally rebelled against that which was reminiscent of the slave past. The fiddle not only evoked "old plantation days," it was also identified with the presumed enemies of the African Americans, the southern poor whites. Exceptions existed, of course, such as could be found in the family of DeFord Bailey, one of the early members of the Grand Ole Opry, the musical bastion of southern poor whites. Bailey, an African-American harmonica player, had a grandfather who was a contest fiddler. He recalled how black and white musicians shared string-band tunes, incorporated them into his harmonica repertory, and bemoaned the fact that "black hillbilly music" got overwhelmed in the 1920s by the "blues craze."[11]

Musical interchange among southern working people did not take place in a cultural vacuum independent of either commercial or cultivated sources. Folk musicians did not simply learn from each other. They also absorbed songs and musical ideas from professional entertainers and from formally trained musicians. Little is known concerning the extent to which the southern lower classes were exposed to the fine arts during the colonial period or even during the nineteenth century. While some formal education was available for the children of the poor, only rarely did they gain admission to musical conservatories. Plain folk sometimes attended concerts given by such musical luminaries as Jenny Lind and Ole Bull, but opportunities for them to have heard concerts or recitals of high-art music during the eighteenth and nineteenth centuries would have been uncommon. The difficulties of travel and the veneer of social elitism associated with the music naturally inhibited attendance at these events.

Music audiences in the South, as elsewhere in the United States, were divided very early between people who clung to the idea of music as a formal, academic art that could only be appreciated by an educated elite and people who thought that music was an informal, emotionally perceived expression accessible to the masses. High-art music, defined in such terms, was not only aesthetically elitist, it was also inherently class-conscious. Musical preference became, and remains, a means of distancing oneself socially and economically from one's neighbors. During the colonial era the southern upper classes did not yet possess a cultural sense of mission that encouraged inculcating musical appreciation among the lower classes. On the contrary, Charleston's Saint Cecilia Society, founded in 1762, the first organized group of music devotees in the South, rigorously limited its membership to 120 men, each of whom paid dues of twenty-five pounds a year. The society, which sponsored concerts and recitals and organized its own troupe of instrumentalists, was above all a socially exclusive club of gentlemen. There is no reason to believe that the "lower orders" ever heard any of the concerts sponsored by the organization. Other concerts, such as those given by touring groups of French musicians at the end of the colonial period, were also oriented primarily to the upper classes. Social extravaganzas sponsored by planters were exclusively upper-class affairs too, for the most part, although black house servants certainly heard the music performed at these functions, and slave musicians were encouraged to learn the varieties of music featured there. Lower-class whites normally were not invited to the plantation balls or to the other gala social affairs conducted by the planters, but on very special occasions such as weddings or political barbecues, the social barriers might come down, and poor white neighbors or relatives might be invited to partake of the festivities.

Music of high-art origin, however, did insinuate itself into the consciousness of the southern folk, if not through direct contact then through the performances of popular entertainers who had somehow absorbed music from the cultivated tradition. The first incidence, of course, of the interrelationship between the cultivated and folk traditions may very well have been the cherished British ballads. No problem of folk scholarship has been more hotly debated than that of ballad origins,[12] and it is not known whether such beloved old songs as "Sir Patrick Spens," "The Wife of Usher's Well," and "The Lass of Roch Royal" originated among the anonymous folk or were the creations of sophisticated writers who intended them for a literate audience, though both sources probably played a part in the process. Regardless of where they began, ballads were adopted by the folk, who reshaped and preserved them and then bequeathed them to their American descendants.

Folk dances of the southern United States, both black and white, clearly demonstrate the interplay between the cultivated and folk traditions. At least since the mid-nineteenth century, when minstrel performers popularized such folk forms as jigs, clogs, hornpipes, and "patting juba," dance steps of presumed folk origin have persistently made their way into the realm of popular entertainment. The origins of such dances as the Charleston, the Black Bottom, and the Bunny Hug are generally well known, but it is less well known that many "folk dances" were survivals or imitations of formal or even courtly dances. The cakewalk, so important in the development of ragtime music, may have originated among slaves as a parody of formal plantation dances, although their white masters may not always have recognized the satire.[13] Square dancing, strongly identified with frontier America, appears to have been a survival of the early-nineteenth-century upper-class fascination with cotillion dancing. Cotillions were popular with members of the English upper class who adopted them from continental European sources, especially French.

Country dancing moved back and forth across the English Channel, popularized among the upper classes in France and England by John Playford's book of 1651, *The English Dancing Master.* When the English country dances moved to France, they became fashionable, were renamed "cotillions" and "quadrilles," and were published along with printed instructions for the dancers. From France they were re-exported to England and North America. The terminology of square dancing—promenade, allemande, dos-a-do, sashay—suggests its French associations.[14]

Though mostly identified in recent decades with Scottish Highland dancing and Irish step dancing, solo dancing was quite common both in the British Isles and in North America until well into the nineteenth century. Until then, a hornpipe was a solo dance, a fact long forgotten by most folk dancers and musicians. Probably the ancestor of the tap dance, it was featured by stage entertainers and nimble equestrian performers. The dance was brought to North America by French and English dancers in the eighteenth century. Rural southerners no longer remember the dance, but they have preserved some of its accompanying tunes. Virtually every country fiddler knows "Sailor's Hornpipe," familiar to many people as the theme song of the cartoon character Popeye, "Rickett's Hornpipe," and "Durang's Hornpipe." Probably only a few of them, however, know that John Bill Ricketts gained his fame, and inspired the tune named for him, by dancing hornpipes on the backs of galloping horses or that John Durang of Philadelphia, the greatest dancer in the United States in the early nineteenth century, earned the honor of having a dance tune written to commemorate his exploits.

It may never be known how such material found its way into the backcountry South, but enough circumstantial evidence is available to suggest the manner in which the process occurred. In the years following the War of 1812, several troupes of actors and musicians moved into the South bringing their various brands of culture and entertainment to the most remote regions. The dramatic companies of Noah Ludlow and Sol Smith, which were combined after 1834, made regular annual circuits from Louisville to St. Louis to Memphis to New Orleans to Mobile and thence to Nashville. They, and other groups similar to them, typically offered songs and variety entertainment, in addition to dramatic presentations running the gamut from farce and melodrama to Shakespeare. In 1822, for example, Ludlow gave the first public performance of "Hunters of Kentucky," the famous song celebrating the Battle of New Orleans that had taken place just downriver from that city in 1815. "Serious" dramatic performers learned to give audiences what they wanted, especially if they hoped to compete with an expanding list of entertainers whose central aim was to amuse and not to elevate. Before the Civil War blackface minstrels, singing clowns, Punch and Judy shows, which often had accompanying fiddlers or other musicians, equestrian performances by trick riders such as John Bill Ricketts, showboats, and the omnipresent medicine shows roamed far and wide through the towns and villages of the South. These performing units, along with the scores of tent and vaudeville shows that toured the region after 1865, created and circulated vast numbers of songs, dances, performing styles, and comedy routines. These remained popular long after their original creators had been forgotten, though it must be pointed out that the "original creators" can never be known conclusively because so much of this material arose from folk sources.

Phineas T. Barnum, the great humbug, was the first promoter to realize that with the proper ballyhoo the American people could be encouraged to patronize the highest forms of art as well as the low. When Jenny Lind, the "Swedish Nightingale," visited the United States under Barnum's tutelage in 1850 and with a guarantee of $187,000, she encountered a tumultuous reception everywhere she visited, including such southern cities as Memphis and New Orleans. The size and enthusiasm of the crowds that responded to her presence suggest that the Jenny Lind mania was not confined to the upper classes. Ole Bull, the flamboyant Norwegian violinist, also attracted large, enthralled audiences during his southern tours of 1843–1844 and 1853. Whether the reception of such musicians indicates a genuine hunger for, or appreciation of, high culture among southerners is open to question. In the days before phonograph records, radio, or television, many audiences starved for entertainment thronged to whatever was available. They could alternate easily between a melodrama and a Shakespearean tragedy, a minstrel show and a concert by Jenny Lind.[15]

New Orleans may have been atypical of the South in its devotion to music and in the breadth of its cultural interests, but chroniclers of its music history argue that people of all social classes patronized opera there. Operas were performed in the city as early as 1791, and at least three opera houses flourished there before the Civil War, mounting productions by French, English, and Italian companies. Beginning in 1827, a New Orleans-based opera company staged well-received productions in such northern cities as Philadelphia, Boston, and New York. Many of these early productions were ballad or light opera, but several of the grandest of operas, such as *The Barber of Seville*, were presented in New Orleans before they were performed anywhere else in the United States. Opera has certainly become separated from the masses in New Orleans, as it has elsewhere in the United States, but at least two scholars of the New Orleans music scene, Ronald Davis and Henry Kmen, argue that attendance at opera performances in the antebellum era was much more socially diverse than it became after the war. According to Davis, "opera became an integral part of the city's life not for just the wealthy and elite, but for the humblest citizen as well." Street vendors and draymen hummed melodies from the latest productions, and Kmen contends that some elements of this music may have made its way into jazz.[16]

While attempts to separate music into categories reflecting social distinctions have generally succeeded, various forms have often intermingled in unexpected ways. Even the most "serious" music has occasionally been adopted and reshaped by folk communities, and devotees of high-art music are well aware that some of the world's great music has a folk basis, such as the peasant music borrowed and adapted by Liszt and Bartok. In the United States, many high-art proponents have supported the utilization or exploitation of folk music, as long as the composers involved had sufficiently rigorous traditional academic training. Further, they have not necessarily opposed folk musicians as long as those musicians adjusted their styles to the demands of the cultivated tradition. Occasionally, gifted folk musicians found themselves encouraged to abandon their uneducated tastes and cultivate their natural talents in a conservatory or under the direction of a master teacher. Folk music in its natural state was seldom appreciated, and performers of such music were almost totally ignored.

Nevertheless, cultivated musicians in the South occasionally explored the folk resources of their region in order to appropriate them for artistic purposes. This exploration did not assume the proportions of a crusade until about the turn of the twentieth century, but there was at least one major manifestation of it before the Civil War. Louis Moreau Gottschalk, born in New Orleans in 1829, was the South's first great classical musician and composer, and the nation's first musical matinee idol. As a child prodigy, Gottschalk received the best formal musical education available, studying under such European-born masters as Francois Letellier, the organist and choirmaster at the Saint Louis Cathedral in New Orleans, and then traveling to Europe at the age of twelve for further study. His ability impressed his European teachers and Frederic Chopin, who heard him in concert, and he won great acclaim in Europe before he became widely known in his own country. Impressed by Jenny Lind's earlier success, he came back to the United States in 1853 and made a whirlwind concert tour of major cities, including New Orleans. Like most crowd-pleasers in American musical history, Gottschalk achieved fame with more than just splendid musicianship. Dramatic stage presence, dark good looks, and an exotic Latin charm all contributed to the charisma that earned Gottschalk his international reputation. He also learned to give his audiences what they wanted to hear: patriotic songs, "classical" arrangements of popular melodies, and genteel, sentimental airs such as his own most en-during composition, "The Last Hope."

Gottschalk was more than an entertainer, however. He was also a com-poser, and in his role as songwriter he tapped, at least partially, the folk re-sources of the South. In compositions such as "Bamboula," "Le Bananier," and "La Savanne," written during his European sojourn in the late 1840s and early '50s, Gottschalk drew upon the African, Creole, and Caribbean resources of New Orleans music. Gottschalk's first principal biographer, Vernon Loggins, points to his subject's childhood experiences in New Orleans as the primary factors that motivated such compositions: the drumbeats accompanying slave dances at the Place Congo, now known as Congo Square, the site of the city's Municipal Auditorium; the rhythmic chants of street vendors; and the lulla-bies and other snatches of tunes sung by his slave nurse, Sally.[17] Gottschalk's second principal biographer, S. Frederick Starr, discounts the role of Congo Square in the making of the young Gottschalk's music, saying he learned his Creole songs "in his own home" from his grandmother as well as from his nurse: "The music of old Saint-Domingue formed an essential element of the Gottschalks' family life."[18] Folk music of various kinds was certainly available to Gottschalk during his formative years, but so was the popular music of the traveling entertainers who often visited the city. Blackface minstrelsy was still in its early stages when Gottschalk sailed for France in 1841, but "Negro music" as conceived by white men was already the rage of both the United States and Europe by the time he returned to this country twelve years later. Although Loggins refers to "The Banjo" (1853) as Gottschalk's most enduring black composition, the piece seems more obviously modeled on Foster's "Camptown Races," just as "La Savanne" had earlier drawn on the frontier dance tune "Skip to My Lou."[19]

Thoroughly grounded in the European art tradition, Gottschalk was also a highly eclectic musician who scarcely could have avoided either con-sciously or unconsciously drawing upon the varied musical forms that so vig-orously interacted in the middle years of the nineteenth century. In addition, according to Starr, he was a thoroughgoing American nationalist and demo-crat. Several of his uncles fought with Andrew Jackson at the Battle of New Orleans in 1815 and, though he was an ardent regionalist, he emphasized national themes over regional ones. Although he was greatly cosmopolitan, he resisted the tendency prominent at the time to segregate classes according to presumed cultural attributes. It so happened that the peak of Gottschalk's artistic production came during the first great flourishing of popular culture in the United States.[20] The boundaries between folk and popular culture al-ready were so thin that it is next to impossible to determine the origin or "authenticity" of much of the music of the era. Gottschalk's work only served to obscure those already hazy boundaries. His sensitivity to the unique presentation of the varieties of music available, especially that of the people of New Orleans—slaves, free people of color, Creoles, Jews, the Irish, "Americans"— and his ingenuity in translating these musical forms into his own compositions demonstrated the potential that the southern folk tradition already held for musicians, both high-art and vernacular. Whatever the precise sources of his compositions, their imagery and rhythm captivated the popular imagination in a way that anticipated a continuing fascination with romantic southern themes.

Chapter 2

NATIONAL DISCOVERY

The South as a source of romantic images and ideas exerted a powerful influence on American popular music long before the region developed musicians with national reputations. As a land of violent contrasts, picturesque terrain, and exotic peoples, the South proved irresistible to poets and songwriters who saw in its lazy rivers, wagon-rutted roads, and old folks at home endless material for art. Stephen Foster was not the first, nor has he been the last, American composer to seize upon the endlessly appealing romantic myth of the South.[1] American musicians, from the blackface minstrels of the 1830s to the popular entertainers of the recent past, have persistently exploited southern images and have drawn upon southern-derived instrumental and vocal styles in order to shape and enhance their own careers.

Blackface entertainment after the 1830s provided the first dramatic evidence of the fascination exerted by the South on American performers. Blackface entertainers, of course, had been popular long before the rise of the minstrel show, but their acts did not typically include music until the Jacksonian era. The early minstrels were itinerant song-and-dance men who traveled widely throughout the United States. Most of them had a strong familiarity with the South and an acquaintance with southern folkways. Northerner Thomas D. "Daddy" Rice, the creator of the "Jim Crow" character and the man who inaugurated the craze for blackface comedy in Louisville in 1829, was only one of several entertainers who had picked up themes in his rambles through Ohio and Mississippi river towns. Daniel Emmett, the composer to whom "Dixie" is commonly attributed[2] and one of the most popular of the minstrels, told of the old circus people such as himself, whose thoughts had always turned toward "Dixie Land" when the icy blasts of winter ravaged the North.

Early minstrels, then, were certainly familiar with the South, and they demonstrated through their stage garb and makeup that they were particularly fascinated by the African Americans of the region. Nevertheless, it is quite uncertain how much of the minstrel music was derived from southerners. Considering the close identification blackface minstrelsy had with the

South, it is remarkable how few prominent minstrels before the Civil War were southerners. LeRoy Rice's reminiscence of his minstrel days, *Monarchs of Minstrelsy*, included a lengthy list of blackface entertainers. It showed a heavy preponderance of New Yorkers and Pennsylvanians, with an occasional exception such as Joel Walker Sweeney, the banjoist from Appomattox, Virginia, who toured with his own troupes in both England and the United States. A fairly sizeable number of New Orleans-based minstrels were virtually the only southerners who made their living in minstrelsy.

The long-held presumption that blackface minstrelsy was a direct borrowing from plantation slave music has considerable merit. The banjo and the rhythm instruments—the tambourine and bones principally—most likely had their origins in Africa and/or in African-American slave experience. Some of the dance forms, such as the juba or jumba, sometimes called "patting juba"— a dance done by one person using hand clapping as a rhythmic accompaniment—probably originated with persons who were enslaved in the West Indies and moved to southern plantations. But even the juba was popularized in northern entertainment in the 1840s by the black stage dancer William Henry Lane, billed as Master Juba, one of the great dancers of the antebellum period. Lane's career suggests that white minstrels may have learned many of their techniques from the commercial urban stage entertainers of their day or from urban blacks, rather than directly from plantation folk sources. Daddy Rice, for example, received inspiration for the Jim Crow character from a crippled black stable worker whom he saw in Louisville. Henry Kmen, in his study of New Orleans music, further alludes to the probable influence of urban blacks on antebellum popular music when he describes the immense popularity of a black street vendor named Old Cornmeal, who took his street routine onto the stages of New Orleans.[3] The itinerant song-and-dance men of the antebellum era were more likely to visit southern towns and cities than they were rural areas, and the folklore they appropriated, though perhaps rural in origin, came through urban contacts. Certain songs, rhythms, and dance steps definitely came from rural black sources, but, as Robert Toll has argued, the minstrels absorbed material wherever they traveled in the United States.[4] Furthermore, folk styles so often interacted in America that it is difficult to determine the ethnic origin of a piece of folklore. Minstrel music was an amalgam of all the rural folk styles—British, German, African, West Indian—and urban popular forms the minstrels encountered, plus the original routines they were busily creating. Through it all, however, ran the constant factor of racism, which pervaded the art of the minstrels in their parodies of African Americans, and white working-class values, which thrived on keeping blacks in their place, whether that place happened to be in the North or in the South.

By the time of the Civil War, minstrelsy had become such an overpowering factor in organized entertainment, in the United States and abroad, that it moved far beyond its folk roots and spawned a large contingent of professional musicians and independent composers who had little or no relationship to rural folk America. Such songs as "Jordan Am a Hard Road to Travel," "Old Dan Tucker," and "Old Zip Coon" may have had folk origins, or they may have been the original brainchildren of such composers as Dan Emmett and Stephen Foster, who merely imitated folk styles. Foster, of course, was the most important, if not necessarily the most popular, product of the minstrel school of songwriters. Robert Toll argues that minstrelsy as a whole presented to northerners a "non-threatening picture" of blacks, but Stephen Foster specifically must be given much of the credit for implanting the romantic image of the Old South in American popular culture.[5] Foster's conception of the South represented a victory of the imagination because he had little firsthand acquaintance with the region. He spent a short time in central Kentucky and took one trip down the Mississippi to New Orleans in 1852. No doubt he saw some of the great houses along the river, but he seems to have seen little else, and he did not acquaint himself with the lives of the plain people who lived inland from the river's banks.

Like Harriet Beecher Stowe, Foster painted descriptive pictures of southern characters and themes, but his music did not come from southern sources. According to William Austin, Foster's music came from the general and diverse body of influences available to most popular songwriters of his era. He absorbed some influence from German music, but more came from American hymnody and the international body of genteel popular music, including that of the Irish composer Thomas Moore.[6] Much of Foster's success, again like that of Harriet Beecher Stowe, came from his immersion in the sentimental tradition. Like much of the popular music of the antebellum U.S., as well as the developing American literature of the period, Foster's music drew on a set of staple themes, the appeal of faraway places and times, the lure of the homeplace, and the recurrent sense of loss that accompanies these two opposite attractions. People responded to his music not so much because it presented a realistic picture of southern blacks or of life in the South in general, which it did not, but because it reinforced the values of the family fireside and featured the stereotypical characters of nineteenth-century sentimental literature: the beautiful but doomed maiden, the dying child, the departed mother, the saintly old man.

Foster's reputation steadily grew in the years after the Civil War, but his real enshrinement as America's greatest popular composer came at the end of the nineteenth century when Czech composer Anton Dvorák essentially anointed him by applauding some of his songs, thus suggesting their affinity with high-art music.[7] Foster's songs seemed particularly appropriate in the late-nineteenth century, when the country was still trying to heal the wounds of the Civil War. The appeal of Foster's nostalgic songs cut across regional lines, for a complex set of emotional reasons. Northerners and southerners alike, even westerners, could identify with the themes of domestic sentiment and a pastoral society that now seemed to be succumbing to the inroads of industrial progress. Whatever the bases for its appeal, notions of an unchanging, placid, yet exotic Southland with gentle manners and contented, nostalgic "servants" became a perennially enduring myth of life in the United States.

Foster was but one of several minstrel-derived songwriters who contributed to the myth of the Old South. Others, in fact, may have been more popular than he, with compositions that have more readily endured in folk tradition without the support accorded to Foster by the high-art establishment. Such writers as Septimus Winner ("Listen to the Mockingbird," "Whispering Hope"), Daniel Emmett ("Old Dan Tucker," "Jordan Am a Hard Road to Travel," "Dixie," supposedly), and Henry Clay Work ("Kingdom Coming," "Father, Dear Father," "Grandfather's Clock") produced songs that were cherished by nineteenth-century Americans who bequeathed them aurally to their descendants.

The writer who had the closest relationship to the South, though his characterizations of it never went beyond the romantic, was Will S. Hays. A native of Louisville, Kentucky, and for a time a riverboat pilot on the Ohio River, Hays spent most of his life as a reporter for the *Louisville Courier-Journal*. He was also a prolific songwriter whose lyric themes were highly reminiscent of Stephen Foster's. Hays was a gifted melodist and an effective composer of gentle, Victorian lyrics, and several of his songs remain singable even though their messages seem alien to modern ears. He wrote comic songs occasionally, but his general repertory was saturated with the sentimentality typical of so much of the popular music of the nineteenth century, including that of Foster. Sentimentality, in fact, often descended to bathos, as in the tale of the penniless orphan girl in "Nobody's Darling on Earth." Many of Hays's songs swelled with Victorian sentiment: faithfulness, unrequited love, domesticity, passion devoid of eroticism. Such songs as "Molly, Darling," "I'll Remember You, Love, in My Prayers," and "We Parted by the Riverside" told of tender but broken love affairs that ended among scenes of pastoral charm. The moon forever shone, dewdrops kissed the roses, and rivers murmured to the sea as lovers parted. Hays also wrote an occasional song of nostalgia, plaintive reminiscences of the departed village or farm or evocations of a vanished way of life with which many could identify. One such song, perhaps the most enduring in the Hays repertory, was "Little Old Log Cabin in the Lane," long a staple of country music. The song was typical of the "faithful slave laments" often heard in minstrelsy, depicting the sadness of a poor old slave who surveyed the decay of his once-happy cabin as "ole massa and missus" slept nearby. Such lyrics could be used to defend the idea of a racially harmonious Old South or of the inability of those formerly enslaved to adjust to freedom. But, like many of the songs that came out of minstrelsy, "Little Old Log Cabin" ceased to be merely a "darky song" and became a lament for the departed rural home.[8]

Sentimental parlor songs in the nineteenth century, though generally northern in origin and aimed at an urban, middle-class audience, often dealt with romantic southern themes. Though they appealed immediately to audiences everywhere, they found a natural, and seemingly permanent, home in the rural South. Such songs are known in the North, if at all, as amusing, quaint relics of an unsophisticated era. Southerners, on the other hand, are more likely to cherish and preserve such "regional" songs as "Mid the Green Fields of Virginia," "My Little Home in Tennessee," or "Carry Me Back to Ole Virginny" (written by a black northerner, James Bland), as well as such weepers as "The Dying Girl's Message," "The Blind Child," "The Little Rosewood Casket," "The Letter Edged in Black," and "Baggage Coach Ahead," also written by a black composer, Gussie Davis.

Although minstrelsy may not have been of southern origin, the phenomenon made a great impact on the region, and it left a long-lasting legacy in southern music. Minstrel troupes still visited southern cities as late as World War I, and by that time several of them had made their headquarters in the South and staged their shows with southern-born entertainers. Minstrel songs, styles, dances, jokes, even the corking of the face, became central facets of southern folk and popular culture. Exhibiting the continuous interflow between folk and popular music, minstrels adapted material from folk sources, reworked it to appeal to urban audiences, and fed it back to the folk through the traveling shows. Nowhere was such material more deeply cherished, or longer preserved, than in the rural South. With their continuing tendency to retain social phenomena that had lost favor in the industrializing North, rural southerners absorbed minstrel ideas and made them the bases for their own personal and localized musical expressions. Commercial black entertainment, for instance, owed a large debt to minstrelsy. African Americans had little access to professional entertainment before such all-black troupes as the Georgia Minstrels took their shows to towns and cities all over the United States. The early black minstrel groups corked their faces, as custom demanded, and generally performed in a self-mocking manner that was degrading to their race. Nevertheless, these pioneer performers created the commercial route that later black entertainers were able to follow and modify, and the original black minstrels included some of the most gifted song-and-dance artists American audiences had yet witnessed, performers such as Sam Lucas, Billy Kersands, Bert Williams, and James Bland. Black entertainers carried the burden of minstrelsy with them into the twentieth century, and southern black performing groups still called themselves "minstrels" through the World War I period. These latter-day groups—such as Mahara's Minstrels, headed by the young W.C. Handy, and the Rabbit Foot Minstrels, led by the great blues singer Ma Rainey and featuring Bessie Smith—playing the "chittlin' circuit" of the South finally forged independent forms of black musical expression in the South and elsewhere in the United States.

White rural musicians, on the other hand, did not move into professional show business as early as southern blacks, but they also strongly displayed the lingering influences of minstrelsy. Early hillbilly music especially is filled with evidence of this indebtedness. The five-string banjo, a fixture of minstrelsy, became an integral component of white rural instrumentation, particularly in the Southeast, and some minstrel-derived banjo styles remained common in country music until Earl Scruggs introduced the three-finger bluegrass style in the 1940s. The major link between nineteenth-century minstrel music and modern country music was Uncle Dave Macon, an outstanding five-string banjoist and member of the Grand Ole Opry from 1926 to 1952. Uncle Dave was born in McMinnville, Tennessee, in 1870 but was exposed at a very early age to minstrel entertainers when his parents moved to Nashville and opened a theatrical boardinghouse. He learned banjo techniques and stage patter from the minstrels, as well as numerous songs that later appeared in both his recordings and personal appearances, such as "Rise When the Rooster Crows," "Hold That Woodpile Down," "Rock about My Sara Jane," and "Jordan Am a Hard Road to Travel."

Many of the more rousing minstrel tunes and routines, those suited for comic, dance, or instrumental purposes, regularly found their way into country repertories. The early hillbilly string bands of radio and recording—such as the Skillet Lickers, Al Hopkins and the Buckle Busters, Charlie Poole and the North Carolina Ramblers, and the Fruit Jar Drinkers—often featured fiddle-and-banjo-dominated versions of old minstrel songs with the same rollicking spirit that probably characterized the original performances. The "rural skits" recorded by the Skillet Lickers on the Columbia label—comic dialogues interspersed with music—also reflected the influence of earlier minstrel routines. The comedy of minstrelsy, in fact, long remained a feature of country music. The blackface comics Jamup and Honey appeared regularly on the Grand Ole Opry and headlined a popular touring tent show through the World

War II period. Musicians from Uncle Dave Macon to Lew Childre, Grandpa Jones, and Roy Clark—as well as stand-up comics such as Rod Brasfield and Benny Ford, who played a character known as the Duke of Paducah—persistently delved into minstrel-derived humor to bolster their routines. Television's syndicated hillbilly variety show "Hee Haw," which premiered in 1969, dispensed a considerable amount of minstrel-like material, even including a variation of "patting juba." The sentimental songs of minstrelsy—such as "Sweet Allalee," "Away Down upon the Old Plantation," "Listen to the Mockingbird," a virtuoso fiddle piece, and "Yellow Rose of Texas"—also appeared with great frequency in the repertories of country musicians. The minstrel performers had drawn so much material through the years from the folk culture of the South that it was only fitting that much of it should be returned to its home.[9]

While serious doubts can be entertained about the legitimate southern, folk, or African-American content of minstrel music, the authenticity of another musical form that came out of the South after the Civil War, the spiritual, is undeniable. Spirituals, unlike minstrel tunes, were introduced to the world at large by bona fide southerners—the Fisk Jubilee Singers from Nashville. The music was first circulated in printed form by northerners, the teachers and missionaries who came south during and after the Civil War to work among former slaves. As in the case of minstrelsy, moreover, the perception and reception of this music were affected by external, especially northern, images of both African Americans and the South. While the minstrels often exploited for its entertainment potential a demeaning caricature of blacks based on their supposed hedonism, promoters of the spirituals either stressed the innate religiousness of blacks or sought to repress their sensuality by trying to turn them away from dancing and "sinful music." Advocates of the latter viewpoint intended that southern blacks should emulate the decorum and propriety of middle-class evangelical Protestantism. Northern observers were generally impressed or intrigued by black spiritual singing, but, as Dana Epstein observes, "very few were able to dissociate themselves from European norms of musical performance and to evaluate Afro-American music on its own terms."[10] Too often former slaves were encouraged to replace their own songs with the "more dignified" hymns of the evangelical churches, or they were urged to adopt the more sedate and conventional performing styles of their benefactors.

Individual spirituals began to appear in northern magazines as early as 1861, when "Go Down, Moses" was printed, but the first significant collection of spirituals, *Slave Songs of the United States,* came in 1867. Although it is now recognized as one of the foundational works of American folk scholarship, the book was generally ignored in the music periodicals of the day, and there was no immediate explosion of interest in spirituals, either by musicians or by the public. When the Fisk Jubilee Singers took their versions of the spirituals north in 1871, they sparked the first real national flurry of interest in southern-derived folk songs. These young black singers were genuine products of folk communities, even though their performing styles were far from representative of folk tradition. Nevertheless, the vogue they inspired for the spirituals did not diminish until well into the twentieth century. They also encouraged a major excursion by high-art musicians into the realm of southern folk culture. The choir was organized in 1867 by George White, the white treasurer of Fisk University, in order to raise money for the Nashville school. The singers, it was believed, would be particularly effective among middle-class white Americans interested in the "cultural uplift" of the black race. The young black students were to demonstrate both the potential and the docility of ex-slaves, and, incidentally, reinforce the already deep-rooted assumption that, whatever else their limitations, music was something at which blacks excelled.

Students who went to Fisk, Hampton, Tuskegee, and other southern schools that were products of northern religious philanthropy certainly did not go there to be reminded of the humiliation of their enslavement experience. They hoped they were on their way to the world of the middle class. Understandably, the Fisk Jubilee Singers did not at first feature the performance of slave-derived religious music. But after audiences at Oberlin and elsewhere in the North made clear their desire to hear such music, the Fisk Jubilee Singers made the spirituals the nucleus of their repertory. They sang to the enthusiastic acclaim of genteel audiences all over the North and then made a highly successful tour of Europe in 1872, the first of several such trips. Though their subject matter was indigenous and rooted in black folk experience, their style of performance came directly from the European cultivated tradition. On recordings made in 1913 of a later version of the Fisk Jubilee Singers, the singing is in a restrained, highly polished manner, with none of the swinging, uninhibited, emotional style associated with the southern, downhome black churches.[11] Nevertheless, they made the world conscious of the spirituals, and after the example of Louis Moreau Gottschalk, they initiated the first real excursion by African-American high-art music advocates into the folk resources of the South.

Public fascination with spirituals, and the subsequent popularity of other types of southern-derived folk music, should be considered, at least in part, as a facet of the larger quest for a national music. This quest, of course, was not new. It had been pursued at least since the mid-nineteenth century when Lowell Mason had sought to create a music that would represent America's distinctiveness while also winning the respect of the world. Implicit in this search was the belief that a true national music must embody "native" American material, that it must rest upon an indigenous folk basis. During the last decade of the nineteenth century, and increasingly in the years immediately following World War I when nationalism was at a peak, high-art music advocates vigorously debated the merits of various folk traditions. Some people, of course, denied the existence of any type of indigenous folk music in the United States, while others stressed the usefulness of Indian, black, and Anglo-Saxon themes, or even commercial materials such as ragtime or jazz, as the raw stuff from which a finished American musical product could be built. The spirituals, though not the raw secular or downhome gospel material of southern blacks, obviously appealed to some musicians because they were both beautiful and presumably of American origin.

The person who did the most to promote the high-art potential of the spirituals was Antonin Dvorák, who came to the United States in 1892. Settling into a New York apartment and on a farm near Spillville, Iowa, during the summers, Dvorák began producing a number of musical works said to be based on American themes. Although Dvorák was an ardent and outspoken advocate of the utilization of African-American themes,[12] there is still some question about whether or not he actually used black melodies himself. The appealing theme of the symphony *From the New World,* "Goin' Home," indeed sounds like a spiritual melody, but it seems to have no precise analogue in African-American music. Dvorák had been inspired to create "folklike" melodies, but, much as Stephen Foster before him, he exhibited a larger indebtedness to the cultivated musical traditions of the world.

In the years following Dvorák's American sojourn, numerous singers, instrumentalists, and composers became enamored of spirituals, though there were limits to the form's popularity. Frequent instrumental and vocal concerts of spirituals were given well into the 1920s; these performances launched the careers of such great American singers as Paul Robeson and Marian Anderson. At least one of these singers was a southerner, the Georgia-born Roland Hayes, who built a very successful first career singing spirituals and then moved on to another career as one of the country's leading opera singers. The composers who dealt with spirituals were usually white men who arranged the material to fit the tastes of white middle-class concertgoers. But a few black composers, such as Harry Burleigh and Nathaniel Dett, specialized in spirituals, and William Grant Still, from Mississippi, wrote concert pieces based on spirituals or adaptations of them and achieved considerable fame and success. Despite the rage for spirituals, however, many musicians and composers denied that they were legitimate sources for a national music. The spirituals, so the argument ran, did not spring from the majority of Americans and therefore could not represent the soul of American experience. One of the leading scholars of southern religious folk music, George Pullen Jackson, denied the originality of the spirituals and asserted that they were borrowed from older white religious music.[13] Proponents of a national American music and critics of the spirituals argued that they should look elsewhere for a folk basis for the high-art form they wished to create.

Considering the American social context at the turn of the twentieth century, it is not surprising that an Anglo-Saxon school of folk music emerged. The country's decisive turn toward imperialism at the time of the Spanish-American War and thereafter helped renew the sense of mission many of its "Anglo-Saxon" people felt, to use their God-given talent and energy to help re-form the world in the image of a Christian USA. This missionary impulse to spread the American Way to the unenlightened peoples of the world was accompanied by the disquieting concern that the Anglo-Saxon core of "American" culture was disintegrating or being dangerously diluted by urban industrialism and immigration. Such fears, at least among scholars, partly explain the resurgent interest in folklore at the end of the nineteenth century, a phenomenon marked by the founding of the American Folklore Society in 1888 and by the collecting of British ballads by the Harvard scholar Francis James Child. A sense of urgency accompanied the collection and classification of folklore in this country, as if the scholars had only a short time to work before the folk tradition succumbed to the processes of modernization. Folklore was not only equated with peasant pastoralism, but in this country the best of that folklore was presumed to be of Anglo-Saxon origin. The Anglo-Saxon rural peasantry was presumed to be disappearing, through urban migration, adjustment to industrial occupations, increasing literacy, and intermarriage with outsiders, and this meant the disappearance of the purest forms of American folklore. Burdened by these biases, then, early folk song scholarship in the United States became infused with a heavy strain of romanticism. Gazing through the misty lens of this myth-tinged scholarship, it was difficult to see the folk as they actually were.[14]

When looking for survivals or remnants of the Anglo-Saxon past, the scholar-romantics naturally turned their attention southward. It had long been assumed that in a nation characterized by ceaseless change the South was a land of stability and a repository of traditional values. Furthermore, the region was already being described as the most Anglo-Saxon part of the country. This view was reinforced by interest in the music of the West because the agrarian nature of so much western enterprise called to mind southern rather than northern associations. The publication of John A. Lomax's *Cowboy Songs and*

Other Frontier Ballads in 1910 sparked a great surge of interest in folk songs of all kinds, and, in fact, inspired a search for folk material in all regions of the nation. It also suggested links between the downhome music of southern whites and the folk music of western settlers, especially that of cowboys, most of whom had come from the South. These links, both real and imagined, profoundly influenced country music, which for a time in the twentieth century was prominently known as country-*and-western* music. Cowboy culture actually was a composite of many racial and cultural groups, with invaluable Mexican and African-American, even northern, contributions to its creation. But in the popular imagination in 1910 the man on horseback more closely resembled characters in the old dime novels or in Owen Wister's *The Virginian.* In short, he was a latter-day Anglo-Saxon knight. To many people, the cowboy's commemoration in popular culture could not have come at a better time, when Americans needed such a symbol to counter their anxieties concerning the disappearance of rugged individualism in modern society. They were aided in their quest by the Wild West shows that arose around the turn of the twentieth century, which helped create the myth of the cowboy and popularized a stylized form of attire considered appropriate for performing or stage cowboys. Depictions of cowboys in vaudeville routines, popular song lyrics and the cover art on the sheet music by which they were distributed, and silent films were strongly influenced by the Wild West shows. Oddly enough, the shows seem not to have used "western" or "cowboy" music at all.[15]

If the cowboy symbolized what many white people in the United States would like to have been, the southern mountaineer was, many of them felt, a living reminder of what the archetypal American once was. Isolated from the currents of social and economic change, the mountaineer remained "our contemporary ancestor," a self-reliant frontiersman who clung to Elizabethan ways. Mary Noailles Murfree, writing under the pseudonym Charles Craddock, made a powerful contribution to the romantic myth of the mountains with her short stories and novels of the 1880s, but the most decisive entry of the mountaineer into American popular culture came with the novels of John Fox Jr., written just before World War I. By the time the folklorists began venturing into the mountain regions in the early twentieth century, many people in the United States were already predisposed to think of mountain people as quaint relics of a bygone era or as simple conservators of an archaic tradition. The fact that they sang songs no one else remembered was not surprising to anyone. Mountaineers were of special interest to the teachers in the mountain settlement schools. These Protestant missionaries, predominantly women, had come south in the years after the Civil War to educate mountain children, to bring "cultural uplift" to them, replacing the rough edges of mountain culture with something approximating the New England middle-class ideal. The settlement women's interpretation of the fine arts was much influenced by their northern genteel upbringing, and their concept of folk music was naturally shaped and limited by their high-art sensibilities. They were clearly not prepared either to understand or to appreciate the rural music that enveloped them in their adopted mountain surroundings and, in fact, fostered images of Appalachian music that ran counter to what mountain folk actually sang and played. Furthermore, many of the mountain families who sent their children to the settlement schools wanted to have their sons and daughters exposed to that finer world outside. They and their children were sometimes embarrassed by their culture and were actively seeking "improvement," a sign of which was abandonment of their traditional music. Still, some settlement workers conceived of the schools as "folk schools" where mountain people were encouraged to preserve their own culture in the form of traditional ballads, folk songs, and dances. In some cases, students learned about these traditions or had a chance to think seriously about them for the first time. The teachers' biases, however, ran toward the oldest and rarest British songs and against the newer songs that had long been moving into the mountaineers' repertory, including, among others, gospel and parlor songs. Moreover, like the academic folklorists of their day, the settlement teachers had a static view of folklore, and in the moral fervor of their mission they rejected songs they considered "unsuitable," such as "Frankie and Johnny" or "The Birmingham Jail."[16]

One of the settlement women, Olive Dame Campbell, wife of John C. Campbell, director of the Southern Highland Division of the Russell Sage Foundation, contributed directly to bringing the folk music of Appalachia to the attention of the nation. An experienced folk song collector, she wrote to English folk dance authority Cecil Sharp and encouraged him to come to the southern mountains where, she predicted, he would find a body of folk songs larger than that in his own country. From 1916 to 1918, Sharp spent a total of about twelve months in the hills, talking to local singers and, with the assistance of Maud Karpeles, transcribing in his notebooks both words and melodies of traditional songs. Many of these songs were included in *English Folk Songs from the Southern Appalachians,* which Sharp and Campbell first published in 1917. Sharp suggested in his commentary that folk singing in the mountains was far from being an archaic practice confined to a few oldtimers, that indeed it was common among both young and old, a vigorous, living force. He confirmed, therefore, much of what the literary romancers had long said about the Southern Appalachians. The region was indeed a land of ancient values, a cultural outpost of England, a preserve. Other students followed Sharp's example, and in subsequent decades they explored the resources of a number of folk communities in the United States, both mountain and lowland.

Sharp's contributions to the broadening of understanding of America's cultural history were many and positive, but his conservative, academic approach to folk music created a false impression about the breadth and scope of southern music that later scholars have never really overcome. Sharp traveled to the United States to find "English" songs, and, like most literary folk song scholars of his day, he was much influenced by the scholarship of Francis James Child. In his *English and Scottish Popular Ballads,* Child had selected 305 ballads and their variants, a corpus of material presumed to be literary in origin and the most valuable surviving examples of the British tradition. Folk scholars ever since have searched eagerly for specimens of the Child canon extant in oral tradition, and they have generally described their collected ballads or variants by the numbers ascribed to them in the Child volumes (as in the case of "Barbara Allen," Child 84). Sharp was understandably quite pleased to find such songs still being sung in the mountains, but he was not nearly so delighted with the other varieties of music that he heard. Consequently, Sharp's book did not present to its readers the total picture of folk music preferences in the southern mountains, omitting religious music, for example, while reinforcing prevailing romantic ideas about the Upland South as the isolated repository of old English ways.

Largely inspired by Sharp's scholarship, a host of folk-song enthusiasts descended upon the Appalachians: not just scholars, but amateur collectors, seekers after local color, and musicians and composers searching for concert material. The 1920s witnessed a vigorous exploitation of mountain folk music by concert performers, men and women who "interpreted" the music for their sophisticated urban audiences. Elaine Wyman and Howard Brockway, for example, compiled a 1920 book called *Kentucky Folk Songs,* consisting of songs they had originally collected for use in recitals. Some of the folk-song performers of the period specialized in costume recitals, wearing clothing of the time period or ethnic group from which the music derived. Grace Wood Jess, a Kentuckian, gave concerts all over the United States dressed as a slave, a plantation mistress, a Creole belle, a Mexican maiden, or whatever the occasion or song dictated. Ethel Park Richardson, a long-time performer of folk songs who had her own radio show, "Hillbilly Heart Throb," and the compiler of *American Mountain Songs* (1927), sometimes dressed like a mountain woman and churned butter or shelled peas as she sang. Oscar Fox, a former ranch boy from Burnet, Texas, who had studied classical piano in Germany, arranged cowboy songs such as "Rounded Up in Glory" he found in John Lomax's collection and presented them to his concert audiences. He was sometimes assisted by Woodward Maurice Ritter from Murvaul, Texas, appropriately attired in cowboy regalia, who went on to win fame and affection among fans of western movies and country and western music as "Tex" Ritter.

Of the costume recitalists, the most active and probably the most successful was Edna Thomas of New Orleans. Thomas had performed classical and semiclassical compositions in New York around the time of World War I, but she began concentrating more heavily on folk material in the 1920s. Usually dressed in the costume of a gracious plantation lady, she carried southern folk songs to genteel audiences in the United States and Europe. Such audiences had never heard these songs before and would not have listened to them at that time had the songs not been presented in a cultivated, semiclassical style.

Edna Thomas and her folksinging colleagues of the 1920s, including Carl Sandburg, who published *The American Songbag* in 1927, were the first of that breed of collectors and entertainers who eventually were termed "urban folk singers." Thomas, Elaine Wyman, Grace Wood Jess, and such later singers as Richard Dyer-Bennett, Burl Ives, Theodore Bikel, Pete Seeger, Bob Dylan, Judy Collins, and Joan Baez were not folksingers at all, but interpreters of folk traditions with which they had only remote connections, if any. Their material was taken from the folk, but whether presented in a concert or recital hall, a university student center, or a coffeehouse, it was performed for a nonfolk audience and in styles compatible with either cultivated or popular tastes. Geographically closer to the folk and probably closer in spirit, though not socioeconomically, was North Carolina folk song collector and festival organizer Bascom Lamar Lunsford. While pioneering the collection of folk songs in the South, Lunsford worked very hard to preserve and present traditional songs in the most authentic manner possible and made many invaluable recordings for the Library of Congress even as he was contributing to the establishment of the commercial hillbilly music business.[17] Generally, though, while audiences for the Fisk Jubilee Singers or Edna Thomas came away with a broader perception of the kinds of songs that circulated among the southern folk, they received scarcely any inkling of how the folk themselves actually sounded.

Cecil Sharp's research and that of the folklorists who followed him quickened the interests of those who believed that "Anglo-Saxon" folk music should be the basis of a national American music. It did not matter to them, if they ever realized it, that the music of the mountains was a composite of the heterogeneous groupings of people who had settled the Appalachians—English, Scots-Irish, Irish, Welsh, Germans, Indians, and even a few blacks—and was therefore anything but purely Anglo-Saxon. It did not seem to matter that the mountains had never been the totally isolated sanctuary of Elizabethan folk-ways so celebrated in romance. What seemed important for the Anglo-Saxon theorists to believe was that they had found at least one bastion of racial purity in a society increasingly given over to racial and ethnic diversity, religious pluralism, and cultural amalgamation. Henry Shapiro argues, in fact, that to many Americans beset by unsettling changes in the 1920s, mountaineers "now appeared as the conservators of the essential culture of America" and "Appalachia seemed to provide a benchmark against which to measure how far the nation had come from its essential self."[18] The romantics never mentioned the irony of all this, if they ever pondered it, that the people they were promoting as the most "American" were those they were also promoting as the most British.[19]

Anglo-Saxon nationalists extracted from the Appalachian repertory the music that best reflected a romantic view of mountain life, marked by social conservatism, fierce individualism, simplicity, and morality, a general set of characteristics that many Americans liked to ascribe to themselves. The songs chosen for concert adaptation usually included the oldest and most pastoral items in the body of Appalachian music. The emphasis on such material was not false; it was merely incomplete. Indeed, mountaineers preserved much British folklore, including some of the famous Child ballads, and they had created their own store of songs reflecting their pioneer inheritance. But newer songs and styles had been gradually moving into the mountains for at least a century before Sharp came to the United States. Despite their supposed cultural conservatism, mountaineers assimilated this new music with no sense of contradiction or inappropriateness.

Mountain people had been learning about the outside world through various means long before Cecil Sharp and the others "discovered" Appalachia, and their music reflected this fact. Young mountain men had seen service in all of America's wars, one of the most common ways young people of limited means encounter other cultures. By the early 1900s, too, the industrial revolution had touched the mountains. Highways and railroads were penetrating the most isolated hollows, and the timber, coal, and textile interests were blasting the image of a wilderness paradise as they robbed the land of its resources. Long before the radio and recording industries accelerated the process of acculturation, new songs, styles, and instruments had moved into the mountains, and mountain musicians had created their own songs to deal with the changing socioeconomic realities of their region. Mountain singers knew and loved the old "lonesome songs" such as "Little Matty Groves" and "The Wife of Usher's Well," but they were equally fond of the more recent sentimental songs of pop origin such as "Bury Me Beneath the Willow," "Kitty Wells," and "Little Rosewood Casket." They saw nothing at all wrong with mixing these two types of songs, even if the academic folklorists abhorred the sentimental tunes and only reluctantly included them in their printed collections.

Proponents of theories of Anglo-Saxon purity in mountain culture recognized the threat to that culture represented by the encroachments of industrialization. That realization gave their campaign a great deal of its sense of urgency. Also, their disapproval of the newer songs grew in part from the belief that these songs were signs and agents of cultural corruption. In fact, a dual purpose often characterized the folk-song ventures of both the Anglo-Saxonists and the academic folklorists: the need to preserve the old songs and to combat their strongest competitors, the hillbilly songs, which were, in fact, largely folk songs disseminated for commercial purposes via radio and phonograph recordings. Part of the hostility the collectors and scholars felt toward commercialization of folk music, from the period of exploration through the various folk music crazes of the twentieth century, stemmed from their belief that the folk would remain pure only if they remained poor. These well-to-do outsiders did not think it corrupt or impure that they were enriched to varying degrees by the music of the people they met in the mountains.

Chief among proponents of the Anglo-Saxon folk-song school was John Powell, a Virginian and one of the South's leading classical musicians. In addition to being a composer and prominent pianist, Powell lectured, wrote articles, and sponsored associations and festivals designed to promote the preservation of the folk music of the South. Although he had decidedly racist views, his work in southern vernacular music was not limited to that of white mountaineers. He had made piano arrangements of African-American spirituals before he ventured into the field of Anglo-Saxon balladry, and he submitted an article to the first issue of the *Southern Folklore Quarterly* in which he noted the survival of ancient British songs in southern locales outside the mountains.[20] But in the 1920s, Powell was a dedicated evangelist of Anglo-Saxon balladry and its suitability for classical artistic expression.

Powell, David Guion, and Lamar Stringfellow were the three most active classical arrangers of southern folk music. But significant work along these lines was done by Oscar Fox and Aaron Copland, a New York native who in the 1930s and '40s adapted various American folk music motifs for his piano and orchestral compositions based in part on his experiences visiting relatives in Texas. Guion, a composer and pianist from Ballinger, Texas, was more catholic in his approach to folk music than most of his academically trained peers. His arrangements included elements of African-American tunes, fiddle tunes such as "Turkey in the Straw," and cowboy melodies such as "Home on the Range." Stringfellow, a North Carolinian, was the director of the North Carolina Symphony Orchestra, the first state-sponsored orchestra in the nation.

His most important work drawing upon southern folk music was his Pulitzer Prize-winning *Suite from the Southern Mountains,* composed in 1930.

Powell was often associated with Texas native Annabel Morris Buchanan in the campaign to promote an appreciation for folk music in the South. Together they founded the White Top Mountain Folk Festival in Virginia in 1931. Though it was not the first festival in the South, White Top seems to have inspired the first collaboration by people with a background in high-art music in the direction and control of such an event. It reflected the sense of cultural mission of the southern upper class to teach and elevate the masses. Annabel Buchanan was director of the folk music section of the Federated Women's Music Clubs of America and a "serious" musician. She and Powell occasionally wrote articles conveying their theories of folk music and revealed their ideas about the proper cultural and moral implications of such music, which mixed cultural uplift with social control.

Buchanan and Powell were more tolerant toward the folk than were most high-art advocates. That is, they encouraged the singing of old songs by the folk themselves, rather than by cultivated singers who came from outside the tradition. But Buchanan and Powell manipulated the performance styles exhibited at the festival, seeking to reinforce their ideas of how traditional music should be performed. They also tried to restrict the kinds of songs making their way onto the festival stage. They might exclude a song on the basis of its age, but more likely because of its nature and tone. They seemed to be trying to transfer the cultural mission of the mountain settlement schools to the festival setting. In an article in the *Southern Folklore Quarterly,* Buchanan described the songs that would never gain admittance to a White Top Festival: "products of the streets . . . the penitentiaries . . . the gutter." Songs from the paperback gospel hymnals and songs about carousing and getting into trouble, such as "Birmingham Jail," she said, would "beg admittance to the White Top programs in vain." Buchanan and Powell excluded more than just songs. They also went to great pains to keep black musicians from performing at the festival, reflecting especially Powell's nativist and white-supremacist notions. White Top's part in the efforts of the cultivated elite to use traditional southern mountain culture as the basis for a distinctive (white) American "national culture" historian David Whisnant calls "systematic cultural intervention," a conscious effort by outsiders to affect a culture, not preserve it.[21]

In rejecting certain types of music, the White Top Festival people were also rejecting major historical developments in the lives of the plain people of the South. The festival conception of southern folk society was that of a static, racially homogeneous, pastoral, and isolated people. This projected idealization had some basis in fact. The South was overwhelmingly rural and its people tended to be socially more conservative than people in other parts of the United States. But change had come to the mountains and to other parts of the South, and newer songs and styles persistently made their way into the repertories of the folk. Southern singers still occasionally sang ballads that were already old when the first American settlements were made, but they also composed and sang songs that reflected a commercial-urban-industrial order slowly supplanting agriculture in the South. The distorted White Top Festival point of view failed to recognize that the folk music of the South was an organic reflection of the changes in the world of the southern folk and that their music mirrored their grappling with the emerging social forces that challenged the whole of their existence.[22]

By the end of the 1920s, the proponents of high-art music had discovered three general types of southern folk music and had appropriated them for artistic purposes: the spirituals of African Americans, the ballads of the mountain folk, and the cowboy songs of southerners and others presumed to have affinity with southern culture. But in each case, members of the cultural elite romanticized the music so heavily that the lives of its creators were distorted, sometimes beyond recognition. The country as a whole, while enriched by these borrowings, received a decidedly limited view of the cultures of black and white southerners. The total richness and diversity of southern music remained largely hidden.

Meanwhile, these same black and white southerners had been building their own forms and styles of music, largely unaffected by what the high-art advocates did or believed. Southerners in increasing numbers became aware of the high-art philosophy and agenda, through schoolbooks and musical programs that they tolerated, assimilated, or ignored as their interests dictated. Furthermore, hillbilly singers such as Carl Sprague from Texas and Ernest Stoneman from Virginia recorded songs that they learned from the Lomax, Sharp, and other folk song collections. But southerners of modest means went on having their fiddling contests, singing conventions, and house parties distinct from the attempts of high-art advocates to reorient southern music. Some southerners, such as the family of singer Jean Ritchie of Kentucky, learned from the settlement schools with deep appreciation. Others took what they wanted from the encounter with the settlement workers and festival organizers and set about fashioning forms that they thought might enable them to use their music to improve their economic straits. The result was a change of a sort unintended by the high-art advocates and of a magnitude unforeseen by anyone. These musical forms, disseminated to the American audience through commercial means, became in the twentieth century the bases for virtually every style of popular music in the United States. Instead of being used artificially to fashion an outsider's version of a national musical culture, southern music appropriated for itself, with the help of a number of talented producers and marketing professionals, a vast section of the nation's musical culture in ways and with results John Powell and his compatriots could scarcely have imagined.

Chapter 3

EARLY COMMERCIALIZATION

RAGTIME, BLUES, JAZZ

With the emergence of ragtime in the late 1890s, southern-born singers and styles first entered the realm of American popular culture. The ragtime craze, which did so much to make the popular music business a major industry in the United States, was only the first of several vital infusions of southern-derived folk styles into mainstream popular music. But like the other forms that continually followed it, such as blues, jazz, gospel, rhythm and blues, rock 'n' roll, and country, ragtime lost its unique regional and racial identities as it became absorbed into the national mainstream.

Ragtime was only one product of the African-American search for musical individuality in the decades following emancipation, and the style reflected the rise of the city and the entrance of blacks and "ethnics" in general into American popular culture. To an even greater degree than blackface minstrelsy, ragtime represented the most serious threat that the genteel tradition of popular music had yet faced in the United States. With Scott Joplin and other blacks providing the initial impetus for making the music nationally popular, and Jewish firms such as Shapiro and Bernstein dominating the publishing business, it is no wonder that such an Anglo-Saxon nationalist as Henry Ford could later charge that Tin Pan Alley was a Jewish conspiracy to "Africanize" America's music.

Although white publishers and promoters contributed to the making of ragtime at every stage of its evolution, black composers and performers provided its driving force during the style's formative years. The roots of ragtime lay in African American dance music, in the fiddle-and-banjo music of the plantations and its accompanying rhythm of foot stomping and hand clapping. In the latter decades of the nineteenth century, ragtime became intimately associated with the piano, an instrumental adaptation that constitutes a major innovation in American black music. The late nineteenth century was the great age of the piano in the United States, and blacks differed little from whites in their desire to purchase an instrument whose ownership was equated with social standing and respectability. Few blacks, however, could afford pianos, and as Eileen Southern has argued, many black musicians received their introduction to keyboard instruments on the little parlor organs their families bought on lifetime installment plans.[1] Other musicians learned by watching pianists in restaurants, saloons, honky-tonks, brothels, churches, or music stores. A few managed to receive formal musical instruction. Most of the ragtime pianists, however, were itinerants, roaming through towns and cities from New Orleans to Chicago or along the East Coast, playing in the flimsy barrelhouses of the lumber camps, in the sporting houses of New Orleans, Memphis, and St. Louis, and in saloons, gambling establishments, and bars everywhere. The instrument they played was new to the black folk experience, but the music to which it was adapted, and the styles that became identified with it, came out of the older traditions of black dance music. Although the piano soon became a valuable component of instrumental ensembles, the early pianists had to simulate the sound of a band themselves. Consequently, they used the left hand to beat out a percussive, often march-like rhythm, while playing a syncopated melody with the right hand, a technique perfected by Scott Joplin.

Although he neither created the music nor coined the term "rag," Joplin became most clearly associated with the developing art form. He strove mightily, but with tragic frustration, to gain acceptance for the genre as "serious" music. Joplin was born into a family of self-taught musicians near Texarkana, Texas, in 1868. His father, a railroad worker, somehow managed to buy a piano, and Scott soon picked up the basics of the instrument. He received some training in classical music from a German immigrant piano teacher believed to have been named Julius Weiss, but his first sustained experience as a pianist came in the honky-tonks and brothels of the Mississippi Valley. Joplin and other early ragtime composers absorbed the music they heard in the black communities, like the folk music collectors in other parts of the South, and organized it into "brief suites or anthologies which they called piano rags."[2] Some of these suites featured sections that amounted to variations on themes while some passages developed entirely new themes, although they usually kept the same rhythm throughout the entire rag. Many of Joplin's compositions had dance annotations following their titles such as "A Ragtime Two Step" for "Sunflower Slow Drag" (1901) and "The Entertainer" (1902) and "Cake Walk March" for "Something Doing" (1903). By the time he published his first composition, "Please Say You Will," in Syracuse, New York, in 1895, Joplin had already served about a ten-year apprenticeship in the honky-tonks, as well as more reputable establishments, of St. Louis, Chicago, and Sedalia, Missouri. Joplin's most popular song, "Maple Leaf Rag," named for the Sedalia club where he often played, was published by John Stark, his partner until 1909. "Maple Leaf Rag," which consists of an elaborate series of passages, choruses, bridges, and variations, was one of the biggest sheet music sellers in popular music history.[3] Along with other ragtime compositions that began pouring out of the publishing houses, "Maple Leaf Rag" helped to fuel the first great boom in the popular music industry.

In the late nineteenth century, the urban-industrial revolution created an audience hungry for musical innovation. As the principal source of music in urban residences in the days before the development of recording technology and the appearance of radio, pianos appeared in thousands of American homes. A corresponding unprecedented growth in demand for sheet music appeared. The ragtime craze lured songwriters from all over the nation, and the syncopated rhythm was often fused in the 1890s with the "coon song," a very popular type of song of minstrel origin that stereotyped African Americans as shiftless, dishonest, sex-crazed buffoons. The form became so pervasive and lucrative a force in American show business that even a black writer, Ernest Hogan, composed a song called "All Coons Look Alike to Me."

After 1900 the term "rag" became affixed to many kinds of songs, such as Irving Berlin's "Alexander's Ragtime Band," which had only the remotest relationship to real ragtime music, and "Ragtime Annie," a fiddle tune that probably dates from the nineteenth century. Joplin was frustrated by his inability to get his music accepted as serious art—his rag opera, *Treemonisha*, had only one performance in Harlem in 1915—and he died in a mental hospital in 1917. But he, Tom Turpin, James Scott, Eubie Blake, and other composers had made the nation ragtime-conscious, and in so doing they had "brought attention to black musicians, either as serious artists or as capable and inventive entertainers."[4] They had also demonstrated once again the persistent appeal of southern images to a nation moving rapidly toward the complexity of urban society. This time, however, the image was not necessarily one of stability or security. Although one is struck today by the gentle or innocent sound of ragtime, in 1900 "respectable" patrons of cultivated music were scandalized by it, while its adherents found escape in a music that suggested the reputed gay charm and sensuality of black and/or southern life.

Ragtime's challenge to Anglo-Saxon supremacy and the genteel music tradition was reinforced by another product of the folk South, the blues. Developing and maturing since the Civil War, the blues emerged from the tradition of field hollers, work shouts, and spirituals common among southern rural African Americans. Emancipation brought a new freedom to articulate grievances or desires and permitted black music to develop in something other than a communal setting. Indeed Lawrence Levine argues that the blues were "the first almost completely personalized music that the Afro-Americans developed" and therefore "represented a major degree of acculturation to the individualized ethos of the larger society."[5] Blues musicians became famous as solo performers, but they were not merely voicing their own private feelings. They were entertainers who sought also to divert, amuse, and provide escape for their listeners. The blues arose out of pain, poverty, and injustice, which many of the songs address directly, but the general mood of the music was not exclusively sad or self-pitying: "Like the spirituals of the nineteenth century the blues was a cry for release, an ode to movement and mobility, a blend of despair and hope."[6]

As innovative as the blues might appear to be as a solo expression, the form continued to demonstrate its indebtedness to and interrelatedness with older African-American folk music forms. Vocal mannerisms of blues singers were not original to the new music, nor was the classic twelve-bar, three-line aab stanzaic formula of the blues. Even the most pervasive and group-oriented black musical trait, the call-and-response pattern, was borrowed from earlier folk music forms and perpetuated by solo blues stylists as singers interacted with their audiences or carried on dialogues with themselves or with their instruments. Much of the foundation of the blues was built on skillful guitar playing. During the concluding years of the nineteenth century and in the early years of the twentieth, black musicians achieved a mastery over the guitar that they had never exhibited during the days of slavery. In the hands of a skilled blues musician the guitar became, in effect, a second voice, punctuating the singer's remarks, or responding to them. The blues also benefited from both personal and communal feelings. An individual singer might utter a very personal message, but it was one that his or her listeners could easily understand and share, and it drew upon the total body of black folk experience. In a sense, improvising blues singers "composed" songs each time they performed, but the lyrics of these songs, as Samuel Charters maintains, were a distinctive language that had the "inflection and richness of the spoken language . . . the way people talked to each other on the street, the way men and women talked to each other."[7] The lyrics of blues songs floated freely from singer to singer and from one part of the South to another and on to the ghettos of the North. The blues were the common possession of the African Americans of the South and then of the United States as a whole.

While it is accepted that the blues were rooted in the black experience in the South, there is considerable disagreement concerning where exactly in the

South the form began. Several researchers, including Samuel Charters, who wrote the first general study of the rural blues, postulate a genesis in the Mississippi Delta, where a heavy concentration of black field workers built "a strongly developed tradition of rhymed work song material" in the context of almost total isolation from white society.[8] Jeff Todd Titon suspects that blues had multiple sources, but he agrees that "the tradition developed most fully in east Texas and the Mississippi River Delta region during the first decades of the twentieth century. Other authorities have proposed East Texas origins for the blues, as well as the area around Atlanta.[9]

Many of the most famous early Mississippi bluesmen of commercial recording fame such as Charley Patton, Sam Collins, Tommy Johnson, Son House, Skip James, and John Hurt began their careers playing for plantation social functions such as fish fries, picnics, and Saturday night dances. They learned from each other and bequeathed much of their music to younger musicians who often heard them only on recordings, which became one of the central means of popularizing and modifying blues styles across the South. Strong vocal and instrumental similarities exist among Mississippi bluesmen, but the migration of musicians began so early after the Civil War, and the influence of other forms of music, such as ragtime, was so pervasive, that it is dangerous to make hard and fast judgments concerning musical style or the purity of its origins. It is also easy to underestimate the role played by songsters in the development and distribution of blues music. The itinerant musical jacks-of-all-trades incorporated blues into their repertories, catching the attention of certain members of their audiences who were captivated by the blues numbers more so than by the popular and sentimental songs that appeared in the same performances. Some of those audience members went on to become blues performers of renown. The style of Mississippi Delta singers was often "hard and unrelenting," melodically limited, and marked by growling tones that sometimes ascended into falsetto. But John Hurt, from Teoc, Mississippi, one of the state's most beloved singers and one who made its name part of his own, sang in a gentle, relaxed, and almost lyrical style.[10] Similarly, Mississippi blues performers generally favored "harmonically ambiguous and polyrhythmic" guitar styles, but so did such musicians as Blind Lemon Jefferson and Blind Willie Johnson who came from Texas.[11] The use of devices to make a guitar simulate the sound of a human voice—the sliding of bottlenecks, pocket knives, or other objects along the strings, or pushing a string to one side of the fingerboard, called "choking" the string or "bending" the note—was most common among guitarists in Mississippi but appeared prominently in the playing of artists from other places, such as Blind Willie Johnson.

Texas blues, by and large, exhibited a greater stylistic variability than did the Mississippi blues, suggesting Texas's greater cultural complexity. Alger "Texas" Alexander confounds generalizations because this highly respected Texas bluesman sang in a rough wail suggestive of the field holler origins of the blues while Blind Lemon Jefferson achieved fame with his high-pitched, almost ethereal singing. Some of the variety in Texas blues style can be attributed to the decentralization of the black population of Texas. It was much less concentrated than that of the Deep South, and it evolved in proximity to a number of important musical traditions, those of rural Anglos, Cajuns, cowboys, Hispanics, and Central Europeans. Texas blues singers in eastern and southeastern Texas sang for parties and other rural social functions and in the barrelhouses of the lumber camps. Singers who grew tired of working local functions ventured into nearby towns to sing on street corners or in bars or for crowds that assembled at county fairs, political rallies, trades days, or medicine shows. Musicians also wandered into the bigger towns and cities of the region such as Austin, Shreveport, Fort Worth, Dallas, and Houston, and several of the best of them were heard on phonograph recordings in the late 1920s and early 1930s. Texas blues also exerted an influence beyond state lines, exhibited by the emulation of artists such as Blind Lemon Jefferson by performers from other parts of the South. While Alan Lomax calls the legendary Delta bluesman Robert Johnson "one of the two or three great originals of the blues," he says that Johnson's recordings of the 1930s suggest that he was "one of Lemon's brilliant disciples."[12]

Although the rural blues were widely known throughout the South to whites as well as blacks in the years before World War I, Americans elsewhere scarcely knew of the music, or vaguely conceived of it as "songs of the Southern underworld."[13] The blues in its rawest form did not get a national hearing until the mid-1920s. Like most manifestations of folk music, the southern blues moved into the American consciousness by a circuitous route. They were first popularized by professional, nonfolk entertainers who arranged, or watered down, for respectable, urban consumption. The agents through whom the blues revolution was inaugurated were two southern black men, William C. Handy and Perry Bradford, both of whom had absorbed musical material from the grassroots but aspired to better things.

As he describes it in his autobiography, Handy's first encounter with the raw, rural blues was a revelation, a turning point in his career.[14] One day in 1903, while he and his Knights of Pythias band were stopping in Tutweiler, Mississippi—in the heart of the Delta country—Handy heard a black rural bluesman strum his guitar and wail that he was going where "the Southern cross the dog," a reference to the junction of the Southern Railroad and the

Yazoo and Mississippi Valley line, locally nicknamed the "Yellow Dog," at Moorhead. The song eventually became the basis for Handy's own "Yellow Dog Blues," but it also inspired his larger campaign to seize upon the ingredients of the southern rural blues for his own artistic purposes. Like Scott Joplin, Handy was a trained musician who sought to rise above his humble origins seeking his musical fortune in urban settings using more elevated types of music. But, again like Joplin, he was an unwitting folklorist who absorbed and revitalized the musical styles he heard during his wanderings through the South and Midwest. When he made his fateful contact with the rural blues in 1903, Handy had thirty years behind him of varied experiences and exposures to virtually every kind of music available in the United States, from classical to ragtime. Born in Florence, Alabama, on November 16, 1873, Handy had to combat the prejudice of his father, who believed that stringed instruments were tools of the devil, and that of his first music teacher, who told him that professional musicians were wastrels and drunkards. But the irrepressible Handy could not be kept away from music. He played cornet in a local band, sang first tenor in a quartet, toured with a small Alabama minstrel unit, played in a brass band, and in 1896 went to Chicago and joined W.A. Mahara's Minstrels, a large organization playing everything from marches and overtures to Stephen Foster songs. This diverse background in popular music, along with a stint as an English teacher and band leader at the Agricultural and Mechanical College in Huntsville, Alabama, where he encountered a strong prejudice against music written by U.S. composers, lent an eclecticism to his music that few musicians possessed.

After another short period with Mahara's Minstrels, in 1903 Handy became director of a Knights of Pythias band in Clarksdale, Mississippi. From this date until 1914 Handy became immersed in the blues, hearing the form often during appearances throughout the Delta, and then in Memphis where he relocated. When Handy moved there, Memphis was a hub of musical energy, and Beale Street had already become the fabled center of saloons and brothels where such bands as the one led by West Dukes played for the nightly enjoyment of the rural African Americans who had been pouring into the city since emancipation. In 1909 Handy made his first contribution to the emerging blues genre when he wrote, at the request of the organization promoting Edward Hull "Boss" Crump's mayoral campaign, a song whose tune became known as "Memphis Blues" but was originally titled "Mr. Crump." ("Mr. Crump don't 'low no easy riders around here.") He sold the song for only fifty dollars, but it was immensely popular in the Memphis area and established his reputation as a songwriter. The tune was followed by other blues compositions, but the one that did most to make the nation blues-conscious was "St.

Louis Blues," which Handy wrote in September 1914, inspired by memories of an 1893 visit to Targee Street in St. Louis. "St. Louis Blues" well illustrates Handy's eclecticism, the sophistication lent to a rural-derived form by a professionally trained, urban-oriented musician, and his gifts for marketing. The tune features a Latin-influenced introduction and bridge, which Handy included, he said, because "the tango was in vogue. I tricked the dancers by arranging a tango introduction, breaking abruptly into a low-down blues."[15]

Between 1914 and 1920 people throughout the United States gradually became introduced to the blues, but usually in a sophisticated form largely shorn of rural characteristics, both written and performed by people who knew the form only secondhand. Many of the songs that gained popularity in these years were vaudeville blues composed for torch and cabaret singers. W.C. Handy, for instance, inspired many imitators, white and black, who churned out songs for the emerging city blues singers. One such successful blues composer was Perry Bradford, born in Montgomery, Alabama, in 1895, but by 1919 a resident of Harlem, where he produced musicals, played the piano, and wrote songs. Bradford fought valiantly in those years to gain national acceptance for African-American entertainers and their music. When he moved to New York, he entered an active black show business scene in Harlem that was vigorously breaking away from the constricting influences of minstrelsy. Bob Cole and others were producing all-black revues, and the Johnson Brothers from Florida, J. Rosamond and James Weldon, were busily producing songs such as "Under the Bamboo Tree" that competed favorably with the music of the white composers of Tin Pan Alley. The Johnsons, who were well educated, worked strenuously to eliminate grotesque black stereotypes in popular music that were left over from the days of the coon songs. Bradford sought to move black music out of Harlem and into the national limelight, while also expanding the performing horizons of African-American singers. In the years immediately after World War I, the most effective means of quick and expanded exposure appeared to be phonograph recording. Black entertainers had been conspicuously absent from recordings, and Bradford set out to correct the imbalance. He approached recording company officials at both Victor and Columbia and tried to persuade them to record Mamie Smith, a young singer from Ohio who had become well known in New York because of her singing in the 1919 production "Made in Harlem," an all-black revue. Those two companies rejected his requests, but the General Phonograph Company, owner of the Okeh label, recorded Smith's singing of two Bradford compositions, "That Thing Called Love" and "You Can't Keep a Good Man Down." Neither song was a blues tune, but they were among the first examples of a black singer recorded in solo performance, and they were soon followed, on August 10, 1920, by

Smith's recording of another Bradford song, "Crazy Blues," the first vocal blues recording.[16] Significantly, Okeh had renamed the song, once called "Harlem Blues," in order to attract white as well as black customers. Bradford had told the Okeh people that southern blacks would enthusiastically buy records by members of their race and that southern whites, who had heard such music all their lives, would buy them "like nobody's business."[17]

"Crazy Blues," as well as subsequent recordings by Mamie Smith, sold well indeed and set a precedent quickly followed by other recordings. Smith, however, was a cabaret singer rather than a blues stylist, and many of the women who emulated her, recording for other companies that quickly followed Okeh's lead, were "overnight converts from pop music who learned the form but lacked the feel of the blues idiom."[18] Regardless of the diluted nature of some of the recordings, the black population of the United States was hungry for black music, and the recording industry, after decades of neglect, began to satisfy the demand. In the years following 1920 an extraordinarily wide array of African-American talent was recorded, on major labels such as Okeh, Victor, Brunswick, and Columbia, on small labels such as Gennett and Paramount, and occasionally on black-owned labels such as Harry Pace's Black Swan. The music recorded ranged from primitive blues renditions that echoed the field hollers or work shouts to sophisticated and complex jazz arrangements. Despite the diverse nature and style of the material, black recordings for many years were categorized as "race records," a term coined by Okeh's Ralph Peer and used by that label as early as January 1922 and for years thereafter in racially segregated catalogs and brochures put out by various record companies. The term *race* was used widely before 1920 to describe the emerging and self-conscious black population of the United States, so when militant newspapers such as the *Chicago Defender* advertised or endorsed "race recordings," they meant that such songs sprang from or represented the feelings of African Americans. It became a matter of racial pride, and an example of incipient black nationalism, to support such musical expression. Pullman porters brought armloads of records south on their runs out of Chicago, and African Americans everywhere purchased records in great quantities. Phonographs were highly prized pieces of furniture in black tenant farmers' homes, and even those farmers who did not own them often bought records that they played on their neighbors' machines. Surveys of African-American families in the late 1920s and early '30s routinely showed more ownership of phonograph machines than radios. Partly because radio reception was still somewhat unreliable, especially in rural areas, phonograph records remained the key means of distributing black music during that period.[19]

Mamie Smith's recording of "Crazy Blues" in 1920 represented a milestone in the cultural transformation that made folk music in the United States available to the general populace. She was neither southern, folk, nor rural, and "Crazy Blues" was really a sophisticated imitation of the rural blues. Paul Oliver refers to her as a "professional singer on the vaudeville stage," but she helped spread the blues, including more authentic versions of it, throughout the country by inspiring the recording of singers whose voices carried both the inflections and the feeling of the southern blues. The greatest of these singers was Bessie Smith, "the Empress of the Blues," who made her first records for Columbia under the direction of veteran talent scout Frank Walker on February 16, 1923.[20]

Born in Chattanooga, Tennessee, in 1894, Bessie Smith was the youngest of seven children. Both of her parents died before she was nine years old, by which time she was singing for nickels and dimes on Ninth Street in Chattanooga to the guitar accompaniment of her brother Andrew. About 1912 she became a member of a show that included her brother Clarence and the legendary singer Gertrude "Ma" Rainey, who, like Mamie Smith, sang blues songs but became best known for her minstrel work in vaudeville. Only a few months later Bessie Smith joined another traveling troupe along with Ma Rainey and her husband, Will. Gradually she gained extensive popularity in the South, and in some of the northern ghettos, traveling with all-black troupes, some of which still carried the "minstrel" tag, and appearing in far-flung clubs and theaters. Many of the theaters, which included the 81 Theatre in Atlanta, the Frolic in Birmingham, the Bijou in Nashville, and the Palace in Memphis, were part of a chain of white-owned vaudeville houses that catered to black audiences. Organized in 1911, the chain was called the Theatre Owners Booking Association (TOBA). Because of the low pay and grinding performing schedule associated with it, black entertainers often said TOBA stood for "tough on black artists" (or "asses"). Smith continued to play the southern circuits throughout her career, but by 1920 she had moved to Philadelphia. By 1923, when she made her first records, she had amassed a large following in most northern communities where blacks had congregated. Ted Gioia states that after her hit "Down Hearted Blues," she was earning $2,000 a week, a far cry from the $2.50 a week she earned with TOBA.[21]

In all likelihood, no singer before Bessie Smith communicated so effectively with a mass African-American audience and none achieved such a heroic stature among them. As her commercial appeal broadened, her repertory also expanded to encompass songs well outside the blues idiom, including the newest popular hits of the day. But she invested even the most sophisticated songs with the moaning, soulful quality of the downhome South. Although her personal life would have shocked many church members, her style was strongly suggestive of religious singing, and she, in turn, influenced the style of some later gospel singers, including Mahalia Jackson. Smith's reputation became such that many of America's greatest musicians, especially from the developing jazz field, sought to be associated with her on recordings and in personal appearances. In addition, the careers of several fledgling musicians were enhanced by being identified with the great Empress. Fletcher Henderson, for example, began recording with her in 1923, and on January 14, 1925, the young Louis Armstrong participated in three recording sessions with Smith, one of which included her great recording of "St. Louis Blues." Smith's personal career, thus, is closely intertwined with, and largely responsible for, the popularization of both the blues and jazz.

After the mid-1920s Bessie Smith was usually in command of her own touring shows, some of which were highly organized and elaborate operations such as the 1925 Harlem Frolics. These shows featured a large orchestra, a group of dancers, a stage crew, and stage equipment. Smith, too, was highly conscious of her image and lived the blues queen role, dressing regally, spending money lavishly, and traveling in grand style. In the mid-1920s, for instance, she traveled in a private railroad car equipped with a kitchen and a bathroom. She won fame and fortune that lasted at least until the mid-1930s; but her personal life was often fraught with tragedy and pain, marital distress, drugs, and alcohol. She was only forty-three when she died on a lonely road near Clarksdale, Mississippi, the victim of an automobile accident on the night of September 26, 1937. Tragically, but perhaps fittingly, the Empress of the Blues died in the region where the blues was born and not many miles from where W.C. Handy first heard the form.

Commercial successes enjoyed by Bessie Smith and other "classic blues" singers, a term that came to be used for women who sung with jazz accompaniment, awakened the recording industry to the existence of a large black audience that wanted to hear real blues music performed by its own people, and not the watered-down adaptations composed and arranged for white audiences. The rural blues, however, the music that provided the basis for the entire blues genre, experienced a relatively brief recording history. It was not recorded with any frequency until 1926, and it suffered a drastic decline after the onset of the Great Depression. The rural or country blues, in contrast to the classic or city blues, was essentially music performed by men to their own guitar accompaniment. Jeff Titon describes the rural material as downhome blues, whether performed by a singer living in a southern city or in a northern ghetto, because the music reflected, or reminded the listener of, the old southern rural home and the associations it brought to mind and to heart.[22] Titon argues that the first downhome singer on records was Daddy Stovepipe, who recorded two songs on May 10, 1924, but the singer usually credited with the first recordings was an ex-minstrel entertainer, Papa Charlie Jackson, who recorded with his own guitar accompaniment in August 1924. Although it began to take on characteristics of the urban blues as the 1920s went on, the downhome blues style flourished on recordings from about 1926 to 1930. During that time, approximately two thousand titles were issued and the entire range of rural blues material, if not the total preference of the musicians, was recorded on 78–rpm discs. Echoes of unaccompanied nineteenth-century field hollers (epitomized by "Texas" Alexander), the songster tradition (Henry "Ragtime Texas" Thomas), Delta blues (Charley Patton), gospel blues (Blind Willie Johnson), hillbilly blues (Coley Jones), jug band blues (Cannon's Jug Stompers), and sophisticated blues (Lonnie Johnson) were only a few of the styles available to the record buyer.

Blind Lemon Jefferson's recording in April 1926 was the catalyst for the first major search for downhome talent by the phonograph companies. Jefferson was born in 1897 in Couchman, Texas, not far from Wortham. Blind from birth, he was already singing on the streets of Wortham well before World War I and soon was a fixture at country dances throughout the county. In about 1917 he moved to Dallas, where he remained for almost ten years, using that city as a base for his performances in north central Texas and becoming a fixture in Dallas's Elm Street "Deep Ellum" music district. Occasionally Jefferson worked with another musician, but usually alone, often playing all night for dances. Jefferson was a physically striking man. He was grossly overweight and, though totally blind, wore wire-rimmed glasses on the end of his nose. But he had an uncommon power over his listeners, especially women, who fawned over him. Some of the most famous blues singers, such as Huddie Ledbetter (Leadbelly), Josh White, Lightnin' Hopkins, and T-Bone Walker later claimed to have had a close association with him. Long before he made his first records for Paramount, evidently after a Dallas record dealer named Sam Price told the company about him, Jefferson had already built a regional reputation and had developed the individualistic style that made him a popular recording performer on both the Paramount and the Okeh labels. Jefferson sang in a freewheeling, wailing manner that set him apart both from his Texas contemporaries and from the Mississippi Delta singers. His guitar playing also contributed to his popularity, providing an expressive second voice that complemented rather than repeated the shouted lyrics. Jefferson was already virtually a legend among his fans and fellow blues artists when he died of exposure on a Chicago street one wintry night in 1930. He was buried in an unmarked grave in a country cemetery near Wortham. Other performers carried on the tradition of the downhome blues, in the city of Jefferson's death

and elsewhere. Leroy Carr, Lonnie Johnson, and others created urban derivatives of the form that spoke to the feelings and experiences of African Americans in the North as well as the South. They all contributed to the creation of
a sense of cultural autonomy among black people in the United States at a
time when they had little independence of any other sort.

Downhome blues reminded African Americans of their humble, rural origins,
even as it moved into such places as Chicago and other cities. In contrast, from
its beginnings, jazz suggested the aura and liberation of the beckoning cities.
Jazz moved into the national consciousness as a southern-derived music, but its
roots lay in many places in Africa, in the Caribbean, in Europe, and in the
United States and its most extensive development occurred in the urban centers
of the U.S. and Europe. The songs in the jazz repertory came from a multitude
of sources including folk music, religious music, minstrelsy, ragtime, blues, marching and concert band music, and modern high-art compositions. But jazz was
overwhelmingly an instrumental style, and it developed when musicians welded
these various musical forms into ensemble instrumental patterns.

Although jazz drew from many sources, nowhere were these diverse
musical influences so concentrated as in New Orleans. Some interpreters of
jazz who emphasize its African origins posit a simple progression from Africa
to the Caribbean to New Orleans, where it became concentrated in the brothels of Storyville, the red-light district that flourished from 1897 to 1917. Then
with the closing of Storyville by the U.S. Navy Department, jazz musicians
took the music up the Mississippi and to Chicago and ultimately to the rest of
the United States. But the musical culture of New Orleans put its stamp on
the development of jazz in complicated ways, and the northern migration of
African Americans took more forms than simply going up the river. For one
thing, the city was peculiarly situated to receive music from many places in
the world. It had a close relationship with the Caribbean, but it also had a past
under French and Spanish as well as American rule. As a seaport, it also received visitors and cultural and economic influences from all over the world.
Furthermore, like the great port cities of the East, New Orleans received large
waves of Irish, German, and Italian immigrants in the nineteenth century.
Throughout that century the city was known for the breadth and variety of its
music. As previously mentioned, light opera was performed there from the
1790s on and grand opera after the 1830s. In addition balls and street parades
occurred constantly, and virtually all fraternal and benevolent organizations,
black and white, had marching bands ready to perform at the slightest provo-
cation. One could hear their music in the parks on weekends, as well as a
myriad of musical styles from street entertainers and vendors.

Jazz bands borrowed their instruments and many of their songs, what has been called "the bedrock of the New Orleans jazz repertoire," from the marching street bands. According to William J. Schafer, the street bands also introduced the African-American technique of syncopation to jazz in its formative stages: "The process changed the plodding, walking march measure into a varied dance rhythm. The march beat shifted from the stiff 1-and-3 accent of military cadence to the springy 2-and-4 of Afro-American music."[23] The real transition to jazz came at the turn of the century when small groups of musicians, drawing on marching-band experience, began playing what was generally called ragtime for the hordes of partygoers caught up in the great national vogue for social dancing. The ingredients that made jazz distinctive—syncopation, antiphony, improvisation, polyrhythm, the use of "blue" notes—came from black musicians drawing upon the African-American, and not solely the African, experience. Jazz did not develop in Africa; it emerged in the United States when Americans of African descent drew upon their total experience to create a new musical style out of a multitude of older ones. Several musicians, including the white bandleader Papa Jack Laine, spoke of "ragging" tunes before 1900, but the performer who is often viewed as the "first man of jazz" was Charles "Buddy" Bolden. Between 1895 and 1907 Bolden became "the key figure in the formation of classic jazz and his personal cornet style, one of a shouting, incredible power, established one of the two main jazz trumpet styles," the other being that of Bunk Johnson, which was characterized by a light touch and precise phrasing.[24]

Bolden made no phonograph recordings and was not mentioned in the New Orleans newspapers until he was committed to a state mental institution in 1907. Consequently, he had always been a shadowy figure in the history of early jazz until the appearance of Donald M. Marquis's myth-shattering and meticulously documented biography.[25] Although he seems to have been little known to the white community, Bolden became a heroic figure to blacks through his performances in the local parks and in the string of bars and dance halls in the area intersected by South Rampart and Perdido Streets. Encouraged by the enthusiasm of his listeners and by the fierce competition of other musicians, Bolden continually strove to create distinctive sounds and rhythms. This kind of creativity sparked the transition to jazz. In the peak years of his activity, 1900–1905, Bolden built the most popular dance band in New Orleans and pioneered in the employment of the "classic" jazz ensemble: a front line of horns and a back line of rhythm instruments. This great pioneer of jazz spent the last twenty-five years of his life in the state mental hospital in Jackson, Louisiana. His death on November 4, 1931, was scarcely noticed or mourned, and he now rests in an unmarked grave in New Orleans.

Like all early jazz musicians Bolden drew upon the total musical environment of New Orleans, and his performances took him all over the city and into a wide variety of entertainment formats. Only rarely, however, did he play in Storyville, the one area that in the popular imagination has been most associated with the birth of jazz. No facet of the jazz story has had a more tenacious or romantic hold on the popular imagination than that of its supposed Storyville origins. This notorious haven of legalized prostitution was named after Sidney Story, the New Orleans alderman who suggested its creation, but described in the press as "the restricted district." It abounded in bars, dance halls, and cabarets as well as bordellos, and in all of these places music was a constant backdrop for the diversions of the flesh. Many fine musicians played the Storyville establishments, including the great "professors" of the piano, Clarence Williams, Tony Jackson, and Ferdinand "Jelly Roll Morton" Le Menthe, and such groups as the Olympia Band, Bunk Johnson's Superior Band, Freddie Keppard's Creole Band, Kid Ory's Brownskin Band, and Manuel Perez's Imperial Orchestra. When the district was closed down, many of them departed for other cities, although as Kathy Ogren and other scholars have pointed out, the demise of Storyville only accelerated a jazz exodus from New Orleans already under way.[26] Furthermore, jazz began before the district was established by statute in 1897, and "the majority of black musicians of outstanding ability in New Orleans never worked so much as a single night" in the area. Al Rose placed the Storyville-jazz relationship in the proper perspective when he said that "jazz was not born in Storyville, nor was it even reared there. Storyville was just one part of the passing scene in which this great art form happened to thrive," although Linda Dahl has observed that many early female jazz singers started their entertainment careers as Storyville prostitutes.[27]

Though the closing of Storyville contributed to the exodus of musicians from New Orleans, their departure began considerably earlier than 1917. Jazz, or at least the forerunner of what came to be called jazz, began moving north by railroads at the end of the nineteenth century and on the excursion steamers to Memphis, St. Louis, and other points on the Mississippi River by the 1910s. The showboat bands were not always jazz groups, but they included such great jazz personalities as Warren "Baby" Dodds, George "Pops" Foster, Johnny St. Cyr, and Louis Armstrong. Furthermore, the Original Creole Band was already making vaudeville tours to such far-flung points as California and New York by 1912, and other black musicians were playing in obscure bars on the south side of Chicago by 1915. Burton Peretti points out that New Orleans jazz bands also migrated in significant numbers to the West Coast, finding especially receptive audiences in Los Angeles, San Francisco, and Oakland.[28]

Despite the vital contributions made by African Americans to the creation and shaping of jazz, white New Orleans musicians introduced the form into the national consciousness and first popularized the term "jazz" or "jass." In June 1915 Tom Brown and his New Orleans band took a job at Lamb's Club in Chicago. They were derided by the local musicians' union as a "jazz" group, a term associated with whorehouse music. As might have been expected, the notorious connotation attracted, rather than repelled, public interest, and people attended the New Orleans group's performances in great numbers. The band soon began calling themselves Brown's Dixieland Jass Band. In 1916 another group of white performers moved from New Orleans to Chicago, playing first at Schiller's Cafe and then at the Del'Abe Cafe. At the latter job they adopted the name Dixieland Jass Band. After their move to New York in January 1917, the spelling was changed to "jazz," and the band made recording history. An initial record for Columbia was filed away and not immediately released, but on February 26, 1917, the band recorded "Livery Stable Blues" and "Dixieland Jazz Band One-Step" for the Victor Talking Machine Company. The record experienced an extremely large sale, and white imitators began to spring up all over the country. The national vogue for jazz music was under way.

Although they did much of their path-breaking work in northern cities, southern white musicians ushered in the jazz revolution, borrowing and adapting a musical form developed by African Americans. It was another five years before the first black jazz records were issued. Therefore, the music that made the revolution in jazz and first captured the attention of the American public was "dixieland," a style of music imitative of black music. In his book on the Original Dixieland Jazz Band, H.O. Brunn discusses the pervasive musicality of New Orleans and tells how ODJB leader Dominic James "Nick" LaRocca absorbed such music from infancy, but mentions African-American musicians hardly at all. Certainly, no black New Orleans band is cited as having had an influence on LaRocca's or the other ODJB members' styles. Virtually all other writers, however, described the ODJB as a band imitative of black musicians, and Rudi Blesh calls it a weak imitation at that.[29]

Almost immediately jazz, like rock 'n' roll about forty years later, became the center of controversy, and the term came to be applied to an entire decade. Many people saw it as an exciting art form and a healthy liberation of musical styles. Few high-art people recognized any art in it, and many other Americans thought they saw in it, and in the lifestyle it supposedly represented, a force potentially destructive not only of good music but of decency itself. Even the *New Orleans Times-Picayune* said that "jazz music is the indecent story syncopated and counterpointed" and that "its musical value is nil." An editorial in the *Times-Picayune* in 1918 referred to it as "the dime novel or the grease-dripping doughnut," although some writers of letters to the paper's editor defended jazz. Donald Marquis asserts that no friendly accounts of jazz appeared in the New Orleans newspapers until 1933.[30] It is not surprising that, given its rhythmic abandon and African-American origins, jazz was soon denounced by Henry Ford's *Dearborn Independent* as a threat to public morals and as further evidence of a Jewish conspiracy designed to debauch American music.[31] The inherent conservatism of so much of U.S. culture in the 1920s, however, could not stem the rising tide, the sea change in music being wrought by jazz. If not everyone in the United States was being swept away by the Jazz Age, there certainly were those who believed and behaved as though that were the case.

When they finally became available, actual recordings of black jazz musicians added incredible energy to the force of jazz. The public had to wait for this development until 1923. Joseph "King" Oliver, born in New Orleans about 1885, came to Chicago in 1917 or 1918 and played his cornet in several bands before organizing his own Creole Jazz Band in 1920. After a short sojourn in California he returned to the Lincoln Gardens Cafe in Chicago where, in 1922, he added a second cornetist, the youthful Louis Armstrong. The following year the band recorded for both Paramount and Gennett, the Gennett records being the first to appear on the market. These recordings, along with others released by the band on the Okeh and Columbia labels, were described by Blesh as "the first definitive records of the Negro's classic jazz."[32] This music attracted imitators as immediately as had the earlier white Dixieland recording groups. In fact, Europeans began to be jazz-conscious almost as quickly as did Americans. The Original Dixieland Jazz Band went to Britain in March 1919 and played to standing-room-only crowds. While jazz was winning international acclaim, in the U.S. it was also making inroads into the "better music" audience, though in a greatly diluted form. On February 12, 1924, Paul Whiteman held his "Jazz Concert" at Aeolian Hall in New York. This concert of "symphonic jazz," which featured George Gershwin's first public performance of *Rhapsody in Blue,* was designed to give jazz respectability and to break down the opposition of its more refined critics. Already, in a pattern that had been demonstrated earlier in the case of ragtime and blues and that surfaced repeatedly in the twentieth century, a black-derived folk art was taken over by whites who moved it away from its folk moorings. Although jazz quickly expanded in style and popularity and often merged its identity with other forms of popular music, its classic style endured. By and large, its direction was shaped by black southern musicians, with some of the greatest coming from New Orleans, such as Jelly Roll Morton, Sidney Bechet, Johnny Dodds, and Louis Armstrong. Morton was a pianist of great diversity and skill who, despite the fact that his claim to have invented jazz was exaggerated, was the first successful composer and arranger in jazz music, a key figure in the transition from ragtime to jazz, and one of the leaders in infusing jazz with Latin rhythms. Bechet, a Creole of Color, as was Morton, helped popularize jazz in Europe through highly praised appearances throughout the 1920s, established the soprano saxophone as a jazz instrument, and achieved great acclaim as a composer. Dodds was a great, though sometimes overlooked, clarinetist. Armstrong, the most beloved of all jazzmen, was virtually a national institution at the time of his death in 1971.

Daniel Louis Armstrong was born in New Orleans in 1901. He was introduced to music at the Negro Waifs' Home for Boys, where he was placed at the age of thirteen after celebrating New Year's Eve by firing his stepfather's gun on the street, a New Orleans tradition. Although he had broad-ranging musical interests as a young person, studied music, and became the leader of the waifs' home's brass band, his real introduction to jazz came from the music he heard floating out of the Storyville establishments and from his membership in the Kid Ory and Fate Marable bands. He took his style to Chicago in 1922, and then to New York in 1924, as a member of Fletcher Henderson's band. After 1925, when he returned to Chicago, he usually led his own bands, including the Hot Five and Hot Seven groups with such preeminent musicians as Johnny Dodds, trombonist Kid Ory, banjoist Johnny St. Cyr, and pianist Lil Hardin Armstrong, his wife. Armstrong was the first genuine star to emerge from the burgeoning throng of jazz musicians and the first of them to forge a reputation as a great soloist and innovator. Though jazz fans praised him for his brilliant cornet and trumpet playing, the populace at large came to know Armstrong as much for his singing. His gravel-voiced style was peculiarly effective, and his "scat" singing, the use of nonsense phrases to simulate the sound of horns, influenced other jazz and pop singers. Through his personal appearances in the United States and on many foreign tours, the first of which came in 1932, as well as through a prolific outpouring of recordings going back to his work with King Oliver in 1922, Armstrong became virtually the symbol of jazz, its U.S. ambassador, to people around the world.

From the time of its early commercialization, jazz established itself, like blues, as a form with long-lasting power. While ragtime remained largely frozen in the form it had taken by the time of World War I, jazz and blues went through many stylistic changes and became international phenomena. Ragtime helped African-American performers establish their credibility and marketability, but the entire popular music industry profited from the jazz explosion after the 1920s. For its part, blues formed the basis of several forms that emerged after World War II and had a profound effect on jazz, as it had from the beginning. As blues became the possession of the U.S. as a whole and inspired fervent devotion in other countries, it became less southern. Jazz lost its southern identity more completely, although many southerners, such as Fletcher Henderson, Lester Young, Nat "King" Cole, Ella Fitzgerald, John Birks "Dizzy" Gillespie, Charlie Christian, and Thelonius Monk played pivotal roles in its periodic reinvigoration or reshaping. In the years since jazz burst onto the national scene, its various forms, ranging from the traditional to the most progressive and experimental, built identities somewhat apart from mainstream popular music and attracted adherents unwilling to listen to or play any other kind of music. Furthermore, jazz as a whole influenced virtually every other kind of American music, from country to classical. Most mainstream pop performers showed the influence of jazz in one way or another, and in so doing they demonstrated the tendency of popular music to absorb and dilute all musical genres while also deregionalizing them. Alongside blues, however, jazz showed the immense creative, and market, potential of black southern music, running parallel to and occasionally mixing with the South's other great stream of musical culture, that of rural white southerners.

Chapter 4

EXPANDING MARKETS

TEJANO, CAJUN, HILLBILLY, GOSPEL

The decade of the 1920s witnessed the first full-scale commercialization of rural southern folk music, made possible by the developing giants of musical distribution, phonograph recordings and radio. In that decade, the two industries were not as intimately related as they later became. Radio stations rarely played recorded music over the air, broadcasting live performances instead, often by regularly appearing local groups or soloists or "staff" musicians who played at different times of the day or night on shows underwritten by local sponsors. On some programs, musicians promoted recordings they had made, but just as often they promoted upcoming local or regional live appearances they planned to make at dances, school shows, or store openings and the like. Although the record industry predated the broadcasting industry, the growing popularity of radio, a free medium requiring only the purchase of the receiving set, forced the recording field to seek means of remaining commercially competitive. The introduction of electrical reproduction in 1925–26 promoted better recording quality, and recording industry personnel took various steps to reach broader audiences, which stimulated the search for ethnic and folk performers. In searching for these performers, representatives of the electronic mass media sought to provide musical entertainment that was familiar to people living in an age before the homogenization or nationalization of vernacular music in the United States, a process to which these media contributed greatly.

Radio stations appeared in southern cities as early as 1922. Almost immediately they began featuring live local talent, including fiddlers, string bands, mandolin and guitar clubs, Hawaiian groups, yodelers, quartets, and blues singers. Usually such entertainers performed on an irregular basis, but by the mid-1920s a few stations, such as WBAP in Fort Worth, WSM in Nashville, and WSB in Atlanta, offered regularly scheduled "barn dances" on a week-to-week basis. The barn dances were inspired by the rural dances of the American frontier and were composed almost exclusively of string-band music. The most famous of these radio shows, ultimately, was the WSM Barn Dance, inaugurated in 1925, and soon to be called the Grand Ole Opry. WSM used talent found in Nashville and in the immediate surrounding area. The performers, according to Charles Wolfe, the chief historian of the Grand Ole Opry, were generally amateurs who had played only in the area of their homes. Occasionally, Opry performers such as Uncle Dave Macon had had some experience on the southern vaudeville circuits or had built at least minor reputations playing in medicine shows or entertaining at county fairs, political rallies, or fiddling contests, or merely singing and hawking their song sheets wherever a crowd gathered.[1]

Commercial potential had never been totally absent from southern rural music, but radio provided a means of immediate and widespread exposure far more advantageous than any medium yet created. Folk entertainers on the radio played for increasingly large audiences, built up a string of personal appearances within the listening range of the stations, and increased both the size and scope of their performing repertories. Newly composed songs inevitably, and successfully, competed with traditional material, but folk performance styles demonstrated a remarkable endurance. Since its inception in 1888, the recording industry had been preeminently a city-oriented phenomenon and had generally ignored rural folk music. Folk songs or dance tunes had appeared on records, usually performed by urban professional musicians. Except for occasional groups such as the Dinwiddie Colored Quartet, hardly any bona fide southern rural music, performed by southern rural entertainers, had appeared on disc or cylinder recordings prior to the 1920s. Mamie Smith's recording of "Crazy Blues" in 1920, however, generated an interest in African-American music and the subsequent discovery of a large black audience for recordings of it. Record companies discovered other previously neglected markets among the nation's ethnic and grassroots groups. Much of this music—Finnish, Irish, Polish, and so on—was aimed at northern and big-city audiences. But the rural South was also found to have its enclaves of unassimilated ethnic elements—especially Hispanics, Cajuns, and hillbillies—and their folk music forms were also recorded.

Although the blues music of African Americans in Texas had a great impact on the musical culture of the state and beyond, people of Mexican descent have long been the largest ethnic minority group in Texas, and they have produced a vigorous and exciting body of music. Described variously as *Tejano, música Norteña, música Tejana,* sometimes even Tex-Mex, the music has roots deep in the time before Texas was part of the United States. It grew out of the cultural-ethnic mix of Spanish and French parlor or salon music and Mexican dance traditions, drew instrumentation and stylistic innovation from encounters with German and Czech immigrants, and reflected in South Texas the same freedom and experimental spirit the frontier experience inspired elsewhere in North America. The music had two streams, so to speak, a working-class variety whose musical groups were called *conjuntos,* and a middle-class variety whose bands were called *orquestas Tejanas.* Commercially recorded for the first time in the late 1920s, the music of Tejanos has always shared some of the stylistic traits of the music produced south of the border, including frequent use of *corridos,* narrative ballads having historical or romantic associations, a form with a long tradition in Mexico. The music was formed, however, in the Texas experience of people of Mexican descent and of their interrelationships with other cultural groups in the diverse region south of Austin. Joe Nick Patoski goes so far as to say that the music is "wholly Texan and is considered foreign even in Monterrey."[2]

Many musicians contributed to the wondrous blend of Tejano music, but Lydia Mendoza's career was the longest and most distinctive. Born in Houston in 1916, she first performed with other members of her family (La Familia Mendoza) but by 1934 had embarked on a solo career, accompanied often only by her twelve-string guitar, and recording for the Bluebird label. With such songs as "Mal Hombre" and "Pero Hay Que Triste," she built a close bond with her working-class listeners and proudly declared that she "sang for the workers." Her devoted fans described her as "La Alondra de la Frontera" (the Meadowlark of the Border). Not only did such music become the chief cultural staple of working-class Tejanos, it also served often as a symbol of racial pride for Latinos at other socioeconomic levels. In the same ways that jazz and blues moved with African Americans from the South to the Midwest and to California, as Tejanos migrated to Southern California, the Pacific Northwest, the Great Lakes region, the Upper Midwest, and other regions, they took their music with them.

While adhering to the Spanish language, especially its South Texas version, Tejano musicians built up a peculiar composite of musical styles, drawing heavily on the accordion and on the rhythms of the polka music of their Texas-German neighbors. From the time of Lydia Mendoza in the 1930s, Selena Quintanilla in the 1990s, and Little Joe Hernandez and Flaco Jiménez in between, such performers became sources of immense pride to their compatriots and won recognition within the larger Anglo population. Les Blank's 1970s documentary film *Chulas Fronteras,* Chris Strachwitz's ten-record collection of music ranging from 1928 to the 1970s, and the Spanish-language crossover hits by mainstream pop artist Linda Ronstadt in the 1980s and '90s indicated growing interest in *la música Tejana.*[3] Its popularity, however, mainly remained a phenomenon within the community that gave rise to the music, a community that often also supported country-and-western music, rock 'n' roll, and pop music drawn from the Anglo market and whose own artists sometimes engaged in these forms. The country hits of Johnny Rodriguez and Freddy Fender (Baldemar Huerta), the country/rock/Tejano styles of the Texas Tornados, and the incandescent popularity in the 1990s of Selena, whose promotion and staging borrowed heavily from mainstream pop figures such as Madonna, point to the musical diversity and creative freedom of life in a borderland. The South Texas region was not the only cultural transition zone, however, where southern music blended with other forms. The regional popularity of *la música Tejana* was paralleled in several ways by the music of another cultural borderland, the Cajun-French territory of southwestern Louisiana and southeastern Texas.

Cajun music was discovered commercially, and somewhat inauspiciously, in 1928 when a singer and accordionist from Rayne, Louisiana, was recorded in New Orleans. Joseph Falcon, accompanied by his guitar-playing wife, Cléoma Breaux Falcon, recorded a song called "Allons a Lafayette" (Let's Go to Lafayette), a reference to one of the principal cities in Acadiana. Falcon was neither the best nor the most representative of Cajun musicians, but his recordings were immensely popular among Cajuns, and Falcon contributed mightily to the popularization of the accordion in southwestern Louisiana. Speculation has arisen over the years about how accordions came to that area. Barry Jean Ancelet and colleagues propose that they may have been brought to the region by German merchants. In ways probably similar to Tejano musicians' incorporation of accordions into their musical lineups, Ancelet, Edwards, and Pitre say, "The accordion arrived without instructions or cultural baggage. Acadian and black Creole musicians began experimenting with it, discovering how to coax familiar tunes out of this new music-making contraption."[4] The fiddle, which had long been a fixture at fais-do-dos, the all-night country dances so beloved in Cajun territory, was temporarily eclipsed by the accordion's popularity and did not really resume its prominence until the 1930s. Despite the prominence on early Cajun recordings of the accordion, which went into its own decline in the 1930s, the fiddle was never totally absent. While there was no single style of Cajun fiddling, the musician who did the most to revitalize the instrument, and who also played a central role in the 1930s in both the popularization and modification of Cajun music, was Leo Soileau of Ville Platte, Louisiana. Soileau began his recording career in 1928, playing a duet with Mayuse Lafleur, a young accordionist who met his death from a stray bullet in a tavern brawl in October of that same year. Not only did Soileau contribute to the development of enduring fiddle styles, he was also partly responsible for popularizing the high-pitched, wailing vocal style so typical of Cajun music.

Cajun culture exerted a powerful impact on all who came into southwestern Louisiana, whether "American," Hispanic, German, or African American. Lauren C. Post possibly overstates the case but says, "the newcomers lost all contact with their original groups and had no feeling of belonging to any but the Acadian population."[5] As a result, several musicians of mixed ancestry attained great prominence as Cajun entertainers. Among them were Lawrence Walker, Dennis McGhee, Harry Choates, and the black accordionists Amade Ardoin and Clifton Chenier. Early Cajun recordings were probably limited in circulation to those areas inhabited by people of Cajun-French extraction or by people who had grown up in the Cajun culture, in the region extending from southwestern Louisiana and along the Gulf Coast eastward to Mobile and westward through Beaumont and Port Arthur to Houston. But increasingly in the 1930s people outside of Cajun culture began to learn about the music. John Lomax made field recordings of Cajun musicians for the Library of Congress in the 1930s, and Cajun performers appeared at the Texas Centennial celebration in Dallas in 1936. The western swing craze of the 1930s drew many Cajun musicians away from their own music and toward more Anglicized forms, probably because of the prominence of the fiddle in western swing and other forms of country music. After World War II, segments of the populace at large discovered Cajun music in its hybridized country-and-western form, particularly through Moon Mullican's very popular "cover" of Harry Choates's "Jole Blon," or as Zydeco, the blues-influenced dance music of the French-speaking black Creoles.[6] Clifton Chenier did most to popularize the fusion of r & b and French music now known as Zydeco. Born in St. Landry Parish in 1925, Chenier began his career as a singer and accordionist playing mostly blues music in western Louisiana and southeast Texas, particularly in an area of Houston called Frenchtown. By 1965 he was freely mixing the Cajun French patois with his blues tunes. On May 11, 1965, he recorded "Zydeco Sont pas Sale" ("The Snap Beans Aren't Salty") and therefore contributed greatly to the circulation of a label that was already being used by folklorist Mack McCormick to describe such music. Chenier was extremely popular in the region that extended from Cajun Louisiana to Houston, and he well deserved the title that he proudly bore, "the King of Louisiana." Cajun music before 1930 had been very strongly rooted in the rural French culture that gave it birth, even though that music had itself borrowed heavily from German-, African-, and Anglo-American sources. The music had not lost its identity, however, even after World War II, when it began to be known outside the area of its origins. After the war, according to Barry Jean Ancelet,

"Cajuns began to show signs of learning to better negotiate the American mainstream in a way that would allow them to preserve their own cultural identity. Musicians were among the first to announce the change by returning to traditional sounds."[7] They were able to do so in large part because record company officials were more interested in expanding markets than in regulating minority cultures.

In its competition with radio the recording industry also began to exploit other varieties of southern white rural music, much of which was recorded after it first gained exposure through the broadcasting medium. The earliest recordings of such music were made by oldtime fiddlers, including Alexander Campbell "Eck" Robertson, an Arkansas native who made his mark as a fiddler in Texas. Others soon followed. Much of the rural talent heard on WSB in Atlanta soon after the station began operating in 1922 made its way onto recordings later in the decade. The first of such entertainers to record, and the one who did the most to illustrate the commercial potential of what came to be called hillbilly music, was Fiddling John Carson from Georgia. Although the Okeh talent scout Ralph Peer was intensely skeptical of the marketability of the material he heard, describing Carson's singing as "pluperfect awful," Fiddling John's recording of "The Old Hen Cackled and the Rooster's Going to Crow" and "Little Old Log Cabin in the Lane" sold several thousand copies. Peer had greatly miscalculated the tastes of the Georgia farmers and millworkers who had enjoyed hearing Carson at fiddle contests and political rallies for many years. Peer apparently failed to realize as well that millions of working-class southerners yearned to hear music performed by entertainers much like themselves. Despite Peer's personal predilections, many people enjoyed Carson's formal, hymn singing style. Nevertheless, it seemed archaic to twentieth-century urbanites, a dialect that came straight out of the plain folk, "redneck" South.

In the wake of Carson's success, rural singers who represented a host of occupations began to appear on recordings: farmers, millworkers, railroad workers, coal miners, cowboys, and barbers, even doctors and lawyers. But regardless of background or status, these musicians, and the music they performed, were destined to be labeled "hillbilly," a catch-all term that branded all southern white grassroots music as culturally inferior. Ralph Peer seems to have been the first to apply the term to southern rural music when he called Al Hopkins's string band the Hillbillies in 1925, but given the social context of the twenties, it is not surprising to find such a label popularly affixed to a rural-derived music coming out of the South. As George B. Tindall has shown, the image of the South as a "benighted" region—a land of backwardness, decadence, violence, superstition, and racism—gained greater strength in the

1920s, a decade characterized by national progress and social change.[8] In the minds of many observers and social critics, the people who gave the nation the Scopes monkey trial, the Ku Klux Klan, sharecropping, and prohibition had also produced hillbilly music. The music thus began its commercial evolution laden with negative connotations that it never really overcame, presumed to be the product of cultural degenerates and a projection of their demented values. The fact that the music was commercial also influenced the reactions of some people. Hillbilly music, the creation of the folk, did not conform to the romanticized conceptions of folk music so prevalent in the '20s, and it certainly did not square with the self-images that many upper-class and for-ward-looking southerners held of themselves and their region. If anything, the music seemed to represent the victory of the Snopesian South, the distasteful fusion of poor white music with the boorish business culture of the United States. The radio hillbillies seemed far different from the prevalent conception, held by both scholars and the public alike, of the folk as the isolated and unchanging descendants of Elizabethan settlers, and the music they performed could hardly be accepted as the remnants of medieval and pastoral balladry.

If some people rejected hillbilly music because of what they considered its crassness, others may have gravitated toward it because it represented to them an image of an older and simpler America and an alternative to the frenetic dance music of the 1920s. Henry Ford was not alone among Americans in deploring the rise of jazz and the subordination of the less complex and more restrained dance music of earlier, rural America. He struck a receptive chord in the hearts of many people when he sponsored a series of oldtime fiddling contests after 1926 in several cities of the United States. If people in the United States yearned to hear the good old songs of the nineteenth century or earlier, they were most likely to hear them on the radio barn dances or on the hillbilly recordings. The barn dances tried hard to project an aura of wholesome, down-to-earth, family-style entertainment, and radio program directors and advertisers often insisted that hillbilly performers affect rustic attire and rustic names, even though the performers might have preferred to dress in a more urban manner.

Issued beginning in the mid-1920s, 78 rpm hillbilly records are valuable documents depicting song material that urban America had forgotten: variants of British ballads and love songs, frontier fiddle tunes and play-party songs, camp-meeting songs and tunes from the shape-note hymnals, and a very large body of songs that originated as pop songs in the nineteenth century, such as "Put My Little Shoes Away," "Over the Garden Wall," "The Fatal Wedding," and "I'll Twine 'mid the Ringlets," later known as "Wildwood Flower." Lovers of old-time sentimental songs had no need to despair about their disappearance, for they could hear such numbers, or similar ones, on hillbilly recordings, albeit with southern rural accents. In the newly composed songs found on hillbilly records one could also find a reaffirmation of traditional religion and conventional morality, but in many of the songs of rural white southerners, old and new, one could also detect voices of concern for the present or the future, of dissatisfaction, and of protest.

Country music, whether in its hillbilly form, or in its more recent sophisticated manifestations, has always been a music of social commentary. Blind Alfred Reed, for instance, voiced a concern felt by many conservative Americans in the 1920s when he sang "Why do you bob your hair, girls?" A very popular type of song found on hillbilly records in that decade was the event song, a type reminiscent of the broadside ballads that commented on topical events of the day. Such songs as "The Sinking of the Titanic," "The Wreck of the 1256," "The Fate of Edward Hickman," "Bruno Richard Hauptmann," and "The Death of Floyd Collins" invariably pointed out morals that could be drawn from tales of tragedy and disaster. Floyd Collins, according to the ballad of 1925, met his death in a sandstone cave because he had not followed his father's advice. Hillbilly music, as the product of the rural South, conveyed the conflicting impulses and images of the region that gave it birth.[9] It was a melding of rural and urban influences; it was simultaneously southern and American; and its performers and audience were torn by opposing desires, clinging to a self-image of rustic simplicity while at the same time striving to be accepted in an urban, middle-class milieu. Consequently, the music encompassed widely divergent strains. Hillbilly singers alternately condemned and celebrated demon rum, for instance. Some of the heaviest drinkers were the most ardent advocates, in song, of abstinence, prohibition, or both. Many hillbilly songs defended law and order on the one hand and on the other glorified outlaws such as Jesse James and Billy the Kid. On occasion, the music applauded humanity's mastery over the machine, as in the classic "John Henry," the story of a black steeldriver that was more popular among hillbillies than among African Americans. But hillbilly songs just as often lauded the machine itself, as in Uncle Dave Macon's paean to the Ford automobile, "On the Dixie Bee Line." Hillbilly singers might extol the virtues of the old home place, and the sense of security it represented, while conversely romanticizing the rambling man who refused to be tied down to such a life. Country music's first two great influential acts, the Carter Family and Jimmie Rodgers, embodied the conflicting impulses of love of home and fascination with the wanderer both in their lives and in their repertories.

During the same short time span in the first four days of August 1927 the Carters and Jimmie Rodgers were recorded for the first time in Bristol,

Tennessee, by a crew of Victor recording engineers directed by Ralph Peer. A.P. Carter, his wife Sara, and A.P.'s sister-in-law Maybelle, came from nearby Maces Spring in southwestern Virginia to inaugurate a family career that endured as such until 1943 and, in various other manifestations, for generations after that. Maybelle Carter, who came to be called Mother Maybelle, performed with her daughters as part of her son-in-law Johnny Cash's traveling show until her death in 1978.[10] The Carter Family built up a large following through their Victor, Columbia, and Decca recordings, as well as by personal appearances and transcribed broadcasts over the legendary Mexican border station XERF. Even though their reputation spread, the Carter Family never moved very far stylistically from their origins. They always sounded like a group singing for a small circle of friends gathered in a family parlor or at a church social, and the bulk of their songs came from the paperback hymnals or from the nineteenth-century song sheets. Even when they moved toward the inclusion of newly composed songs, as all hillbilly performers did, their choices still reflected the values, aspirations, and fears of the rural Protestant South and its longings for stability in a world succumbing to change. A.P. and Sara were divorced during much of their performing career, so when the Carter Family sang "Will the Circle Be Unbroken," one of their most enduring songs, they sang with an acute consciousness of family dissolution, something many of their listeners knew too well but longed to forget.

Jimmie Rodgers, on the other hand, had never enjoyed the advantages of a settled home life. Born near Meridian, Mississippi, in 1897, he lost his mother before he was four years old, and because his father's railroad work often took him away from home, the boy lived in a succession of relatives' homes. Rodgers became a railroad worker when he was fourteen years old and remained one until 1925, when a worsening case of tuberculosis forced his retirement. By late 1927, when he became a full-time professional musician, Rodgers had seen more of the world and had sampled a broader range of experiences than most rural southerners could have imagined. His railroad work had taken him to Texas and the Southwest, and he had lived for a brief period in New Orleans. Before he made his first records for Victor, Rodgers had played in a dance band in Meridian, had toured the southern mountains as a blackface entertainer with a medicine show, and had played briefly with a string band in Asheville, North Carolina.

While the Carter Family was a repository of nineteenth-century popular music, Rodgers was more responsive to the popular currents of his own day, and his recordings were important vehicles by which such forms as yodeling, Dixieland jazz, and Hawaiian music moved into the country genre. The enduring and eclectic nature of his music is evidenced by the diverse character of artists who offered recorded tributes to Rodgers in the last decades of the twentieth century, including Merle Haggard, Leon Redbone, and Bob Dylan. One hundred years after Rodgers's birth, even the Rock-and-Roll Hall of Fame in Cleveland prepared a special tribute to him because of his influence on early expressions of that form. Eclecticism was only one of his contributions to country music, however. Through his songs, his devil-may-care personality, and his early death at the age of thirty-six, Rodgers contributed to an enduringly popular mystique in country music, that of the free, rambling, but star-crossed young man. There was nothing menacing in his personality, and certainly no tinge of the outlaw, but Rodgers projected the image of a man who had been everywhere and who had done everything. He was the worldlywise rounder who loved the women and left them behind, but who also possessed a tender solicitude for children and mothers, as in "Sleep, Baby, Sleep" and "Mother, the Queen of My Heart." Rodgers often sang about hoboes, as in "Waiting for a Train" and "Hobo Bill's Last Ride," rounders, as in "My Rough and Rowdy Ways," and convicts, as in "Moonlight and Skies" and "Ninety Nine Year Blues," both written by a real convict, Raymond E. Hall, then serving in the Texas state prison. Rodgers, in short, drew upon images that had been popular among white southerners' European ancestors and perhaps among poor and oppressed people everywhere. Although the ramblingman image had Old World origins, it gained a new validity during the Depression era among poor, confined, and isolated rural southerners who could find escape, if nothing else, in an identification with the unfettered and footloose characters who populated much of the music they heard on their radios and record machines. Hillbilly music, like the people who produced and nourished it, was typically ambivalent about home, the country, and the South, idealizing them while exhibiting a fascination with rambling. Home was often extolled after it was abandoned, and the wandering life was sometimes glorified because it was unattainable. Ironically, but not surprisingly, Jimmie Rodgers's favorite song among his own recordings was "Daddy and Home."

Another expression of the white grassroots mind that underwent commercialization during the 1920s was gospel music. White gospel music has always been closely related to the rural secular music of the South, with both phenomena drawing from the folk resources of the region. Secular and sacred music represented two different expressions of the same mind, and they experienced similar commercial evolutions. The gospel music business, which became a major facet of the nation's entertainment industry, developed out of two aspects of nineteenth-century American religious history, the shape-note singing schools and the evangelical revivals. But it drew much of its dynamism and much of its personnel from the Holiness-Pentecostal movement of the late nineteenth and early twentieth centuries. By 1900 a great stream of religious songs, fed by the big-city revivals of the era, flowed into U.S. popular culture, and in the South such songs circulated invariably in shape-note form. On an average of twice a year, several publishing houses printed paperback hymnals designed for church conventions and singing schools. The publishing houses were sometimes aligned with religious denominations, or adjuncts of them, but even the independent ones defined their goals in missionary terms. They were intent on evangelizing the nation through the power of song.

While concerns such as those headed by A.J. Showalter and R.E. Winsett made important contributions in popularizing and distributing southern gospel music, the Vaughan Publishing Company of Lawrenceburg, Tennessee, made the most crucial innovations in the marketing of the music. Until at least the late 1930s it was the most effective of the southern gospel publishing houses. The founder of the company, James D. Vaughan, was a devout member of the Church of the Nazarene, one of the principal denominations of the Holiness movement in America. Vaughan never wavered in his commitment to the Holiness faith, and he was acutely perceptive in his ability to advertise his belief while also enhancing the commercial viability of his publishing concern. Vaughan and his gospel cohorts preached an otherworldly message, but they very astutely utilized the techniques of the world to popularize that vision. Vaughan's business was the selling of songbooks, and as a salesman he was an ingenious innovator. He appears to have been the first southern publisher to send quartets to churches and singing conventions to plug the Vaughan songbooks. The members of the early quartets were employees of the company who presumably shared J.D. Vaughan's spiritual mission. Their purpose was to advertise the songbooks and their contents, not their own particular talent. In 1922 one of the Vaughan quartets, of which there were as many as sixteen on the road during the decade, recorded for a Vaughan-owned label. Though the discs were not recorded in the South, "they were the first records designed for a specifically southern audience."[11] Then in 1923, Vaughan opened radio station WOAN, one of the earliest commercial stations in Tennessee, as a medium for advertising his company's religious merchandise.

As important as it was, the Vaughan Company was only one of several publishing houses that carried on the shape-note tradition. A.J. Showalter, a descendant of Joseph Funk of Singer's Glen, Virginia, and the composer of "Leaning on the Everlasting Arms," conducted such a business in Dalton, Georgia, and educated a long list of Southerners who in turn fanned out through the South holding their own music schools. R.E. Winsett published his widely circulated songbooks in Dayton, Tennessee, site of the Scopes trial in 1925. Eugene Bartlett worked through his Hartford Music Company in Hartford, Arkansas. F.O. Eiland and the Trio Company of Texas made a significant impact on regional gospel publishing. The chief competition to Vaughan, however, came from J.R. Baxter, from Tennessee, and from Virgil O. Stamps, from Texas, who merged their concerns in 1926 to create another giant in the field of southern gospel music.

Stamps-Baxter dominated much of the white gospel market until World War II, particularly in the region west of the Mississippi River. V.O. Stamps, the son of a saw mill operator and state legislator in Gilmer, Texas, sent out several quartets bearing the name of "Stamps" and often sang bass and acted as the genial master-of-ceremonies in one of the touring quartets. One of these quartets, the Stamps All-Star Quartet, which included V.O.'s brother Frank as bass singer, achieved a wide popularity and did much to establish a separate identity for the quartets apart from the publishing house, a development quartets representing other houses soon emulated. In October 1927 the quartet made some recordings for Victor under the direction of the ubiquitous Ralph Peer, apparently without the consent or foreknowledge of Virgil Stamps. Peer encouraged them to record some of the older, stately hymns, but one of their alternative, newer selections, "Give the World a Smile," became an immediate hit. In fact, it became one of the best-loved songs in the Southwest, primarily because every Stamps-sponsored quartet used it as a theme song. "Give the World a Smile" featured a bass lead on the chorus, but was made distinctive by the use of an after-beat rhythm in which the other three quartet members made antiphonal, syncopated responses to the lead. The style, obviously borrowed from instrumental jazz, was likely the product of gospel pianists who had absorbed the technique from secular sources. The pianist for the Stamps All-Star Quartet, for instance, was Dwight Brock from Gadsden, Alabama, who expressed an affinity for the work of such pop pianists as Little Jack Little and Whispering Jack Smith.

White gospel quartet music drew considerable inspiration from the dominant secular music forms of the nation. Quartets, in fact, often sang popular songs or "semiclassical" numbers such as "The Lost Chord" during their concerts. Gospel singers learned much of their four-part harmony from shape-note singing schools, but they also picked up elements from barbershop quartets, black gospel quartets, and the other popular quartets of their day. Publishing houses promoted competition among their quartets, and singers adopted mannerisms and techniques that contributed to their public appeal and acceptance. Religious zeal either gave way to show business or made an accommodation to it.

By the end of the 1920s the white gospel quartets had taken long strides away from both the publishing houses and the singing schools and had become more thoroughly immersed in the world of commercial competition, using the same methods of marketing and distribution—radio, recording, and personal appearances—that were available to secular singers. As the nation descended into the depths of the Great Depression, the quartet business suffered drastically, but the messages of the gospel songs brought succor and relief to millions of Americans, especially those in the South. No music was ever more cherished by southerners than such songs as "Precious Memories," "Farther Along," and "If I Could Hear My Mother Pray Again." No amount of market innovation, sophisticated production techniques, or borrowing from secular forms could turn southern lovers of gospel music from the artists who brought it to them. Like the people of the other relatively unassimilated subcultures of the South, rural whites and their plain-folk cousins in the cities and towns of the region or the nation as a whole faced a time of trial indeed during the Depression. It changed their lives, and it changed their music.

Chapter 5

THE GREAT DEPRESSION AND NEW TECHNOLOGIES

The Great Depression was a cultural as well as an economic event. Along with the distress it brought to virtually every segment of the U.S. economy, including the entertainment industry, it also wrought serious changes in the nature and structure of the various forms of commercialized southern folk music. For the most part, the period from 1929 to 1941 was far from disastrous for southern musicians. It was a transitional era during which southern regional folk styles evolved and matured, becoming more professionalized and gaining greater national recognition and acceptance. The record industry severely curtailed its operations under the impact of hard times. Some of the smaller companies collapsed, while a few were consolidated with other companies. RCA Victor responded to the economic crisis by introducing a budget label called Bluebird, specializing in hillbilly and race recordings. In 1934 Decca came into existence with a thirty-five-cent record that proved so successful that it encouraged other companies to introduce cheaper subsidiary lines and to lower the prices for other records.

In the urge to economize, record companies dropped from their rosters some of the folk talent that had shown little commercial appeal. Traditional songs, or adaptations of them, did not disappear from recordings, but their numbers declined during the 1930s. While record companies retrenched economically, performers sought fresh and commercially stimulating material to satisfy the tastes of their gradually expanding audiences. Performers who began to record for the first time in the 1930s were as likely to have learned their material from commercial recordings of entertainers of the 1920s as the latter were to have learned theirs from the folk sources of their communities. Therefore, many of the folk songs that appeared on recordings, on radio performances, and in personal appearances in the thirties were learned from earlier commercial sources.

While newer and younger personnel affected the nature and scope of southern grassroots music forms, the inexorable force of technological innovation probably did more to alter the character of commercially available folk music in the United States. The replacement of acoustical recording by electrical innovations in 1926 greatly improved the fidelity of recorded sound, and the introduction of electrical transcription in the mid-1930s expanded the radio audience potential for all entertainers. This process of recording radio shows made it possible for performers with regular broadcasting commitments to go on tours, leaving behind recorded shows that could be played in their absence, thus expanding their audience through personal appearances promoting their radio programs. Electrical transcriptions also could be played on other radio stations, further expanding the audience base of the artists. The development of microphones changed both the presentation and nature of music. The amplification that microphones made possible encouraged the development of both "natural" and contrived styles. Singers could be heard, and could hear themselves, in front of large or noisy audiences, and they were also freer to experiment and improvise. Most crucial, however, in the modification of rural or folk-derived musical forms was the introduction of electrically amplified instrumentation. Although musicians had long experimented with electronics, the first commercially successful employment of electric instruments came in the mid-1930s when guitarists, first in blues and jazz and soon thereafter in country music, attached primitive electrical pickups to their instruments. Instrumental amplification allowed soloists, especially guitarists, to develop improvisational styles featuring subtle or intricate note patterns and chord progressions that would have been virtually inaudible on acoustic instruments in noisy settings.

While the recording industry was forced to make serious adjustments in order to survive the Depression, radio was in its heyday. Radio was the cheapest form of entertainment available, and it brought both solace and security to anxiety-ridden Americans who sought escape in its programming. In the South, depending on the location, one could usually begin the day, or spend the noon hour, which radio programmers considered primetime, listening to a program of hillbilly, Cajun, blues, gospel and ethnic styles of music. Radio entertainers generally built their personal appearance schedules on the strength of their radio broadcasts. The size and scope of the listening audience could be estimated by the nature of the correspondence received from fans—hence the hillbilly admonition, "Keep them cards and letters coming in."

Among the most powerful forces in the popularization of hillbilly and gospel music were the Mexican border stations, popularly called the X-stations because of their call letters and somewhat untouchable characteristics. They were powerful, literally, in the days before extensive government regulation of radio broadcasting, using extremely high-powered transmitters to send their signals throughout North America. These stations were owned by Mexican nationals but were often leased or managed by businessmen from the United States who used them to promote their own products or those of other advertisers. The first of these entrepreneurs was the "goat gland man," Dr. J.R. Brinkley, who began the operation of XERA, later XERF, in 1932 in Villa Acuña, Mexico, just across the Rio Grande from Del Rio, Texas. Brinkley became a wealthy man by selling his medical books and advertising his scheme to promote male sexual rejuvenation through goat gland transplants. XERF, and other stations such as XEAW, XENT, XEPN, and XEG, "the Voice of North America," aimed their transmitters toward the United States and blanketed North America with power that sometimes exceeded 100,000 watts. The X stations, furthermore, exerted another kind of power on the musical culture of the South and of the U.S.

Much of the material from their broadcasts became part of the folklore of the twentieth century. Long-winded announcers hawked the virtues of such patent medicines and remedies as Kolorbak and Black-Draught, as well as baby chicks, songbooks, prayer cloths, resurrection plants, and "autographed pictures of Jesus Christ that glow in the dark." Once-in-a-lifetime offers constantly advertised as scheduled to go off the air forever at midnight somehow generally reappeared the next night on another program. X-station broadcasts could be heard occasionally in every region of the United States and in Canada, though it is difficult to know who listened to them. Late-night listeners, particularly people who had car radios and listened while driving in order to stay awake, were most likely to hear these broadcasts because the border stations were often the only ones on the air during these hours. Regardless of who they were, or what their motivations may have been, listeners to the Mexican border stations could hear, usually by transcription, some of the most important acts in hillbilly and gospel music. The Carter Family, the Pickard Family, the Callahan Brothers, Jesse Rodgers (Jimmie's cousin), Cowboy Slim Rinehart, J.R. Hall (the Utah Cowboy, who was really from Texas), the Stamps Quartet, and the Chuck Wagon Gang were among the most prominent entertainers who could be heard on border radio. Something of the rural South thus made its way into the nation at large through the medium of border radio programming.

Radio's exploitation of folk music was, of course, accompanied by the expanded role of commercial advertising. Hillbilly music, for example, reached its first national audience through the sponsorship of certain products that became household words through their association with various hillbilly acts or shows. Crazy Water Crystals, produced in Mineral Wells, Texas, was the premier national advertiser of country music during the 1930s. Although it was ballyhooed as a curative for a wide array of ailments, Crazy Water Crystals was essentially a laxative. Beginning first in Texas with the sponsorship of local radio shows, the Crazy Water Company soon branched out into cities throughout the Midwest, South, and East, aligning its product with all kinds of music shows, but especially those with a country flavor. In the Carolinas and Georgia, the company was particularly energetic in its recruitment and use of hillbilly talent. A Crazy Barn Dance broadcast each Saturday night from Charlotte, North Carolina, with a large roster of performers, and several hillbilly acts in the Southeast carried the term "crazy" in their titles, such as the Crazy Mountaineers and the Crazy Hillbillies. The popularity of Crazy Water Crystals did not extend beyond the 1930s, but some of the products that first gained national recognition through their association with hillbilly music became fixtures in U.S. advertising. Alka-Seltzer, for example, was catapulted toward its status as a ubiquitous household commodity in 1933 when it began sponsoring a thirty-minute segment of the National Barn Dance. The collaboration between hillbilly music and various brand names worked to the benefit of both. The music repeatedly demonstrated its ability to sell products while simultaneously entering millions of homes through its association with popular brand names advertised on radio shows. The Grand Ole Opry, though a fixture on WSM in Nashville since 1925, might never have become a show business institution in the United States had it not attained in 1939 the sponsorship of the R.J. Reynolds Tobacco Company for thirty minutes each Saturday night on NBC. Hosted first by Roy Acuff, and later by Red Foley, the Grand Ole Opry, along with pitches for Prince Albert Smoking Tobacco, moved into millions of homes where it formerly had been denied admittance.

While hillbilly music gained a national forum in the 1930s through radio exposure, race music had widened its geographic range and altered its basic forms through the migration of African Americans. Ordinary forms of population movement slowed during the Depression years, but the "great migration north," which had reached its peak during World War I and the early 1920s, and similar migrations to the West Coast did not really ebb in any significant way until well after World War II. Much of the blues music of the post-1930 era was produced by southern migrants, or by their children, in the communities of black newcomers in the North and in California. The music made occasional references to bygone southern experiences and most certainly evoked images of life "down" or "back" home, but it had a decidedly different quality from the music of the previous decade. Younger musicians, especially, rebelled against sounds that seemed too reminiscent of slavery, plantation life, or rural matters in general, so the country blues, a solo singer with a guitar, was rarely recorded after 1930. Instead, the music became more closely attuned to a generation living in the city and more sophisticated in its arrangements and instrumental accompaniment. Led by such musicians as Eddie Durham, Charlie Christian, and Aaron "T-Bone" Walker, blues performers everywhere after 1934 began electrifying their guitars. They also increased the size of their combos, adding pianos, saxophones or other horns, basses, and drums. By the end of the 1930s, the term *race* was passing out of usage and blues as it had been known was being replaced by a form more consonant with the city, what came to be known as "rhythm and blues." Like race music before it, rhythm and blues served as an umbrella phrase for a large number of black styles that were often very different from each other and were played by a diverse set of musicians. It drew energy from the boogie-woogie jazz rhythm developed by the late 1920s and prefigured even in certain ragtime pieces. Its progenitors ranged from Count Basie and Lionel Hampton to Leroy Carr, Scrapper Blackwell, Lonnie Johnson, and the Hokum Boys with Georgia Tom Dorsey. But, as the name implies, rhythm and blues was much more oriented toward dancing than country blues ever had been. It was urban, aggressive, electrified, and youth-oriented. It projected an image of hipness that was far different from the emotional qualities of the often rough-edged country blues and the rusticity to which hillbilly music still clung at the end of the '30s. Rhythm and blues also helped bring about the music revolution known as rock 'n' roll. Part of the reason this hip new set of styles emerged was that in the late 1930s and '40s, the four main record labels had such a stranglehold on the market that they inhibited creativity. The small, independent labels, and the artists drawn to them, were freer to experiment, to reach across the artificial barriers between styles. T-Bone Walker, for instance, perfected his single-note electric style in the early 1940s playing with Freddie Slack and His Orchestra and recording for Capitol, but he really made a name for himself when he began headlining with Marl Young, Jack McVea, and Al Killian and recording for such labels as Rhumboogie, Mercury, and Black & White.[1] He provided a great deal of inspiration for B.B. King, who drove the blues forward in the 1950s and said of Walker, "If I could have played like him, I would have."[2] Walker and King, like Charlie Christian, inspired guitarists and other musicians who went in a dizzying array of directions, from standard jazz to boogie to r&b and bebop, "rockabilly," and rock 'n' roll, as a result of the increasing musical freedom that flowed out of the Great Depression. B.B. King also quoted something T-Bone Walker once said, "Blues is just gospel music turned around. It's feeling great, and feeling sad right on, besides." Paul Oliver notes that much of Walker's musical inspiration, along with much of his style, came from the rhythms of church pianists, saying that the first time Walker heard boogie-woogie piano playing was "in the Holy Ghost Church in Dallas, Texas."[3] Furthermore, many r&b singers employed a shouting singing style reminiscent of many gospel soloists. Thus, for all the musical innovations underway among African-American artists, and their white imitators, a strong measure of southern traditionalism prevailed. If, as Scott DeVeaux says, "Rhythm and blues . . . became the soundtrack for the urban black experience of the late 1940s and 1950s,"[4] the form still had one foot in the old world of black gospel music.

During the Depression, black gospel music assumed a more independent identity apart from secular music than it had possessed in the '20s. To many black people a clear and unbridgeable chasm separated "sinful" music and "spiritual" music, and some religious singers would not sing a secular song. Gospel singers nevertheless exerted a powerful influence over their secular counterparts. A very large percentage of black blues and pop singers obtained their first experience singing in church and many of them began their professional careers as members of gospel quartets or choral groups. Tony Heilbut argues that many vocal techniques and stage mannerisms associated with blues and soul music actually began with gospel singers.

Several gospel quartets were on the road during the 1930s, some of which, with new personnel, remained active for decades. While their fan base was very strong in the southern states, gospel quartets attracted attention throughout the country, especially in urban areas such as the ghettoes of Chicago, Detroit, and New York. The Zion Harmonizers, the Fairfield Four, the Five Blind Boys, the Swan Silvertones, the Sensational Nightingales, the Charioteers, and the Dixie Hummingbirds were only a few of the popular black quartets that sang in churches, auditoriums, and radio stations. Engaged in intense competition with each other, such singers as Archie Brownlow of the Five Blind Boys, Rebert H. Harris of the Fairfield Four, and Claude Jeter of the Swan Silvertones relied not on beauty of voice alone, but also vocal gymnastics calculated to drive an audience to distraction. To a much greater degree than in white gospel music, where singers tended to sing with physical restraint, black gospel music stressed theatrics, and its singers pulled out all the stops to evoke the greatest audience response. Ascending into falsetto, growling a note, repeating a word over and over, or "worrying" it endlessly by bending it or prolonging it, sometimes unleashing an unearthly, almost primordial, scream, and accompanying their singing with some of the fanciest footwork seen outside of a dance hall, gospel singers pioneered in the use of methods that became commonplace decades later in the performances of such rhythm and blues and soul singers as Ray Charles, Sam Cooke, Fats Domino, Aretha Franklin, and James Brown.

If one individual can be singled out as the father of black gospel music in the United States, it is Thomas A. Dorsey, one of the great names in both southern and U.S. music history. Dorsey was born in Villa Rica, Georgia, in 1899, the son of a Baptist minister. Like many young men of his time, Dorsey was attracted to the sounds of blues and jazz. He worked for a while with Ma Rainey, and as a pianist made records under the name of "Georgia Tom" and, along with Clarence "Pinetop" Smith, the pioneer of boogie-woogie piano, as part of the Hokum Boys. Even during his most secular phase, when he was recording such risqué songs as "It's Tight like That," Dorsey never strayed very far from the faith of his childhood. The compulsion to do the work of the Lord bore fruit in 1929 in Dorsey's decision to perform only religious music. He had moved to Chicago about 1916 where he and Sallie Martin founded the Gospel Singers Convention. This association became a source and training ground for quartets and choirs that fanned out into the black communities of the nation. Dorsey's chief inspiration as a composer came from the works of Charles Tindley, an African Methodist Episcopal minister in Philadelphia in the early years of the twentieth century. Tindley may have been unknown to most southerners, but his songs circulated widely among them and became deeply loved. Such songs as "We'll Understand It Better By and By," "Stand by Me," "Take Your Burden to the Lord (Leave It There)," and "I'll Overcome Some Day," the basis for the great civil rights protest song "We Shall Overcome," were cherished by white and black southerners alike.

Dorsey was the successor, if not the protégé, of Tindley, and his songs, having the advantages of modern marketing and distribution, were even more broadly circulated. His most famous song, "Precious Lord, Take My Hand," written in 1932, grew out of deep personal loss, the death of his wife and infant son, but it became the possession of countless people in the United States. The most compelling interpretations of "Precious Lord" were those of such black singers as Mahalia Jackson, with whom Dorsey worked and toured for years, but the song was also recorded and performed by such white singers as Clyde Julian "Red" Foley, Ernie Ford, Elvis Presley, and others. Another of Dorsey's more famous songs, "Peace in the Valley," gained enormous commercial success through the recording of Kentucky-born Foley, a very popular country singer in the years following World War II. Dorsey's career had enormous influence on the total realm of gospel music, black and white, in the United States. His songs became known to an exceedingly wide spectrum of people in the U.S.; he was a longtime member of the white-dominated National Gospel Singers Convention; and his compositions appeared frequently in southern gospel songbooks.

White gospel music in the 1930s continued to be dominated by quartets. Although the publishing houses no longer monopolized the control of such quartets, the Stamps-Baxter Company still exerted a leading and innovative role in gospel music. Several quartets were on the road bearing the name of Stamps in their performing titles, a practice that enhanced both the company's business and the reputations of the quartets. V.O. Stamps reaped great publicity for his company and his singers when the Stamps "parent" quartet sang at the Texas Centennial celebration in 1936. From that appearance, the quartet earned a regular spot on 50,000–watt KRLD in Dallas, which introduced them to an even larger audience. Members of quartets still understood and explained their work as a religious mission, and their singers generally came out of the gospel singing schools. But show business persistently intruded into the styles of the singers alongside evangelistic impulses, and newer songs replaced the older hymns. Quartets competed with each other to find the lowest bass singers and the highest tenors. A few quartets, such as the Texas-based Chuck Wagon Gang, D.P. Carter and his children, Anna, Rose, and Jim, sang to guitar accompaniment. Most other gospel groups used piano accompaniment, and many quartets were in fact known by the skill and showmanship of their pianists. Such pianists as Dwight Brock and Marion Snider generally faced their audiences as they played, and with great flourishes they clowned and hammed their way through many but the most serious songs, which, of course, took great skill to accomplish while maintaining the rhythm for a high-powered quartet. In a profession that took itself and its mission very seriously, the gospel pianists often provided the only comic relief. Few people complained about the fact that many quartets were mixing great amounts of entertainment, pure and simple, with the earnest purposes of the gospel message.

As professional as their performances might be, gospel quartets were still not sufficiently commercial during the Depression years to achieve extensive economic rewards for their talents. By their very nature they were isolated from most of the performing outlets that were open to blues or country musicians. They were still generally confined to concerts in schoolhouses or auditoriums or to church-related functions where receipts were small and often based on donations. The working-class evangelical churches of the South, particularly those of a Pentecostal persuasion, provided the most receptive arenas for the gospel quartets. Energized by their commitment to "make a joyful noise unto the Lord" and showing a remarkably democratic receptivity to most musical instruments and even to secular-derived styles, the Pentecostal churches furnished enthusiastic audiences for the touring quartets and were the sources of many of the finest quartet singers. Whatever their denominational affiliations, however, the churches had little money to contribute to the singers. A quartet could expect warm hospitality, a sumptuous meal at the home of some good church member, and whatever sum the collection or "love offering" brought in. Anything extra came from the diligent hawking of songbooks, records, and photographs. In response to the preferences of their traditionalist listeners, most quartets made a point of singing many of the old familiar hymns, but within their repertories the newly composed songs always outnumbered the old. Many of these new songs came from the most popular songwriter in the white gospel field, and one of the most beloved musicians in the rural South, Albert E. Brumley.

Born on a tenant farm near Spiro, Oklahoma, in 1905, Brumley began writing songs soon after he attended a singing school near his home community in 1922. He worked as a teacher, singer, and writer for E.M. Bartlett's Hartford Music Company in Hartford, Arkansas, one of the leading shape-note publishing houses in the South, and a company that the Brumley family came to own. His first successful composition, one of the most popular gospel songs of all time, was "I'll Fly Away" (1931), featuring a spirited melody and structure reminiscent of the nineteenth-century camp meeting songs. Brumley songs thereafter entered the repertories of all the gospel quartets, moved into most of the country churches via the shape-note hymnals, appeared frequently on country recordings, and from there came into the permanent possession of the southern folk. Brumley's compositions, memorable because of their simplicity and melodic beauty, were quintessentially southern in tone and theme. They generally fell into two categories: conventional gospel songs, such as "I'll Meet You in the Morning" and "If We Never Meet Again," which stressed the heavenly joys awaiting the faithful Christian, and nostalgic rural songs, such as "Dreaming of a Little Cabin" and "Cabin in the Valley of the Pines," which reminisced about childhood, mother and father, and the old country home. Brumley's religious songs were appealing in large part because they were evangelical but nondenominational. They held no expressions of theology or polity that might alienate performers or listeners, but employed themes and imagery that were the mainstays of traditional southern Protestantism. They posited a conception of a merciful, benevolent God who waited like a shepherd to gather in wandering children amidst scenes of pastoral bliss. Brumley's nostalgic songs, on the other hand, breathed with a consciousness of life's evanescence, affectionately depicting an abandoned and decaying rural world held together only by the steadfast love of mother and father. In his religious songs, the unfulfilled wishes of this world are projected as being realized in the heavenly world to come.

While this otherworldly message was consoling to many southerners during the Depression years, others were less content to wait for economic security and human justice beyond the grave; they sought music that would either voice their discontent or provide escape from the problems of this world.

Hard times inspired protest, and protest often made its way into the messages of both blues and country songs, secular and religious, as in Big Bill Broonzy's "Black, Brown, and White," Slim Smith's "Breadline Blues," and David McCarn's "Cotton Mill Colic." Professional blues, country, and gospel singers often commented on the social and political events of the day, but the most sustained expression of protest, as opposed to commentary alone, came from humble farmers and workers who poured out their anguish in music. The textile strikes in the Southern Piedmont in 1929, the bloody conflict in the eastern Kentucky coal fields in 1931, the organizational efforts made in the Deep South by the Southern Tenant Farmers Union (STFU) from 1934 to 1936, and the southwestern dust storms of the late 1930s all produced their balladeers. As southern labor "stirred,"[5] organizers and sympathizers came in from the North to lend their support to what essentially had been spontaneous uprisings. Communist-dominated unions, such as the National Textile Workers' Union and the National Miners Union, added an explosive ingredient to the situation while also introducing a revolutionary rhetoric that had not been heard in the South since the Populist revolt of the 1890s and scarcely ever among the southern hill-country and mountain folk. According to folklorist Archie Green, "Piedmont mill villages and Cumberland mine camps became meeting grounds for the ideologies of Andrew Jackson and Karl Marx, Abraham Lincoln and Mikhail Bakunin," as conservative southern workers joined in temporary though unlikely alliances with radical northern organizers. One result was the appearance of a body of topical songs that "fused time-worn melodies with strange, revolutionary lyrics."[6]

Though the textile, coal, and sharecropper strikes ended as tragic exercises in futility, they had an unintended effect on the music of the United States. Northern organizers leaving the South took back home with them a large body of songs that helped fuel the incipient urban folk music movement of the '30s. The lifespans of most of these songs were short, but a few of them, such as Florence Reece's rousing "Which Side Are You On?" inspired by police repression in Harlan County, Kentucky, have endured as major documents of the quest for social justice in the U.S. Some of the southern folk balladeers actually became better known than their songs at least among the liberal intellectual community in the North. The murder in 1929 of Ella May Wiggins, the balladeer of the Gastonia textile workers, made her a martyr to radicals in the U.S. and beyond, and the names of Aunt Molly Jackson and her half-sister Sara Ogan and half-brother Jim Garland, from the Kentucky coal fields, and

John Handcox, the black preacher and songwriter for the STFU, were soon known and revered among liberals and radicals far afield from the songwriters' southern homes.

One name eventually came to dominate among protest-song writers, however, that of Woodrow Wilson "Woody" Guthrie, born in 1912 in Okemah, Oklahoma. The shaping of Guthrie's social consciousness began in the early 1930s during his residence in Pampa, Texas, and in his rambles through the oil towns of the Southwest. His reputation as the poet of the Okie migrants and as the Dust Bowl balladeer, however, did not begin to develop until the late 1930s, after he had lived among the Okies in California for several years working as a hillbilly singer on KFVD in Los Angeles. He moved to New York in 1940 in the company of actor Will Geer and became part of that city's labor-radical movement. Guthrie's legitimate working-class credentials, his indomitable courage and good humor, and his facility as a songwriter—"Talking Dust Bowl Blues," "So Long, It's Been Good to Know You," "Philadelphia Lawyer," "Oklahoma Hills," "This Land Is Your Land"—made him the inspiration for several generations of socially conscious singers who were activists, reformers, and/or advocates of radical political and economic change. Guthrie drew from the music of people among whom he traveled—Hispanics, hillbillies, African Americans—and adapted the most traditional melodies and motifs to a call for transformation of the United States. Inspired by the suffering wrought by the Great Depression, he bent his finely tuned ear to the musical and emotional rhythms of the people and turned them into songs with uncanny blends of humor, pathos, fury, hope, and determination. Guthrie's openness and commitment to democratic ideals gave him the freedom to pull from and create music without respect to ethnic or economic distinctions, music that sounded hillbilly but drew on the diverse song traditions of black southerners and Mexican immigrants and migrants, as well as white folk from areas as diverse as the plains of Texas and Oklahoma, southern California, and Appalachia. What practically all of his music had in common was a commitment to social justice, a deep suspicion of the rich and powerful, and just as deep a faith in the good sense and goodwill of the plain folk of the United States.

Beginning in the 1930s with Ella May Wiggins, Aunt Molly Jackson, and Woody Guthrie, the protest music tradition demonstrated its enduring strength throughout the rest of the twentieth century through two vital groups of musicians: urban-born, principally northern singers such as Pete Seeger, Phil Ochs, Si Kahn, John McCutcheon, Joan Baez, and Bob Dylan, who fueled the urban folk revival of the 1960s and later, and rural, southern-born singers such as Nimrod Workman, Hedy West, Billy Edd Wheeler, James Talley,

Anne Romaine, Hazel Dickens, and Steve Earle, whose protest material arose within the context of country music. Dickens came closest to typifying and perpetuating the tradition of Aunt Molly Jackson; she wrote some of the songs and did most of the compelling singing for the sound track of the award-winning documentary film, *Harlan County, USA.* The living tradition of protest song demonstrated one of the most telling ways that southern music has affected both the consciousness and the popular culture of the United States at large.

Those effects were seen in other ways as well. While the songs of Albert Brumley evoked images of a vanishing rural South and held out the promise of a blissful home in the sky, protest singers called for the establishment of economic and social justice in this world. Most people across the country, though, North and South, generally wanted neither heavenly solace nor radical politics in their music; hence the popularity of the thoroughly escapist swing music of the '30s. The big pop bands had large followings in the South, and the region produced some leading swing musicians, such as Tex Beneke, Jack and Norma Teagarden, and Harry James, but southwestern rural musicians made significant innovations to the swing style in ways quite apart from the urbane forms produced by Paul Whiteman, the Dorsey brothers, and Glenn Miller. Musicians in the Southwest fashioned a form of music that became known as western swing, which effectively combined rural and urban motifs by using instruments ordinarily associated with rural folk music to create dance music with a swing beat. The westernmost portion of the South—Texas, Louisiana, Oklahoma—was peculiarly situated to produce grassroots music forms of a hybrid nature because of its ethnic and racial diversity, the influence of nearby New Orleans, the emergence of the oil boom, and the sway of the cowboy culture. The region was heavily rural until World War II, but the presence of alternative cultures and competing economic systems contributed to the breaking down of traditional patterns earlier than in the southeastern states. Texas, for example, has contributed the largest number of musicians to the country music profession and has always had a vigorous tradition of old-time fiddling derived from the migrants who came there from the older southern states. Nevertheless, rural Anglo musicians learned from the blacks, Cajuns, Mexicans, and Central Europeans with whom they came in contact in the sprawling Southwest and drank, sometimes deeply, of the cowboy myth. Texas fiddlers knew and loved the old-time hoedowns, but they tended to play them with greater melodic variation than elsewhere, and they also included in their repertories waltzes, schottisches, polkas, ragtime, and jazz tunes. This musical eclecticism contributed greatly to the formation of western swing.

Although its roots and its principal influences lay in country music, western swing, a term that was not really used until after World War II, was heavily indebted to pop, blues, and jazz, as well as the folk music traditions of white southerners. It evolved out of the fiddle-and-guitar bands of the Southwest, but its most crucial development came with the creation in 1931 of the Light Crust Doughboys, a radio band sponsored by the Burrus Mill and Elevator Company in Fort Worth. Two of the original members of the group, singer Milton Brown and fiddler Bob Wills, who had been performing and gradually building up a following in the Fort Worth area separately and together, joined forces and made the Doughboys wildly popular. Through personal appearances and radio programs, Brown and Wills became familiar to music fans throughout Texas and Oklahoma, a factor of great value to them after they both left the Doughboys and organized their own influential bands. They were not the only beneficiaries of the popularity of the Light Crust Doughboys. A large number of musicians in the Fort Worth area moved in and out of various bands, most notably a longstanding Fort Worth group called the Hi-Flyers, and the pathbreaking work of Brown and Wills greatly stimulated the market for their services and made Fort Worth the creative center for a new musical hybrid. Someone else who profited from the success of the music, though he could barely stand it, was the Doughboys' sometime announcer, Burrus Mill's general manager, W. Lee "Pappy" O'Daniel, who parlayed the fame he gained from the Doughboys into becoming governor of Texas and a member of the United States Senate.

After he left the Doughboys in 1932, Milton Brown formed the Musical Brownies, the most popular band in the Southwest. With Fort Worth as their headquarters, the Musical Brownies toured extensively in Texas, performing their hot dance rhythms for wildly enthusiastic audiences. The Brownies were essentially a fiddle band and played any kind of song that their dance-minded listeners wanted to hear. Although the fiddles usually took the lead, on everything from "St. Louis Blues" to "Sweet Georgia Brown" and "El Rancho Grande," they were supported by a piano and steel guitar, both played in the fashion of jazz instruments. Bob Dunn, the steel guitarist, was one of the truly pioneering musicians of country music history. His technique of guitar improvisation, marked by riffs that sounded like the bursts of a trumpet, was unique in country music, and in 1934 he became the first known country musician to electrify an instrument, an innovation soon copied by other steel guitarists such as Ted Daffan and Leon McAuliffe. Brown's death in April 1936, as the result of an automobile accident, cut short a promising career and stimulated unceasing debate among western swing fans about his and Bob Wills's relative prominence and importance to the music's development. Brown's biographer, Cary Ginell, pays tribute to Wills principally for "popularizing the genre created by Milton Brown."[7]

Born in Limestone County, Texas, in 1905 and reared in West Texas near the Hall County community of Turkey, Wills was descended from old-time fiddlers on both sides of his family. He remained essentially a hoedown or "breakdown" fiddler to the end of his life, but Wills was an eclectic music lover with a special affinity for the blues, and as a boy had been a fan of singers as diverse as Bessie Smith, Jimmie Rodgers, and Emmett Miller. The careers of Milton Brown and Bob Wills demonstrate the strong impact that phonograph recordings had on musicians who emerged professionally in the 1930s. The performances of Brown and Wills, as well as those of other musicians, were often direct copies, stage patter and all, of previous recordings, although Wills's remarks often came from medicine show routines, including blackface, he had learned and performed as a young man in his pre-Light Crust Doughboy days. After Wills left the Doughboys, he formed a band called the Playboys, played for a short time in Waco, and then moved, first to Oklahoma City, and then in 1934 to Tulsa, where he renamed the band the Texas Playboys and remained until 1942. Wills's years in Tulsa defined his particular approach to western swing, produced most of his best-known songs, and made him nationally famous.[8] Wills popularized his music through daily broadcasts over powerful KVOO, dances at Cain's Academy, a Tulsa ballroom that served as his headquarters, personal appearances throughout the South-Midwest, and, of course, phonograph recordings. No band was more revered throughout the Southwest than the Texas Playboys, and its influence on the whole field of country music is incalculable. This success stemmed not from Wills's abilities as a musician, which were famously limited. Though Cary Ginell inaccurately asserts that Wills was "incapable of . . . playing in meter,"[9] it is certainly true that he defied musical convention. Most of his musicians believed that he broke meter when he played, for instance, because he felt constrained by any limitations. He had great appreciation for blues artists who routinely broke meter, and he cared more for creating musical excitement for listeners than for observing formalities. He could not play the jazz improvisations he loved so much, though he could play the melodies of many popular tunes and was able to play some soulful, and meter-breaking, blues solos.[10]

Beginning as a fiddle band, the Texas Playboys expanded in personnel as Wills diversified the instrumentation, adding saxophones, trumpets, clarinets, piano, steel guitar, and drums to the standard guitar, banjo, and upright bass rhythm accompaniment that he used to back up the fiddles he and at least one other member of his band played. The Playboys contributed little to the evolution of jazz, and there is little evidence that the jazz world ever recognized the band's merits. Some jazz luminaries such as Artie Shaw were positively loathsome in their disregard for Wills and his band. Few bandleaders of any description, however, could have avoided being envious of the crowds the Playboys drew. They played country fiddle tunes, "jumped-up" blues, and the popular swing music of the Depression era and early years of World War II, anything Wills wanted them to play as long as people could dance to it, without any fear of inconsistency or incompatibility. In style, size, and repertory the Texas Playboys often resembled the swing bands, but their central use of fiddles and the steel guitar planted them squarely in the country music tradition, and it is there that Wills and his musicians made their most lasting impact. Tommy Duncan, chief vocalist of the Playboys for many years, inspired a host of country singers. Smoky Dacus, the Playboys' first drummer, is commonly believed to have been the first person to play such an instrument in country music. Leon McAuliffe built on Bob Dunn's foundation and played a major role in changing the steel guitar from a pop instrument to one of the dominant sounds in country music. Rhythm guitarist Eldon Shamblin developed a sliding chord/bass note combination technique by changing chords on practically every beat and supplying his own bass line. He not only helped smooth out the Playboys' music but also dazzled generations of guitarists in every field of vernacular music. The influence of such Playboy fiddlers as Jesse Ashlock, Louis Tierney, Johnny Gimble, and Wills himself, was strongly felt in country music, and a large number of songs—ranging from "San Antonio Rose" and "Take Me Back to Tulsa" to "Maiden's Prayer" and "Faded Love"—became standards known to virtually all country singers and, in fact, many artists in the mainstream of popular music in the U.S. and beyond.

Texas bands as a whole, including those that were only loosely related to swing music, began to exert a powerful influence on country music toward the end of the 1930s, although the chief influence of Texas music did not come until after World War II. The music of the western swing bands was heard far and wide on recordings, and several bands circulated their music through personal appearances. Beginning in 1935, Adolph Hofner fronted a band out of San Antonio that remained regionally popular for decades and combined German dance music, especially polkas and waltzes, with western swing. Headquartered in Beaumont, Cliff Bruner, the great fiddler who had once played with the Musical Brownies, worked the southwestern area of Louisiana extensively with his band, the Wanderers. Bruner is thus largely responsible for the spread of the swing style among Cajun musicians. Through attending Bruner dances, and hearing swing music broadcast from Texas radio stations, young Cajuns were prompted to diversify their styles and repertories.

By the end of the '30s, Leo Soileau, who began his recording career in 1928 as a Cajun fiddler, was leading a band called the Four Aces that shifted easily from Cajun to swing. The Rayne-Bo Ramblers and the Hackberry Ramblers were other Louisiana groups that combined Cajun and country music. Founded in 1933 by fiddler Luderin Darbone, the Hackberry Ramblers kept their group intact probably longer than any other string band in the U.S. Like many other Cajun bands that came after them, the Ramblers used both French and English lyrics and employed instruments that permitted them to shift easily from one style to another: fiddle and accordion, steel and standard guitars, plus bass and drums.

Although Cliff Bruner's band influenced other musicians and showed the strong influence of western swing, particularly in Bruner's own jazzlike fiddling, it was significantly different from the Bob Wills prototype. For one thing it was smaller. Costs of maintaining a large band were high, and now that the growing use of electrical instruments permitted a small band to be heard even in the noisiest of places, most Texas bands tended to consist of four or five musicians. Noisy dance halls exerted a powerful force in molding the type of country music that emerged from Texas and spread to other places far and wide.

Particularly after the repeal of Prohibition, hundreds of musicians found employment in bars, taverns, and dance halls where they created a subgenre of music that came to be known as honky-tonk. Honky-tonk musicians established a beat strong enough for dancing, but their music was essentially oriented around lyrics and aimed at working-class listeners. While their songs typically dealt with their listeners' values, preoccupations, and fears, including the problems of drink, illicit love, and divorce, many songs dealt specifically with the milieu in which the performers worked, the honky-tonk itself. Al Dexter, from Troup, Texas, recorded in 1936 one of the first hillbilly songs to carry the word in its title, "Honky Tonk Blues," and during World War II he had a smash hit, "Pistol Packin' Mama," which recalled the turbulent atmosphere of honky-tonk life during the East Texas oil boom of the '30s. He and other Texas cohorts, such as Ted Daffan, Floyd Tillman, Moon Mullican, and, preeminently, Ernest Tubb, wrote or recorded songs that increasingly made their way into the larger world of country music. Furthermore, the music they created soon became essentially the sound of national country music, as the styles of the Southwest fused with those of the Southeast in the 1940s.

As important as style fusion was in the obliteration of regional differences within country music, a common dress or uniform often seemed to be the most apparent unifying factor. Up until the late 1950s, virtually every country singer from the West Virginia hills to the Texas Plains dressed in some

semblance of cowboy costume and called themselves something such as "Tex,"
"Slim," "Hank," "the Lone Cowboy," or "the Girls of the Golden West." The
cowboy image would have been appealing to country singers even without
Hollywood, and the man on horseback was certainly a much more romantic
figure to the people of the United States than was the backward hillbilly. But
the silver screen in the 1930s made a most powerful contribution to the myth
of the cowboy and its identification with country music. In 1934 Gene Autry,
of Tioga, Texas, sang in a Ken Maynard film and ushered in the era of the
singing cowboy. In the following ten years Autry did more to introduce country music to a national audience than did any other country singer. In so
doing, he popularized the guitar among American youth and contributed
mightily to the equating in the public mind of the image of the cowboy with
the country singer. The popularity of the singing cowboy was not lost on
Hollywood moguls, and Autry was soon followed by other cowboy singers,
including Herb Jeffries, a black Hollywood singing cowboy. The fan of Saturday afternoon cowboy movies might see Tex Ritter, Roy Rogers, Rex Allen,
Jimmie Wakely, Johnny Bond, Eddie Dean, the Sons of the Pioneers, or the
Riders of the Purple Sage, all of whom began as country singers and who
maintained singing careers along with their professions as actors. Other country singers, such as Ernest Tubb, Jimmie Davis, and Bob Wills, made occasional appearances in cowboy movies, and a few people who became well known
country songwriters, such as Fred Rose and Cindy Walker, contributed songs
to the screen cowboys. The Hollywood singing cowboy largely disappeared
from U.S. popular culture after World War II, but he left his mark upon
country music. With the exception of an occasional number such as "El Paso,"
cowboy songs declined in the country repertory, but the cowboy mystique
endured in the wearing of cowboy costumes and the sporting of cowboy mon-
ikers, and enjoyed a resurgence in the last quarter of the twentieth century
through the work of Riders in the Sky, Sons of the San Joaquin, Red Steagall,
Michael Martin Murphey, and Don Edwards, who also helped inspire and
often contributed to a boom in popularity of cowboy poetry. Along with the
emergence in the 1930s of other "western" styles such as honky-tonk and
western swing, the music of the Hollywood singing cowboys also contributed
to the shaping of the once-popular term "country and western." Their legacy
evolved into two general streams of behavior and understanding, one that
drew on the real or supposed symbolism of cowboy culture to celebrate such
virtues as steadfastness and self-reliance and one that lauded rebellious, un-
tamed, even countercultural aspects of the cowboy lifestyle. Both manifestations of the continuing appeal of cowboy culture tapped into modern-day
concerns and fantasies; both had their adherents, and their precedents, in the

South; and both generated considerable revenue for the entertainers who popularized them.

As the United States entered World War II, the grassroots music forms of the South demonstrated their regional origins and identification. In various ways, however, the music of the South was already being exported to other regions of the United States and was moving into the consciousness of the nation generally. Population migrations had always played powerful roles in the spread of southern music. Blues, jazz, and black gospel music had traveled north and west with African-American migrations, and although the migration of southern whites was not as extensive as that of blacks or caused exclusively by the hard times of the Depression, the Okie exodus to California in the late 1930s did much to transplant hillbilly music to that state's sunny climes, becoming what James Gregory calls the "language of a subculture."[11] As southerners left the marginal economy of their region to seek employment in other cities, flocking to the auto plants of Detroit, the rubber plants of Akron and Dayton, Ohio, the packinghouses and oil refineries of Chicago, or to industrial work in cities closer to the South such as Cincinnati or St. Louis, they often took their musical preferences with them and permanently implanted them in new southern enclaves around the United States.

Even without migration, southern-derived musical forms would have circulated throughout much of the nation via the media. By 1941, radio had made much of the nation aware of the folk-derived music of the South through the broadcasts of the Mexican border stations, such 50,000–watt domestic stations as WBAP in Fort Worth and WWVA in Wheeling, West Virginia, and the Grand Ole Opry on NBC each Saturday night. The movie industry had given employment to many country singers while also providing them with an audience that might not otherwise have given them a hearing. Furthermore, of course, phonograph recordings made by southern-born entertainers might conceivably wind up in any home in the U.S. The extent of circulation or the sales figures of recordings issued before World War II is hard to gauge accurately, but hillbilly and blues records had been nationally advertised, as in Sears Roebuck and Montgomery Ward catalogs, since the 1920s. Popularity or "Hit Parade" charts were not nearly so common in the 1930s as they later became, but *Billboard* had begun to run its charts by the end of the decade. Even before the war brought enormous changes to entertainment in the United States and exerted its homogenizing effects on the country's musical tastes, records by such southern-born entertainers as Louis Jordan, Nat "King" Cole, Bob Wills, and Jimmie Davis were already appearing on jukeboxes in areas outside the South. Furthermore, songs from such sources were occasionally being "covered" by pop singers. For instance, Bing Crosby, who dipped frequently into the country music songbag, had a huge hit recording of "San Antonio Rose." The music of the grassroots South was gradually making itself heard in the farthest reaches of the nation, in large part because of changes in U.S. society and in the music business during the Great Depression. The explosion of interest in the music of the South and its metamorphosis into mainstream popular music were yet to come, but they were indeed on the way.

Chapter 6

THE NATIONALIZATION
OF SOUTHERN MUSIC

World War II wrought revolutionary changes in the social structure of both the South and the nation at large. While promoting major transformations in the habits, employment, and residence of rural southerners, the war also effectively nationalized their music. The war accelerated changes that had long been under way among blacks, and to a lesser extent among whites. Wartime demands promoted a major shift in the South from agriculture to industry, thereby creating alternative opportunities for rural and small-town people, opening up new sources of wealth, and accelerating the move from the country to the city. The establishment of military bases and defense plants in the South during the war, and the burgeoning of oil, petrochemical, and aerospace centers in the 1950s, brought thousands of outsiders to the South who did not share the cultural affinities of native southerners. People who had spent their entire lives in the South found these new people and the new experiences unfolding in their midst more than a little bewildering.

As was true everywhere during the '40s, southern families confronted social pressures that had never seemed quite so overwhelming in a rural environment. Traditional family solidity was weakened; women were faced with greater pressure to bring in outside income; and children found alternative role models among new acquaintances in towns and cities and among those provided by the media, whose writers and performers knew or cared little about the pressures of change in the South. The new life in the city, especially in an industrial atmosphere, brought both frustration and liberation, and southerners made adjustments with varying degrees of success. Generational, gender, and race relations affected the ways most migrants adapted to life in the cities and in industrial cultures, with profound social consequences on family, regional, and even national levels. These social changes and socioeconomic transformations contributed to events as momentous as the civil rights revolution of the late 1950s and early '60s, but they also changed aspects of life that seemed at first glance not to be so momentous, such as the ways southern youth strove for cultural identity. Social change had always come slowly in the South, and the effects exerted on the youth did not become readily apparent until at least a decade after the war. Among the results were the explosion known as rock 'n' roll and the consequent shattering of older concepts of popular music in the United States.

While important demographic changes took place within the South, the region asserted itself just as dramatically in the nation at large through population migrations. The movement of African Americans from the South to the North and West, which had been significant since 1914, surged to even greater heights during World War II. Black people generally fled the South and the economic and personal oppression they often suffered there, but large numbers of white southerners left the region, too. White migration, much of it from the Upper South, was generally motivated by the desire for improved economic opportunities. By failing to provide economic security for rural poor whites, the South essentially exiled many of its most loyal sons and daughters. Lured by wartime prosperity and new defense jobs, thousands of rural and small-town southerners moved to Detroit, Washington, Baltimore, Philadelphia, Cincinnati, and Los Angeles, as well as to the big cities of the South. In these cities their children ultimately lost most of their rural ways and much of their southern identity. But more immediately, much of the rural South was exported to other regions as the migrants took their cultural preferences with them, continuing and accelerating trends that had begun with the migrations of the Great Depression and before. Storefront fundamentalist churches, "southern" or "redneck" bars, "soul food" or "Dixie" restaurants, and southern accents multiplied in those cities where the migrants congregated, and jukeboxes began featuring greater numbers of songs such as "San Antonio Rose," "Pistol Packin' Mama," "You Are My Sunshine," and "Born to Lose." The migrants absorbed much from their new environments, but they also implanted much of their own culture. Not only did country music attract a strong following in Detroit, Chicago, Southern California, Pennsylvania, and southern Ohio, but the music that became especially popular outside the South, probably reflecting the cultural conservatism of the migrants, tended to be music with a more traditional orientation, rather than the pop country styles that gradually emerged in the 1940s.

While southern civilians took their musical preferences all over the United States, their sons and daughters in the military took them all over the world. Some service personnel merely carried their affinity for music with them. Others performed as blues or country musicians in special service units. Northerners and southerners heard and unwittingly absorbed each other's musical prefer-

ences, from the selections they made on jukeboxes and from picking and singing sessions in barracks, on troop transports, and in battlefield rest areas and
other places where they found themselves thrown together in the kinds of
imposed unions created by war. People in military service were starved for
anything reminiscent of home and delighted at the appearance of any kind of
musical performer, whether jazz, blues, pop, or country. Many people were
therefore exposed to various kinds of music to which they had never before
deigned to listen. Some people no doubt recoiled from the experience of listening to country music with the feeling that it was nothing more than one
long, atrocious, nasal lament, but others developed a liking for it, as did Julian
Aberbach, who came home from military service and founded Hill and Range
Publishers, one of the most important publishing houses for country music.
The spread of such music through Europe caught the ear of Chris Strachwitz,
who emigrated to the United States from Austria at the age of twelve. He fell
in love with grassroots music of the U.S., became a noted record collector,
founded Arhoolie Records and Down Home Music, and became one of the
most influential popularizers of Tejano, Cajun and hillbilly music in the country
and beyond.[1] Musical preferences among people in the service often reflected
their opposing cultural backgrounds, and disputes over radio or jukebox selections, which sometimes descended into fights, often reflected North-South
antagonisms. Military units were not racially integrated until the Truman administration, but after that time barracks and service clubs periodically rever-
berated with violent clashes between black and white servicemen concerning
tastes in music.

Changes in the music industry during the war promoted the growth of
southern-derived music forms. The number of jukeboxes, then a novelty to
many northerners as well as southerners, increased as music entrepreneurs
moved to satisfy the needs of people in the service and defense workers for a
cheap form of entertainment. Jukeboxes may have encouraged the greater use
of electric instruments as musicians noticed how the machines could cut
through the din of crowded cafes, bars, and other establishments. Jukeboxes
definitely expanded the market for the recording industry. In the 1930s, however, record executives in the major companies had discouraged radio stations
from playing records on the air because they believed the practice cut into
their sales. As Cary Ginell points out, for instance, "All of the Musical Brownies' releases for Bluebird and Decca included the phrase 'not licensed for radio
broadcast' imprinted on their labels."[2] The jukeboxes of the '40s stimulated
sales of records to people who heard songs on the coin-operated machines and
then wanted to own their favorite records so they could play them repeatedly
for free.

Two conflicts within the music industry also positively affected the airing of grassroots music. The first of these involved the struggle between two music-licensing organizations, the American Society of Composers, Authors, and Publishers (ASCAP) and Broadcast Music, Incorporated (BMI). ASCAP was founded in 1914 by Victor Herbert and others to protect the performance rights of U.S. composers. It remained a tightly knit group of writers of sophisticated popular music, reputedly biased against folk-derived forms. BMI lent active support to all kinds of grassroots music, having been founded in 1939 by broadcasters during their conflict with ASCAP over the use of ASCAP-licensed material on radio. After the expiration of a five-year contract with ASCAP, broadcasters refused to negotiate an agreement calling for a greatly increased licensing fee and on January 1, 1941, announced a ban on all material controlled by ASCAP. As a new licensing organization, BMI suffered because it had few songs in its catalog and because it had to depend on new and inexperienced songwriters. This shortage created an opportunity for southern grassroots and other writers of vernacular music. Gradually, publishing firms began to join the organization, some of whom, such as M.M. Cole and Southern Music, had extensive catalogs of country and race material. In 1942 the Nashville-based Acuff-Rose company also joined BMI, an action followed by most other new companies. By the time ASCAP and the radio networks had resolved their differences in October 1941, BMI had become securely established and its stable of grassroots-oriented publishers and writers had gained similar recognition.

Right on the heels of the ASCAP-BMI struggle came the American Federation of Musicians' recording ban of August 1, 1942, occasioned by the fear that jukeboxes and radio stations that used phonograph records were putting musicians out of work. The refusal by the recording companies to establish a fund for unemployed musicians led to the strike. The major record companies, such as Decca, Victor, and Columbia, tried to hold out against the strike, but they began capitulating in September 1943. Meanwhile, the small and independent labels, many of which specialized in country, Latin, or rhythm and blues music, signed contracts with the musicians' union almost immediately. As a result, such music gained a foothold in popular culture in the United States that it otherwise might not have enjoyed.

Despite such accidental advantages gained during World War II by southern folk-derived musical forms, they had long been developing on their own, without the encouragement enjoyed by mainstream popular music. Millions of people yearned to hear southern music, and the small record labels moved to meet the demand. Such labels proliferated during the war and on through the early 1950s, and most of them specialized in country, rhythm and blues, gospel, Tejano, Czech, Cajun, and other grassroots music of interest to local fans. Many performers who first attained local popularity in cities such as Houston, Atlanta, or Memphis later signed contracts with major companies and gained national popularity. Most of the labels eventually disappeared or were bought up by the big companies, but a few of them endured to become major companies. Most important, many of the songs that first gained local or regional popularity during this period gradually entered the national consciousness and were subsequently recorded, or "covered," by entertainers on major labels. The route these songs took usually ran through the pocketbooks of young people from middle-class homes who were receptive to music their parents generally ignored.

In the period after 1941 hillbilly music left its regional base in the South, intruded into the national scene, and gained an acceptance that had never before seemed possible. By the end of the 1950s the term "hillbilly" was being universally replaced by "country" or "country and western." At the beginning of the era of national expansion, when the rural origins of country music still clung tightly to it, the singer who dominated the music was a mountain boy from East Tennessee named Roy Acuff. After about three years of performing in his hometown of Knoxville, Acuff joined the Grand Ole Opry in 1938. He rose to immense popularity and commercial success largely on the strength of two songs, "The Wabash Cannon Ball" and "The Great Speckled Bird," both of which he performed each Saturday night for decades on the Grand Ole Opry. Acuff's singing style differed radically from those of the western swing performers and other country crooners, such as Eddy Arnold, who were becoming prominent in country music. His earnest, almost wailing, style suggested the mountain gospel churches, and his songs tended to be either old-time ballads or songs with an old-time flavor. And his popularity was not confined to the Southeast or the Deep South. He drew large crowds wherever he traveled. For instance, when he performed at the Venice Pier in Los Angeles, local promoters feared that the immense crowd who came to hear him, no doubt including many former southerners, would cause the pier to collapse. Acuff's rise to fame, which helped him become, in 1963, the first living performer to be elected to the Country Music Hall of Fame, paralleled that of the Grand Ole Opry and, in fact, contributed significantly to the show's new prominence. The broadcast ran from 7:30 to midnight each Saturday night and because of its presence on 50,000–watt, clear-channel WSM-Nashville, the Grand Ole Opry already had a South-wide audience before it blossomed nationally after 1939 on the thirty-minute NBC segment. Acuff hosted the show while he was at the peak of his popularity, but after the war the program was hosted by Red Foley, a smooth singer and genial master of ceremonies, who was supported by numerous guest artists and two well-known comedians, Rod Brasfield and Minnie Pearl (Sarah Ophelia Colley). Acuff continued to be indispensable to the Opry's image and appeared on the show virtually to his dying day.

Roy Acuff was only the first of several "stars" who came to the Opry during and just before the war years. Bill Monroe came in 1939, Ernest Tubb in 1943, and Lloyd "Cowboy" Copas and Eddy Arnold in 1944. Each of these entertainers built important and influential careers in country music, but Eddy Arnold, the first great country crooner, won the most widespread acclaim. Born the son of a sharecropper in Chester County, Tennessee, Arnold came to the Opry as a member of PeeWee King's Golden West Cowboys. But by 1945 he had embarked on a solo singing career and between 1946 and 1949 became the dominant country entertainer and one of RCA Victor's brightest stars. Though Arnold moved back and forth between the country and pop music fields at various points in his career, in the immediate postwar years he made major contributions to the building of Nashville as a major music center and of country music as an international industry.

Ernest Tubb's affiliation with the Grand Ole Opry in 1943 was the beginning of an association that lasted until his death in 1984. Born in Crisp, Texas, in 1914, Tubb made his first, largely unnoticed, records for Victor in 1936, singing and yodeling in the manner of his idol, Jimmie Rodgers. Tubb sang for about six years on Texas radio stations, ranging from San Antonio to San Angelo to Fort Worth, and in dance halls all over the state, developing a highly distinctive style of his own. When his first big record, "Walking the Floor over You," was introduced on Decca in 1941, he was living in Fort Worth and singing on KGKO and also touring much of the state in a sound truck as the Gold Chain Troubadour, sponsored by Gold Chain Flour. On the strength of "Walking the Floor," "Blue Eyed Elaine," and other songs, he was signed to a Grand Ole Opry contract in late 1942 and joined the show in January 1943. Tubb was the first major performer to take the honky-tonk style to the stage of the Grand Ole Opry. His joining of the show was more than symbolic of the fusion of southwestern and southeastern styles during the war. He was an immensely popular performer, and a large number of country entertainers became singers because of his example or shaped their styles partially in imitation of his. The country music that predominated in the years after 1946 and at least up to 1955 was a composite of styles that drew their strength largely from Texas musicians such as Ernest Tubb.

No performer represented better the multiplicity of motives and emotions, influences and results, the commingling of styles that characterized country music's first boom period after World War II than Hank Williams. The greatest country superstar of the postwar years, Williams was a young singer who acknowledged his two chief influences to be a mountain singer of sentimental and religious songs (Roy Acuff) and a honky-tonk singer from Texas (Ernest Tubb). Hiram King Williams was born on September 8, 1923, near Georgiana, Alabama. Like most rural southerners who grew up during the war years, Williams was torn between the traditional music he had always heard at home and in church and the newer dynamic, electrified sounds that were beginning to predominate in country music. He was already singing in the honky-tonks of South Alabama by the time he was fourteen. He sang in an earnest, emotional style suggestive of Roy Acuff, but drew his instrumentation from the honky-tonk bands and called himself the Drifting Cowboy. His repertory ranged broadly, including gospel songs, blues tunes, beer-drinking songs, sentimental numbers, and plenty of lonesome love songs. He was a member of the Louisiana Hayride in Shreveport when his recording of "Lovesick Blues," an old Tin Pan Alley pop blues tune, became the top country song of 1949. By 1950 he had moved up to the Grand Ole Opry and become the most talked-about performer in country music. The music had reached its highest peak of commercial success to date, and Hank Williams was its acknowledged leader.

In these booming years of country music popularity, songs with country identification increasingly began to be picked up by pop singers. The pop music industry began to be cognizant of the small labels and the "ethnic" styles they recorded. For a few years the mainstream pop singers profited from covering country and rhythm and blues tunes, as with Patti Page's "Tennessee Waltz," Rosemary Clooney's "Half as Much," and Georgia Gibbs's "Dance With Me, Henry." Before long, however, mainstream pop singers found themselves pushed aside by the very artists whose material they had taken, new "pop" singers such as Chuck Berry and Fats Domino. Hank Williams never made the popular charts himself, but his songs crossed into pop territory with great frequency. The legendary Williams, in fact, did most to break the fragile barriers between country and pop music, and his songs were covered by several pop entertainers, such as Tony Bennett, Frankie Laine, and Guy Mitchell. He died of a heart attack on January 1, 1953, and by the time of his death, his life had become much like the tragic songs he often sang. He had been fired from the Grand Ole Opry because of chronic drunkenness and emotional instability and had once again become an unsteady member of the Louisiana Hayride. Marital troubles added to the personal turmoil that shortened his troubled life, which itself came to have powerful significance for country music figures and for artists in other fields who were influenced by them. But part of his influence that also should be remembered is how he helped bring about the decline of mainstream pop music. By the late 1950s r&b, rockabilly, and rock 'n' roll singers had begun to dominate. There was little room for Patti Page and Rosemary Clooney. Country musicians such as Hank Williams did much to bring about these changes.

Country music's emergence as a lucrative industry attracted to it a larger number of entertainers and a consequent realization among industry leaders that the music's scope and image needed broadening. This broadened perspective, augmented by the liberating social trends of the war, produced a more tolerant attitude toward female performers. Some women entertainers, such as Lulu Belle Wiseman, Maybelle Carter, Patsy Montana, Texas Ruby Owens, Molly O'Day, and Rose Maddox, had won a large degree of earlier recognition, but usually they had been associated with family groups and only rarely had achieved any kind of individual identity. The first genuine female superstar of country music appeared in 1952 when Kitty Wells, born Muriel Deason in Nashville, Tennessee, recorded "It Wasn't God Who Made Honky Tonk Angels," the "woman's answer" to Hank Thompson's earlier hit, "The Wild Side of Life." Throughout the 1950s Kitty Wells was the acknowledged "Queen of Country Music." In fact, her live appearances during that decade consistently outdrew those of most male performers. Despite her remarkable success and status, she remained a modest and unassuming person and never gave the slightest suggestion of being dissatisfied with traditional gender roles. Her husband, Johnny Wright, remained her spokesman and manager. Although she helped open doors for other women singers such as Patsy Cline, Loretta Lynn, and Dolly Parton, Wells's private life and values generally conformed to the stereotypical image of the southern housewife.

Until the mid-1950s, country music continued to win commercial success, and its styles remained identifiably rural and southern. Few people could have foreseen that country music, along with the whole field of mainstream pop music as it had been known for three decades, was about to go into a virtual state of collapse. The nation was on the threshold of the rock 'n' roll revolution.

In the years following World War II, young people in the United States gained an influence and buying power that previous generations had not possessed. The values and sensibilities of teenagers and young adults in urban areas were shaped increasingly by television and other mass media. And with largely unprecedented personal freedom because of the loosening of parental restraints during the war, young people all over the U.S. became acutely conscious of their specialness in what was becoming a youth-oriented culture. They consequently sought symbols, models, and entertainment forms that most closely mirrored their own lives and aspirations. The entertainment industry was ready for them. Its leaders recognized the immense potential of the youth market and took steps to shape and satisfy the desires of young people with their own spending money. To take advantage of this affluence, the entertainment industry began to make some adjustments.

As young people in the U.S. groped for self-understanding, they found little with which to identify in mainstream pop culture. Much of the older popular music was too sophisticated, bland, or repressed to satisfy their cravings, and they sought novel or exciting alternatives in the various kinds of ethnic or grassroots material found on small record labels. By 1952 or 1953 they were listening to rhythm and blues material that their parents scarcely knew existed, and some young, white would-be musicians were already experimenting with these songs. In the meantime, many young people also found cultural heroes among such actors and troubled souls as Marlon Brando and James Dean, whose anti-authoritarian manners and disaffected expressions and gestures seemed confusing and inarticulate to parents but spoke volumes to their teenaged children. The dress, hairstyles, and demeanor of Brando, Dean, and other young actors, combined with the alienated vision of the Beat poets and the rocking rhythms of grassroots music, provided many of the volatile ingredients of rock 'n' roll. One of the major sources of the rock 'n' roll revolution was the readiness of people for whom music was an essential part of their lives to combine the music of blacks and whites in ways that assaulted the old order socially, culturally, politically, and economically.

Rhythm and blues was a powerful contributor to the breaking down of racial barriers in the United States. For years, r&b radio shows out of Nashville, Memphis, and New Orleans had been blanketing the country and helping shape the musical tastes of its young people, white as well as black. Even though a number of black performers, including the Ink Spots, the Mills Brothers, Sister Rosetta Tharpe, and Lonnie Johnson, had followings among white people and catered, in part, to that audience, the rhythm and blues that predominated during the 1940s and early 1950s was a composite of styles aimed largely at black audiences. Very little of the older style of country blues remained after World War II. Even such singers as Lightning Hopkins, Muddy Waters, and John Lee Hooker, who adhered to the older ways of singing, generally adopted electrified instruments. The great African-American migration to the cities and the desire to move away from landscapes and experiences that reminded them of earlier degradation led southern-born blacks with rural roots and urban, northern-born blacks to seek musical forms that corresponded to their own values and aspirations. The electrical amplification of instruments certainly divested their music of many of its rural connotations. Not only was the guitar widely electrified, it came increasingly to be played in the single-string flatpick style pioneered by T-Bone Walker and Charlie Christian, with little of the finger-picking style so common in the 1920s. Rhythm and blues bands, despite their emphasis on vocals, were basically dance-oriented, so they partly filled the vacuum left by the decline of the big bands after World War II. But as dance bands, and as groups that played in noisy environs, their sound had to get louder; hence the electrification and the addition of basses and drums. When Fender electric basses became available, they helped establish stronger r&b rhythm sections than had been possible with acoustic upright basses. Fender also introduced several lines of standard guitars that became the rage in vernacular music, especially the famous Telecaster and Stratocaster. Most r&b performers gravitated to cities. Some, such as T-Bone Walker, went to the West Coast, but more went to Chicago or Memphis. Their music appeared on a multiplicity of small record labels, virtually all of them white-owned: Specialty, Peacock, Duke, Aladdin, Aristocrat, Chess, Vee Jay, King, Apollo, Deluxe, and Savoy.

Many of the black performers who were household names in many parts of the African-American community went their entire performing careers known to only a handful of white listeners who might have stumbled upon their records or heard them perform on black radio shows. Blues and rhythm and blues artists played for the black masses, whether they lived in the ghettos of Chicago, Detroit, or Los Angeles, or in the cities or small towns of the South. According to Charles Keil, blues singers became "culture heroes" in black communities and important masculine models for black youth. Keil suggests that the hustler and the entertainer were seen as men who were clever and talented enough to be financially well off without holding traditional employment, though they compromised their identity by taking subservient places in the white-run economy.[3] Although the bluesmen assumed heroic proportions to their listeners and accordingly dressed and groomed themselves in the flashiest of styles, their success derived from the fact that no cultural gap separated them from their audience. While they achieved status and its accoutrements unknown, and largely unknowable, to their fans, African-American performers for the most part did not try to separate or distinguish themselves from their supporters. Like most white country singers, the blues and r&b artists shared the cultural values of their listeners even while achieving a glamor and aura of power that plain folk could generally admire only from afar.

Several of the blues singers of the postwar period were men whose styles and careers dated from the 1930s. Aaron "T-Bone" Walker was born in Linden, Texas, in 1910 and exhibited a strong acquaintance with the country blues tradition of that state. Because it seems almost obligatory for Texas bluesmen to claim an association with Blind Lemon Jefferson, one might respond skeptically to Walker's own claim to such a connection, but it seems likely that he sometimes heard Jefferson during his time in Dallas. What cannot be questioned is Walker's importance as a bridge between the older traditions and the new. In 1935 he became one of the first artists to play an electric guitar; he was a pioneer in the employment of a single-string technique; and he was one of the first to take the blues to the West Coast, playing in Central Avenue clubs in Los Angeles in 1936 and 1937. After World War II, he became a fixture on the West Coast blues scene, noted for his acrobatic stage behavior, and recorded for several labels. In 1947 he recorded his biggest hit, "Stormy Monday."

Howlin' Wolf (Chester Burnett) and Muddy Waters (McKinley Morganfield) were also older bluesmen who successfully adjusted to the newer urban and electrified style. Both were born in the Mississippi Delta, in 1910 and 1915 respectively. Although folklorist Alan Lomax recorded Muddy Waters while on a trip to Mississippi searching for Robert Johnson, neither Waters nor Wolf gained significant recognition until they moved to Chicago after World War II and were discovered by white blues aficionados. As his name suggests, Howlin' Wolf groaned and shouted in a manner reminiscent of the Mississippi field hollers, while Muddy Waters played the French harp and bottleneck slide guitar. Of all the old-time bluesmen who remained active during the 1940s and '50s, Waters seems to have made the best adjustment to rhythm and blues and to have had the greatest international impact. He was sufficiently rural in the early 1940s to record for Alan Lomax and the Library of Congress, but by the end of the decade he was an active and leading member of the aggressive Chicago rhythm and blues scene. He did not have a large white following at the time, but his influence asserted itself in a strange and unexpected way. One of his recorded songs from the latter period, "Rollin' Stone," inspired the name of the famous British rock group. The popularity that such bluesmen as Howlin' Wolf and Muddy Waters enjoyed among some of the performing groups in Britain was a factor in their discovery in this country. When the Rolling Stones, the Animals, and the Beatles came to the United States, they brought with them an appreciation for the southern blues that they passed on to their American fans.

Among the generation of blues singers who came of age during World War II, the name of Riley B. (B.B.) King is preeminent. Born in 1925 on a Delta plantation near Indianola, Mississippi, King moved to Memphis shortly after the war and began playing on street corners and in dance halls. He soon obtained a job on WDIA, a 50,000–watt station, where he sang and worked as a disc jockey. It was here that he became known as the Beale Street Blues Boy, abbreviated B.B., and began building his reputation as a great blues singer.

King refused to capitulate to rock 'n' roll during the 1950s and stuck to his
Delta-born style through successive changes in music fashions. While he did
not share in the adulation that black rock 'n' rollers received from white youth,
King won the passionate devotion of an African-American audience and inspired many people such as Bobby Blue Bland to enter the music profession.
With a schedule that included a staggering number of one-night stands, extending all over the South and to the West Coast and back again, King traveled with his guitar, nicknamed Lucille, and built an enviable rapport with his
listeners. Charles Keil, writing in 1966, asserted that King was "the only straight
blues singer in America with a large, adult, nationwide, and almost entirely
Negro audience."[4] Since those words were written, B.B. King has become
known to a much wider circle of people in the United States, largely because
of the publicity given him and his songs by his British rock admirers.

Although most black singers such as B.B. King were almost totally unknown in this country outside of the black community, a few contributed
songs that gradually began to enter the white consciousness in the late 1940s
and early '50s. These singers, whittling away at the edges of mainstream pop
music, prepared the way for the coming of rock 'n' roll. Louis Jordan, from
Brinkley, Arkansas, was the first black r&b singer to produce songs that were
popular with both black and white Americans. Jordan had been a jazz musician in the '30s, but his postwar recording success came with the production
of comic and novelty songs such as "Choo, Choo Ch' Boogie," "Caldonia,"
"Open the Door, Richard," and "Beans and Cornbread." Jordan's songs seem
to have been popular with all age groups, but the r&b singers who came after
him were more particularly attuned to youth. When white young people began to discover black music, they found in it a freedom, expressiveness, and
sensuality that they did not hear in other forms of music, and they liked what
they heard. Between 1952 and 1955 a succession of rhythm and blues songs
were recorded on the little 45-rpm discs that since their introduction in 1948
had been supplanting the old 78s. These songs competed for the favor of
American youth and included Roy Brown's "Good Rocking Tonight" (1947);
Lloyd Price's "Lawdy Miss Clawdy" and the Clovers' "One Mint Julep" (1952);
Clyde McPhatter's "Money Honey" and Ruth Brown's "Mama, He Treats Your
Daughter Mean" (1953); Joe Turner's "Shake, Rattle, and Roll"; Lavern Baker's
"Tweedle Dee"; and Hank Ballard's "Annie Had a Baby" and "Work with Me,
Annie" (1954); and Fats Domino's "Ain't That a Shame" (1955).

Antoine "Fats" Domino and Professor Longhair, from New Orleans,
Little Richard (Penniman), from Macon, Georgia, and Chuck Berry, from St.
Louis, provided the transition from black rhythm and blues to rock 'n' roll.
Not only were their songs often covered or copied by white singers, but these

black rock 'n' rollers also competed favorably with the white singers and often appeared alongside them on the charts. With his exuberant vocal style and chorded, boogie-woogie piano playing, Domino had done much to create the distinctive "New Orleans dance blues" sound. Domino's recordings were made in the studios of Cosimo Matassa; in fact, virtually every r&b record made in New Orleans from the mid-1940s until the late '60s was produced in studios owned by Matassa.[5] Although not as well known as Fats Domino, another New Orleans pianist, Henry Roeland Byrd, helped establish rhythm and blues as a stylistic force, rather than simply as a catch-all expression for African-American vernacular music. Better known as Professor Longhair, Byrd developed and popularized a piano style featuring a furiously rolling bass pattern and exuberantly syncopated left hand. He also helped establish New Orleans as a city with more going on in it musically than just jazz, especially with his contributions to what is known as "New Orleans funk," practiced notably by the Neville Brothers. Professor Longhair was never widely known outside of the Crescent City during his lifetime, which ended in 1980, but his influence lived on in the careers of the Nevilles, Allen Toussaint, Marcia Ball, and others such as promoter Quint Davis who made sure that their fans knew about "Fess." Fats Domino became so much a part of mainstream rock 'n' roll that he often turned the tables on white musicians and made successful adaptations of their songs. In 1956, for example, he recorded a very popular version of a song introduced by cowboy singer Gene Autry, "Blueberry Hill." Chuck Berry did more to create a separate rock 'n' roll guitar style than probably any other artist, wrote songs based on the interests of middle-class kids, and received criticism from other black performers for being too "country." Little Richard helped reinforce the role of the piano as a rock 'n' roll instrument, infused his music with the vibrancy of gospel, and suffered perhaps the ultimate insult a black rock 'n' roll artist could experience, having his songs covered by syrupy crooner Pat Boone.

Rock 'n' roll was not exclusively southern in origin or manifestation, but it first exploded on the national scene with a southern accent, and most of its early southern practitioners were young men who drew upon country, gospel, and rhythm and blues roots. Sam Phillips, the owner of the Memphis Recording Service and the Sun Record Company, had long recognized the commercial potential that lay in the fusion of southern black and white grass-roots forms. He had often said that if he could find a white man who could sing in a convincing black style, he would make a million dollars. Music history is replete with references to the fact that Elvis Presley was that man, though Phillips seems not to have recognized him immediately, ignoring Presley's first recording tests. Furthermore, Presley seems to have stumbled upon the idea of recording a rhythm and blues tune only after his attempts with other types of music had resulted in mediocre imitations of the pop crooners and country singers of the day.

Presley was born on January 8, 1935, to very poor and religious parents in East Tupelo, Mississippi. His initial exposure to music came at the First Assembly of God Church, but he also listened to country music and gospel quartets on the radio. Although he surely must have heard rhythm and blues earlier, his most direct contact with it came after he and his family moved to Memphis in 1948. By the time he made his first records for Sun in 1954, Presley had absorbed both songs and styles from most of the grassroots traditions of the South, but he seemed to have no exclusive commitment to any of them. In fact, when he made his first test records, he was singing some of the bland pop hits of the day. On July 6, 1954, he and two local musicians, guitarist Scotty Moore and string bass player Bill Black, were jamming in the Sun Studios when, almost absentmindedly, they began "messing around" with a song that excited them and also sparked Phillips's first real interest in their music. This was an old blues tune, learned from Arthur "Big Boy" Crudup, called "That's All Right, Mama." When their first record was released, "That's All Right" was backed with "Blue Moon of Kentucky," a country tune written by Bill Monroe. This choice, too, was the result of somewhat aimless jamming. Never was a revolution launched in such a playful and unplanned manner.

"That's All Right, Mama" became a big hit in Memphis soon after it was featured by white disc jockey Dewey Phillips[6] on his rhythm and blues show, "Red, Hot, and Blue." Presley and his music were such hybrid phenomena that no one could categorize them. Soon after the record appeared, Presley made guest appearances on the Grand Ole Opry and the Louisiana Hayride and then joined the Hayride's regular cast. Old-time country fans were wary, if not appalled, by the young singer some people called the "Hillbilly Cat" and his frenzied, sensual style, but Presley achieved two results that had not occurred among "country" singers before: he mesmerized youthful audiences that had not previously been attracted to country music, and he aroused emotions within them that heretofore had been latent. Presley tapped an enormous reservoir of repressed emotion among young people in the United States, North and South, and the "rebels without a cause" of the 1950s began to find a sense of common identity in a music that reflected their values and fears. They also benefited from something Peter Guralnick observes, that in Memphis, by pure chance, three white men who were musically colorblind—Presley, Phillips, and Phillips—came together and decided to record and play on the radio a new kind of music that drew inspiration from both black and white sources. Coming at the start of the civil rights movement, the rise of Presley's music and the blurring of color lines that it represented gave it special power and meaning in the South, especially, and in the United States as a whole.[7]

As an entertainer, Presley had lost his exclusive regional identification by 1956. Under the astute, if manipulative, management of Colonel Tom Parker, a former carnival man and booking agent, he signed a recording contract with RCA Victor and went on to experience a national success and international recognition unsurpassed by any figure in popular culture. In the twenty years that preceded his death in 1977, Presley's popularity never really declined from the peak reached in the late 1950s. His records did not always dominate the charts, but he successfully adapted to the various changes that came to pop music during those decades, and he maintained an astounding commercial viability through numerous movies, Las Vegas appearances, and television specials. He never lost his original audience, and he picked up a new one among younger people who had never seen him in person. He became so much the property of the people of the U.S., and the mythologized projection of the dreams of so many of them, that he retreated into the isolation of his Memphis mansion and a small circle of friends, bodyguards, and relatives who gathered around him at Graceland.

Even though Elvis became part of the international realm of show business, neither he nor the other young southern singers who followed in his wake could ever escape, even had they desired, the marks of their southern-bred culture. Generally described as "rockabillies" because they supposedly embodied both rock 'n' roll and hillbilly characteristics, such singers as Carl Perkins, Roy Orbison, Jerry Lee Lewis, Charlie Rich, and Conway Twitty carried the dialects and inflections of the Deep South in their speech and singing styles. Their music was also deeply indebted to the varied folk styles of their native region, reflecting a powerful fusion of gospel music, both white and black, country, and rhythm and blues. Growing up in the South, they scarcely could have avoided hearing such music on radio, recordings, or jukeboxes, but they usually had an even more personal form of indebtedness. Charlie Rich, for example, grew up in a family of gospel singers, but he also learned the blues style from an old black singer who lived near his home in Arkansas. Carl Perkins, whose recording of "Blue Suede Shoes" was one of the big hits of 1956, had been born into a tenant farm family on a plantation near Lake City, Tennessee. Perkins was a faithful listener to the Grand Ole Opry and was particularly fond of Bill Monroe, but he credited his guitar style to a black musician who lived on the plantation.

Jerry Lee Lewis, in many ways the most interesting of the so-called rockabillies, often acted as if he had stepped out of the pages of Wilbur J. Cash's *Mind of the South,* the prototypical ambivalent southerner embodying both hedonistic and puritanical traits. Lewis was born in Ferriday, Louisiana, the son of devout Assembly of God parents. He briefly contemplated going into the ministry and enrolled for a time in a Bible school in Waxahachie, Texas. Religious music was very much a part of his life, but "sinful" music exerted a more powerful sway. In Ferriday, he spent a considerable portion of his free time, as did his musical cousins, Mickey Gilley and Jimmie Lee Swaggart, at Haney's Big House, a black club that specialized in rhythm and blues music.

While Lewis's piano style, with its flourishes and rolling chords, is reminiscent of white gospel music, it probably owes a good deal to sounds heard at Haney's. The three cousins, all pianists using much the same style, built prominent careers as professional musicians. Lewis mixed country with rock 'n' roll; Gilley made his name in mainstream country music; and Swaggart skillfully incorporated his musicianship into his appearances as a Pentecostal evangelist, which were seriously curtailed after a sex scandal in the 1980s.

Lewis vaulted into the national music limelight in 1957 with his hit recording of "Whole Lot of Shaking Going On" and with subsequent televised appearances on Steve Allen's "Tonight" show, where he bowled over the audience while almost wrecking the piano. He soon became embroiled in controversy when it became known that the twenty-three-year-old had married his thirteen-year-old cousin. He survived the firestorm of bad publicity and eventually moved into the field of country music, but he never lost the energy, dynamic flair, and swaggering confidence that characterized his early rockabilly days. Neither did he abandon the lifestyle that veered from the sanctified to the sinful. At various points in this career, he announced a recommitment to Christ and declared that he had changed his ways, vowing, for instance, not to perform where liquor was sold. Some people who heard his announcements celebrated his conversion, and others expressed regret at the loss of the good times he provided them. Others stayed skeptical, predicting that his change of heart would not last, and were proven right, as Lewis returned time and again to pounding pianos in honky-tonks and, often, scandalizing the public with new indiscretions.

Artists in the rockabilly style became culture heroes to young people in the U.S., and they contributed at least unconsciously to the youth revolution of the 1960s. In addition, their music was as popular in Britain as it was at home. Charles "Buddy" Holly, the Texas singer and songwriter who died in an Iowa plane crash in 1959, and the Everly Brothers (Phil and Don) from Kentucky, were direct influences on the music and harmony of the Beatles, as well as other groups that made up the "British invasion" in the '60s. The Beatles were often said to have named themselves as a tribute to Holly's group, the

Crickets. But if the artists who performed rockabilly music themselves were rebels, their rebellion was in no way overtly political, nor was it fomented against the traditions of the South. Presley, Lewis, and their cohorts were a whole world and a culture away from the iconoclastic, anti-authoritarian hard rock musicians of the 1960s. When as a Memphis teenager Elvis Presley decked himself out in bright, flamboyant clothing and worked his hair into a ducktail, he was in no sense flouting society's rules but was affirming his identity in a milieu that generally ignored the children of the working-class poor. Likewise his and other rockabilly performers' employment of a sensual performing style was as much an expression of stereotypical masculine imagery deeply imbedded in southern working-class culture as it was a violation of conventional middle-class standards. Presley never intended to antagonize any facet of that southern working-class world from which he came. However, his theatricality, his employment of the emotionalism he had picked up in church, a setting where it was sanctioned and socioculturally "safe," had other implications when carried to the general public. Even preachers of his own denomination denounced his antics, much to Presley's surprise and disappointment. Hell-raisers the rockabillies could be; but radicals they were not. Although he sang with a heavy black-influenced style and helped break down barriers between black and white musical culture, Presley never publicly questioned the racial values of his region. His manners, with a profusion of "sirs" and "ma'ams," epitomized southern courtesy. He willingly, and famously, served in the military and, alarmed by what he considered to be scandalous conduct on the part of many hard rock musicians in the '60s, reportedly offered his services to the FBI as an informer and his allegiance to President Richard Nixon in a well-publicized meeting that both hoped to use to their advantage. Stories about alleged drug use that circulated after his death did not negate his overtures toward conservative law-enforcement officials, but they did place him in the context of ambivalent southern behavior patterns, much like those of Jerry Lee Lewis.[8]

Yet Elvis Presley, Fats Domino, and their fellow southern rock 'n' roll performers contributed to a social revolution that exerted a profound influence on the popular music and youth of the world. Looking back on the music of the period and comparing it to the rock and pop music that followed, the rock 'n' roll of the 1950s seems to represent an innocent and naive phase of U.S. cultural history. The nation's youth merely groped in the 1950s for answers that youth in the 1960s asserted with fury and finality. Regardless of the intent behind the music of the 1950s, and regardless of the social consequences spawned by its emergence, southern rock 'n' roll musicians effectively implanted much of the culture of the working-class South in the nation at large. Their visibility as concert performers and their prominence on the national record popularity charts were the obvious symbols of their impact, something that was also felt in countless less obvious ways. They had taken their music further into the realm of national popular culture than any southern grassroots performers before them.

Chapter 7

THE 1960S AND 1970S

ROCK, GOSPEL, SOUL

Native rock 'n' roll's impact on popular music, particularly its domination by southerners, had already begun to diminish by 1960. As Robert Palmer put it in *Rock & Roll: An Unruly History,* the genre suffered a remarkable rate of "attrition" through the untimely deaths of Buddy Holly and mates in 1959, Elvis Presley's departure first for the Army and then pop stardom, Little Richard's defection to gospel music, and Jerry Lee Lewis's and Chuck Berry's involvement in raging sex-related scandals. Rock 'n' roll became standardized and sanitized by the national market-oriented labels and distributors who thought some of its manifestations were too earthy for middle-class record buyers and offered them, instead, "manufactured 'teen idols'" who would not threaten the sensibilities of nervous parents and community leaders.[1] But the year 1964 saw an even more dramatic turning point in American music with the arrival in the United States of the Beatles, an event that marked the beginning of a much-remarked "invasion" of the United States by British rock 'n' rollers. In a sense, the coming of the British groups meant that rock 'n' roll had come full circle from the recordings of grassroots American entertainers, to Europe, and then back again. The British groups, especially the Beatles, the Rolling Stones, the Animals, the Yardbirds, Cream, and Led Zeppelin, tended to have a deep appreciation for the music of their blues and rockabilly predecessors. The Brits were shocked at the ignorance of people in the U.S. about their own musical heritage and built the familiar blues-based, three-chord format into many of their songs. But this new breed of musicians, especially those from Britain, were more than copyists. They had no interest in simply recreating the sounds of musical forebears from the southern United States. The Beatles did their last cover of an old rock 'n' roll tune in 1965, as Craig Morrison says, after which "rock had dropped the roll."[2] These were revolutionaries, musicians who greatly altered the American music scene and, indeed, that of most of the western world and much of the rest. Through their influence electronics returned to popular music with a vengeance, coming at the apex of the acoustic-dominated urban folk revival in the United States and helping send the folk-music movement into eclipse. They also helped transform rock 'n' roll from largely being a form of dance music to one witnessed at concert venues. While their older brothers and sisters had stories of dancing to rock 'n' roll bands at road houses, young people from the mid-1960s on often spoke of having "seen" bands at various concert halls and sports arenas. With their long hair and "mod" dress, the British rockers fomented a revolution, as well, in style and manners among youth in the United States that never really dissipated. The British musicians, their psychedelic counterparts from San Francisco, and other emulators and innovators from the U.S. introduced the strongest urban tone yet heard in American rock 'n' roll. Their high-powered electric instrumentation, their stage costuming, the sex-and-drugs orientation of much of their material, and their brash performing styles suggested very little of the earlier rural-tinged music of the southern rockabillies. In short, rock 'n' roll was transformed into rock music—hard rock, acid rock, and, later, heavy metal—and most of the innocence and naivete of the earlier form disappeared.

Not only was rock much less derivative of the past than early rock 'n' roll had been, it also seemed much more attuned to contemporary youth, as a product of their urban experiences and their participation in a national musical culture made possible by the electronic mass media. Thus, the rock music of the mid-1960s was as powerful a de-regionalizing force as had yet appeared in U.S. popular culture. Young southerners who were drawn to it, either as performers or listeners, became part of a culture that knew no regional bounds. Rock music in the 1960s made its appeal neither to class, to race, or to region; it was an art form that spoke exclusively to youth, anywhere. The rockabillies of the 1950s often recorded in the South, and even as they were blurring the lines between black and white music, their southernness was very apparent. The rock singers of the 1960s, on the other hand, usually recorded in New York or Los Angeles, and whether they came from Mobile, Des Moines, or Boise, they reflected a non-conformist, anti-establishment youth culture, mostly alien to the South, whose traits became virtually worldwide: long hair, unconventional dress, illicit drug use, sexual freedom, and hostility toward or disinterest in politics or civic and religious authority figures. Rock music's emergence during the turbulent 1960s, when practically all of the nation's institutions were being challenged, further explains the reluctance of some southern rock singers to identify with the South. Ambitious southern rock musicians moved to where the action was, to New York, Los Angeles, or San Francisco, though they could scarcely avoid being embarrassed about the politics, religion, and racism of their home region. The international spotlight that the civil rights movement, especially, helped shine on the South illuminated many unfavorable characteristics of the region, some of which inspired criticisms from rock musicians such as Neil Young, whose bitter denunciations of the South in "Southern Man" and "Alabama" and of government brutality toward Vietnam War protestors in "Ohio," a war largely supported by mainstream southerners, constituted some of the political sentiments many young people felt at the time. Their affinity for rock music may have been sharpened, in fact, by a rebellion against the values of the white majority of the South. Whatever the cause, in the 1960s when all musical roads seemed to lead toward New York or the West Coast, even if a few groups such as the Byrds and Creedence Clearwater Revival drew on southern or country themes and motifs, few had much incentive to create something that might be called southern rock.

Nevertheless, although they might often recoil against an identification with the South, some southern-born rock musicians could not avoid absorbing many of the region's musical traits. The Winter Brothers, Johnny and Edgar, from Beaumont, Texas, were devotees of the blues, but they toiled in obscurity until they left Texas and relocated in New York. Doug Sahm, from San Antonio, drew upon at least three musical sources: blues, Tex-Mex, and country. He had been a child steel guitarist in local country bands, but later spent much of his time playing with Chicano and black groups. Shortly after the British invasion became such a powerful part of the American musical scene, Sahm's producer, Huey Meaux, advised him to grow his hair long, find four other musicians, and prepare to emulate the Beatles's methods. The result was the Sir Douglas Quintet, probably the first American rock band to show the direct effects of the British invasion. The quintet made one successful record, "She's About a Mover," and broke up after a marijuana bust in Houston. Sahm left to become part of the San Francisco scene but later returned to Texas, built a new career in Austin, and became a mainstay in the Texas Tornadoes, the popular Tex-Mex group.

Apart from Louisiana-born Johnny Rivers, who made the transition from rockabilly to rock 'n' roll and enjoyed solid popularity while maintaining fairly pronounced southern characteristics, the most successful southern rocker during the 1960s was Janis Joplin. Her career shows the multiplicity of influences that helped to shape the rock genre, but it also demonstrates how unreceptive the South was, at least initially, to its daughters and sons who would not conform to the prescribed culture of their region. Born to a middle-class family in Port Arthur, Texas, Joplin was a bright and sensitive child whose liberal attitudes and interests in music, art, and literature set her apart from most of the city's youth. Though hardly the ugly-duckling she later recalled herself to have been, her slightly plump physical appearance and awkward self-consciousness meant she would never live up to the teen starlet image young middle-class women were expected to emulate in the early 1960s.[3] She sought escape in music and the company of young people who shared her sympathies.

When Joplin enrolled at the University of Texas in Austin in 1962, the city had not yet become an important music center, but it had an active urban folk scene, which she entered immediately. Joplin, however, avoided the polite, Kingston Trio variety of folk music and immersed herself in the earthier forms of blues, gospel, bluegrass, and country, singing often in a hillbilly bar in north Austin called Threadgill's. Although her clear preference was for the blues, and her idol was Bessie Smith, Joplin had no exclusive style during her Austin days and generally sang a particular song in the style of the person from whom she had learned it. She and her friends became known in Austin as much for their unconventional dress and lifestyles as for their music. Although the term was not yet current in Austin, Joplin anticipated the hippie subculture, and when she heard that San Francisco might be responsive both to her music and her lifestyle, she left for that city in 1963. Joplin found an acceptance in the rock music world that she had never gained at home in Texas, and after her discovery at the Monterey Pop Festival in 1967, her career skyrocketed. With a vocal style partly shaped by her fascination with Otis Redding, and with an aggressive energy that punctuated her stage presence, Joplin was soon touted as the best white blues singer in America and one of its most powerful female performers. Sadly, she self-destructed almost as quickly as she had flourished.

By the time Janis Joplin died on October 4, 1970, the victim of an accidental overdose of heroin, much of the mood of rebellion and angry protest that had characterized the previous decade had begun to dissipate. As the achievements of the civil rights movement and federal legislation brought measurable improvement in the lives of southern African Americans, and as the nation tired of social and political upheaval and began moving to the right politically, race relations improved in the South but seemed to worsen in the country as a whole. The glare of national publicity moved significantly away from the ills of the South to those of the northern ghettos. Northern cities whose newspapers had sent courageous reporters into the South in the 1950s and '60s to cover the civil rights movement as if covering a war found themselves dealing with their own crises in school desegregation and equal employment and housing opportunities. In the South, meanwhile, the election of a new group of progressive governors such as Reubin Askew in Florida, Dale Bumpers in Arkansas, and Jimmy Carter in Georgia inspired a fresh wave of "New South" rhetoric. Carter's election to the presidency in 1976, with its promise of sectional healing and a reunited nation, intensified the feeling of many observers that a progressive South might lead the nation to racial justice and human understanding. With the lessening of the age-old evils of southern society, along with some of the guilt that had accompanied them, young southerners were freed to a great extent to reaffirm or rediscover the good that lay in their culture. Naturally, the conceptions of what was good in the South, or what was indeed "southern," varied considerably. The promotion, sometimes simply music-industry hype, surrounding "southern rock music" in the 1970s was largely a reassertion of the mythic South, but in the context of a heightened New South ideology.

Recording and promotion of southern rock musicians had not been entirely absent in the South in the 1960s, as witnessed by Huey Meaux's operations in Houston and by Bill Lowery's success in Atlanta with the recording of Joe South, Tony Joe White, Jerry Reed, Billy Joe Royal, and Ray Stevens. But until the emergence of Phil Walden and his Capricorn label in 1969, no southern-based company, not even Sun Records in Memphis or the New Orleans producers of the 1950s, had successfully rivaled those in other regions of the United States. Walden, once the manager of Otis Redding, was one of many southern music entrepreneurs who had long resented the failure of the South to hold on to its rock musicians. His establishment of Capricorn Records in Macon, Georgia, was a direct effort to make use of the musical wealth of the South while keeping the region's rock performers at home. Walden literally created the Allman Brothers Band in 1969 when he asked Duane Allman, a gifted session guitarist at the recording studios in Muscle Shoals, Alabama, to recruit some other musicians to make recordings and live appearances. The Allman Brothers subsequently gained great popularity throughout the United States, made Capricorn a nationally known label with a gross of $43 million in 1976, and contributed very largely to the creation of what became known as the Macon Sound. The Allmans used an instrumental format widely copied by other southern rock bands, particularly those who recorded for Capricorn: two guitars, two sets of drums, keyboards, and bass. Theirs was basically a blues-rock sound given shape by Duane Allman's slide-style guitar and by Gregg Allman's white soul singing. But the Allmans sometimes also projected a country feeling through the playing and singing of guitarist Dickey Betts, as in "Rambling Man," in which Betts's solo guitar playing closely resembles that of a steel guitarist.

Some southern rock bands, such as Lynyrd Skynyrd from Florida, the Marshall Tucker Band from South Carolina, and the Charlie Daniels Band (CDB) from Tennessee adhered very closely to the Allman Brothers's instrumental format while often differing widely in the type of material performed.

Others, such as Wet Willie from Alabama, Sea Level, a direct offshoot of the Allmans, .38 Special from Jacksonville (led by Donnie Van Zant, brother of Lynyrd Skynyrd leader Ronnie Van Zant), the Amazing Rhythm Aces from Memphis, and the Atlanta Rhythm Section diverged from the Allman instrumental pattern. Some used backup singers, including women, in a male-dominated musical genre, much the way rhythm & blues bands did. Wet Willie and Sea Level performed basically white blues and r&b with no country admixture at all, though the Amazing Rhythm Aces had a hit, "Third Rate Romance," on the country as well as pop charts in 1976 and Charlie Daniels became known as a fiddler as well as guitarist and lead vocalist in his band. Wet Willie produced a national hit, "Keep On Smilin'," which recreated the r&b sound for the white youth audience. It should be pointed out also that the Marshall Tucker Band was virtually alone, with the British band Jethro Tull, in giving a flute a central place in its music.

Southern rock music was marketed with a self-conscious southernness unknown even at the height of the rockabilly craze. Capricorn distributed thousands of buttons admonishing record buyers to "Buy Southern." Phil Walden made the most of his personal and political friendship with Jimmy Carter. As governor of Georgia, Carter had supported a bill to control tape piracy, a cause dear to Walden, who, in turn, made financial contributions to Carter's political campaigns. During the crucial opening stages of Carter's run for the presidency, when he was little known outside of Georgia—even stumping panelists as to his identity on the popular game show "What's My Line?"—several southern rock bands played at concerts to raise much-needed money for his campaign. Carter's identification with rock bands did not hurt him among the nation's youthful voters, and the bands undoubtedly profited from their association with the successful presidential candidate. Indeed, the Marshall Tucker and Charlie Daniels Bands were featured at the main ball celebrating Carter's inauguration.

Such rock magazines as *Rolling Stone* and *Crawdaddy*, and other types of promotional literature, made constant allusions to the presumed "southernness" of southern rock bands. It was not solely their instrumental style, with its indebtedness to blues, r&b, and country forms, or the images in their lyrics that evoked notions of southern culture and southern identity. Other more intangible qualities concerning attitude, behavior, and lifestyle set southern rock musicians apart from those from other areas of the country and sometimes from images being promoted by advocates of New South ideology. Sometimes this style was projected as nothing more than a musical reflection of an easy-going ambience and an honest, down-to-earth approach to life, but often the emphasis was on the mythical southern machismo with its hedonistic attitude and underlying acceptance of violence. According to Stephen R. Tucker, southern rock "emphasized such traditional [southern] themes as masculine aggression, the superiority of rural life, and unbridled individualism. . . . appeal[ing] most strongly to white southern working-class teenagers . . ."[4] Some bands displayed Confederate flags at their concerts and in their promotional literature, giving rise to questions about whether they were expressing racist inclinations or whether they were simply trying to set themselves apart from rock groups from other parts of the country. Some imagery and behavior seemed to suggest desires for self-assertiveness and self-determination, long-held southern yearnings with respect to the region's place in the United States. One journalist described southern music as "something more than just rock-and-roll south of the Mason-Dixon line. At best, it's the living image of Southern culture; a fusion of the varied and sometimes antagonistic elements of Southern life. At worst, it's awful, a sort of mindless, shake-your-butt disco music for the smash-the-beer bottle-over-the-waitress'-head set."[5] Some southern rock musicians even questioned the notion that the form was a distinctive one when it first came out. Toy Caldwell, leader of the Marshall Tucker Band, was quoted as saying, "I guess to me, Southern music is just a band from the South playing music."[6]

Other musicians lived and performed out of a more focused southern image, if not stereotype. Charlie Daniels probably became the most aggressively southern of all the rock musicians, representing the South of the hell-raising good old boy who lives only to play music, get drunk, make love, and fight if the need arises. Lynyrd Skynyrd also built a devil-may-care image that carried more than a hint of potential violence, though they diverted from some of the more aggressive themes of southern rock in their anti-handgun song "Saturday Night Special." Ronnie Van Zant, the lead singer of the group who died in an airplane crash in 1977 with two other members of the band, was the coauthor of "Sweet Home, Alabama," a militant hymn of praise to the state with at least ambivalent defense for its former governor George Wallace, who was internationally famous for resisting racial desegregation. One line in the song is a reply to singer Neil Young's disparaging remarks about race relations in Alabama: "A Southern man don't need him around anyhow."

Chet Flippo, a southern-born rock journalist, probably spoke for many southern rock fans, at least those with a sense of cultural inferiority, when he said that the Allman Brothers "more than anything else, returned a sense of worth to the South." He may have overstated the point when he said that the Allmans had "moved a whole generation of southern kids uptown" and that "kids in the South finally had cultural heroes of their own."[7] Going "uptown," after all, or at least breaking out of the old impoverishment of the South is something that most southern musicians, and many of their fans in the South, have striven to do all along. Whether they could make the trip without losing much of their cultural baggage has always been the question for such southerners.

Southern-born rock entertainers strongly identified with their native region, and as successful musicians they became personalities many southerners appreciated and regarded with pride. Furthermore, the images that appeal to the southern rockers were often closer to those of the "Austin outlaws" than to scenes or symbols in their own home areas. Charlie Daniels, for instance, spoke of his southern origins with a truculent pride, saying "Be proud you're a rebel" in his song of praise to his fellow southern musicians, "The South's Gonna Do It Again," but he adopted the dress of the cattle drover and nursed a penchant for the western novels of Louis L'Amour. Similarly, the members of the Marshall Tucker Band were products of cotton-mill families in Spartanburg, South Carolina, but their hearts seemed to be in the Old West. Like Charlie Daniels, they too adopted the attire of working cowboys, and became known for their passion for old cowboy movies.[8]

Though ZZ Top made their reputation as a hard-driving rock band whose songs often featured suggestive lyrics, the group also earned considerable acclaim for inventiveness in exploring the seemingly endless varieties inherent in the deceptively simple blues-based rock genre. ZZ Top's lead singer and guitarist, Billy Gibbons, developed a distinctive, black-tinged vocal style, and although the band used only three instruments—guitar, bass, and drums—they became known for producing some of the highest-decibel sounds in American rock music. They also earned a place at least on the edges of southern rock, possibly an appropriate place for them in light of the ambivalent nature of their state's ties to the South. Not often mentioned with the Allmans, Marshall Tucker, or CDB, nevertheless ZZ Top embodied many of the traits of the genre, especially with their strong regional identity. The difference was that ZZ Top focused more on Texas than on the Deep South. The "little old band from Texas" carried the cowboy myth, at least a Texas version of it, to its greatest lengths among rock musicians. As was true of the Allman Brothers Band, ZZ Top was the creation of a music promoter, Bill Ham, a former Houston record distributor. Their concerts were accompanied by an avalanche of publicity exceeded only by that accorded the Beatles and Rolling Stones. At a time when many artists performed at the mercy of quirky sound and light systems in venues around the country, ZZ Top created legendary stage performances using multiple tons of their own equipment, including a 40,000–watt sound system. They performed on their own stage built in the shape of Texas, outfitted with various livestock and wildlife reminiscent of the Old

West—longhorn steers, buffalo, vultures, and rattlesnakes—all before a Texas panorama.

Although ZZ Top continued to flourish well into the music-video era, southern rock began to decline in the 1980s. But it played an interesting, somewhat familiar, role in the evolution of southern music. In a way, the British invasion was one of the best things that happened to southern vernacular music in the 1960s. It helped liberate rock 'n' roll from the homogenized, formulaic sound it had acquired during its nationalized, "safe" period in the very early '60s. The "roll" in rock 'n' roll may have been lost, but its loss helped make possible a new brand of youth-oriented popular music that actually reinfused the possibility for regional variations. Just as surely as the British rock musicians developed a myriad of southern-rooted styles of their own, their revolt against nondescript rock 'n' roll helped make southern rock possible. Whether it lived up to its New South hype, it lived nonetheless. When it went into decline, it did not die, but found new expressions in other forms, as will be seen in the next chapter.

While they did not universally share the values and preoccupations of rock music, all forms of music in the 1960s showed the evidence of heightened commercialization and organization, and all exhibited an awareness of the primacy of youth in contemporary popular culture. Consequently, virtually all entertainers, secular and gospel, understood the importance of displaying a youthful image and vitality, while also keeping abreast of changing fashions and styles. Long hair and modern dress became associated with nearly all musicians, not solely those with an affinity for rock music. Every variety of music in the United States became deeply immersed in the matrix of big business, and each demonstrated a concern for packaging, promotion, and merchandising that showed how far it had traveled from its folk roots. Furthermore, drums and electric instruments, including synthesizers, appeared in every musical genre, and instrumental techniques and even vocal mannerisms borrowed from rock appeared with regularity in other musical forms.

By the beginning of the 1960s gospel music had come to terms with the world and had thoroughly appropriated the techniques of show business, while continuing to infuse much of its own spirit into the field of secular music. The sense of religious mission no doubt still burned brightly in the lives of many gospel singers, but an increasing number viewed the music as just another facet of popular music or as an avenue for entrance into different kinds of performing careers. Singers with rural or downhome flavor still existed. Some of them attained great popularity, both white groups such as the Chuck Wagon Gang, the Sullivan Family, Wendy Bagwell and His Sunlighters, and African-

Mahalia Jackson with Thomas A. Dorsey, 1940. Jackson and Dorsey, through their singing and songwriting, contributed immeasurably to the shaping and popularization of black gospel music. Dorsey is known as "The Father of Black Gospel Music," while Jackson was the genre's most revered singer. *William Ransom Hogan Jazz Archive, Tulane University.*

Above, Kid Howard's Band, 1958. *Photo by Ralston Howard. Hogan Jazz Archive, Howard-Tilton Memorial Library, Tulane University. Below,* Professor Longhair. *Hogan Jazz Archive, Howard-Tilton Memorial Library, Tulane University.*

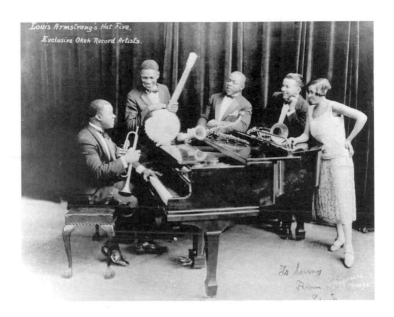

Above, Pictured here in 1926 with his famous Hot Five Band, Armstrong was the greatest southern-born musician who ever lived, and one of America's finest ambassadors to the world. Left to right: Louis Armstrong, Johnny St. Cyr, Johnny Dodds, Edward "Kid" Ory, Lil Hardin Armstrong. *Hogan Jazz Archive, Howard-Tilton Memorial Library, Tulane University.*

Right, Albert Brumley was the most popular white gospel composer, and his songs circulated widely in both gospel and country music through inclusion in paperback hymnals and radio broadcasts. His best known song, "I'll Fly Away," won renewed popularity in the early-twenty-first-century through its performance in the soundtrack of *O Brother, Where Art Thou? Photo courtesy of Albert E. Brumley & Sons.*

Above, B.B. King with his guitar Lucille. The "Beale Street Blues Boy" reshaped his native Mississippi Delta blues style into an electric and electrifying form that captivated listeners here and abroad. The "British Invasion" by rock performers in the 1960s owes much of its form and flavor to King. *Photo by Michael P. Smith. Below,* Shown here in 1936 with the veteran talent scout Eli Oberstein, Lydia Mendoza ("The Meadowlark of the Border") built an intimate relationship with her many Tejano working-class fans. Her music is now known around the world. *Photo by Allee Wallace. University of Texas Institute of Texan Cultures at San Antonio.*

Above, Dolly Parton. This Tennessee mountain girl may be best known for her flamboyance and beauty, but she is also one of America's finest singers and songwriters. *Photo by Becky R. Johnson. Below,* Arthel "Doc" Watson. Since his introduction to folk revival audiences in the early 1960s, this extraordinary North Carolina-born guitarist and singer has built a reputation as America's greatest traditional musician. Each April he hosts in Wilkesboro, North Carolina, a giant festival named for his deceased son, Merle. *Photo by Becky R. Johnson.*

Above, The Hackberry Ramblers. Led by fiddler Luderin Darbone and accordionist Edwin Duhon, this venerable group has taken their blend of Cajun and country music to audiences in America and Europe for over sixty years. *Photo courtesy of Ben Sandmel. Below,* Clifton Chenier, the "King of Louisiana," wears his crown proudly, as is befitting of the man who introduced Zydeco music and his infectious accordion style to the world. *Photo by Philip Gould © Philip Gould 2003.*

Before her death in 1995, Selena Quintanilla had become the most popular Tejano singing star of all time. While preserving her fantastic appeal among Latino fans, she had taken her unique version of the Tex-Mex style to audiences throughout the nation. *Photo by John Dyer ©John Dyer 1992. All Rights Reserved.*

Above, Tish Hinojosa. Few entertainers have more ably illustrated the eclectic nature of southern music than this San Antonio-born singer-songwriter with her Latino, pop, folk, and country blend. *Below,* Robin and Linda Williams. This husband-and-wife duo has introduced southern songs and styles to national audiences for many years through their recordings and personal appearances. As longtime members of the *Prairie Home Companion* cast, they reached audiences that otherwise would not have known about the richness and diversity of southern music. *Photo by Senor McGuire.*

American groups such as the Consolers and Fairfield Four. Almost any night, at least up through the 1980s, on a string of radio stations across the country, one could hear the transcribed broadcasts of the Reverend and Mrs. J. Bazzel Mull as they talked to the "neighbors" and hawked their special offers of Chuck Wagon Gang and other gospel quartet albums.

The world of the Mulls and the Chuck Wagon Gang, however, was a rapidly receding one. The Chuck Wagon Gang endured, surviving numerous personnel changes over the many years of their existence. Longtime member Anna Carter and her husband, former Louisiana governor and Country Music Hall of Fame member Jimmie Davis, continued to perform together as Davis approached his one hundredth birthday. But no facet of American music has been more competitive or more highly professionalized than gospel music. Gospel singers typically dressed in expensive, elegantly tailored suits. While women in gospel groups continued to dress somewhat traditionally, male singers often sported elaborately styled hair and often wore "pencil-thin" mustaches, looking like either stereotypical morticians or professional gamblers, super seded later by longer hair and even, occasionally, beards. The days of simple piano accompaniment disappeared almost completely, and virtually every quartet began performing with drums, electric bass, and a retinue of horns or electric guitars. White gospel groups began to lean toward country and western instrumentation, while black singers adhered to the instrumental sounds of rhythm and blues or soul music, especially being more likely to employ organs than were white groups and being more likely to perform in choirs than whites. The performing styles of black and white singers still differed greatly. The physical presence and prowess of African-American singers distinguished their performances, as they moved all about the stage and out into the aisles of auditoriums and churches where they appeared, often with remarkable energy and endurance. Except for leaning into the one microphone that was usually reserved for singing, the old white quartets traditionally stood rigidly and formally while their pianists clowned, to varying degrees, interacting with and often delighting audiences. Although differences persisted in the ways black and white gospel groups conducted themselves, the gap narrowed greatly in the 1960s when most white quartets began to use multiple microphones and introduced stage routines that essentially amounted to choreography, something of a risky venture among audiences often hostile to dancing. Often this new concern for coordinated movement meant nothing more than the use of synchronized hand gestures or a little swaying. But in the case of a few singers, most notably the Oak Ridge Boys, the routines were not far removed from those of the popular soul singers of the day.

Gospel songs underwent a similar evolution toward homogeneity and predictability as rock 'n' roll did in the early 1960s. In an effort to make their music palatable to the largest possible audience, many gospel singers and composers created a product much like that of the fast-food franchises: generalized, bland, and quickly produced. The songs had little theological or denominational identification, and generally eschewed references to the old themes of death and redemption or images of hellfire and damnation. Their general tone became that of an up-tempoed, yet reassuring, affirmation of the life of the believer. Seldom did groups perform the old-time "blood" songs, referring to the sacrificial death of Jesus, or the songs admonishing his followers to reject the world, such as "Farther Along" and "I'd Rather Have Jesus," that were once so dear to the hearts of southern evangelicals. Devotees of songs such as "Lonely Tombs," "We'll Understand It Better By and By," "Conversation with Death" ("Oh Death"), or "The Blood That Stained the Old Rugged Cross" searched for them in vain in the repertories of the white quartets. They appeared most likely in the performances of the country and bluegrass gospel groups, such as Ralph Stanley and the Clinch Mountain Boys, the Sullivan Family, or in the singing of a downhome black group, such as Iola and Sullivan Pugh, who recorded under the name of the Consolers. Black gospel singers, on the whole, preserved a stronger traditional feeling in their songs than the white quartets. Although they exhibited characteristics derived from jazz, rhythm and blues, and soul idioms, black singers in the 1970s still sang, and made hits of, such songs as "I'm Waiting for My Child to Come Home" and "Don't Drive Your Mother Away," a best-selling sermonette recorded in 1969 by Shirley Caesar.

Whatever the nature of their songs, and regardless of the motives that underlay their singing, gospel performers both black and white have included some of the greatest singers that the United States has produced. Men and women of great vitality, with enormous vocal range and remarkable vocal control, they generally performed for audiences composed exclusively of the faithful, and only rarely became known to the mainstream public.

If gospel music has had an international superstar, it would surely be Mahalia Jackson, born in New Orleans in 1911. She grew up in a home of devout Baptists, but absorbed much of the fervor of the Sanctified people who had a church near her home. She also loved the records of Bessie Smith, and this fusion of blues and gospel music was no doubt a major factor in her appeal. She moved to Chicago in 1927 and entered a community that was already teeming with great solo gospel singers, but she held her own among them even as a teenager. Although she recorded for Decca in 1937, her career did not blossom until after World War II. During the war she joined forces with Thomas Dorsey, with whom she toured the entire United States. She resumed recording in 1946, and her third record, "Move On Up a Little Higher," was one of the best-selling gospel records of all time and the prime force behind her national success. At this stage of her career, Mahalia sang in the freewheeling style of the southern churches, and her popularity was particularly intense among the black southern migrants to the northern United States. Tony Heilbut maintains that she was "unashamedly Southern, roaming and growling like the down-home congregations, and skipping and strutting like the Sanctified preachers."[9]

In the early 1950s Jackson began to build a large following in white America, largely through her appearances on the popular radio shows of Chicago-based Studs Terkel, as many jazz devotees began to notice a resemblance between her and Bessie Smith. In 1954, amid great fanfare, she signed with Columbia Records and began appearing on her own radio and television shows. An appearance at the Newport Jazz Festival in 1958 and a best-selling album recorded with pop icon Percy Faith brought her immense success and demonstrated how far she had traveled from the downhome churches of the South. Although her style and choice of songs came to diverge widely from the music of her childhood—"Silent Night," for example, was her first big international hit—she retained the loyalty of black people everywhere until her death. Because they had both done so much, in their own special ways, to liberate and elevate African Americans, it was only fitting that she should sing in tribute to Martin Luther King Jr. at his funeral, choosing King's personal favorite, the Thomas Dorsey classic "Precious Lord." When Mahalia died in 1972, she was laid to rest in New Orleans, in one of the most heavily attended funerals in the storied history of such events in that city.

No other gospel singer won such acclaim as that accorded to Mahalia Jackson. But Sister Rosetta Tharpe, from Cotton Plant, Arkansas, a guitar playing, Holiness-style singer, made some very popular records for Decca during the 1940s, and saw them go higher in the *Billboard* charts than any previously recorded by gospel singers. Her hot guitar style and swinging, blues-tinged singing of such songs as "Strange Things Happening Every Day" and "Up above My Head," sung with Marie Knight, won a widely diverse audience. Her records, for example, often could be heard on country deejay shows. Still, Tharpe never became a major force in American show business, and even though other singers, such as Bessie Griffin, Alex Bradford, Andrae Crouch, and the Clara Ward Singers, created sophisticated routines and carried them even into the nightclubs, none of them ever achieved the standing in American popular culture attained by Mahalia Jackson. The chief arenas for black gospel music remained the churches where the robed choirs held sway, or the auditoriums in cities around the country that staged package shows featuring the Swan Silvertones, the Dixie Hummingbirds, the Five Blind Boys, Shirley Caesar, or James Cleveland. Most African-American gospel singers or singers who drew heavily from the gospel tradition and became household names did so by leaving the genre, usually for soul music or rhythm & blues. Sam Cooke, a Mississippi native brought up in Chicago and formerly of the venerable black gospel group the Soul Stirrers, not only found success as a soul singer, in the secular use of the term, but also crossover success in the pop music market. Al Green, a native Arkansan who spent most of his teen years in Grand Rapids, Michigan, went the other way, so to speak. He established a huge base of popularity in both soul and r&b and then took his gospel-based style and Sam Cooke influences to the leadership of the Church of the Full Gospel Tabernacle in Memphis, where his singing and preaching epitomized the crossover phenomenon in every sense of the word.

White gospel singers never received the acclaim enjoyed by Mahalia Jackson, nor did they often move away, or at least not far, from music that appealed to their traditional gospel audience. Occasionally the crossover pathway led the other direction, as in the case of performers such as Red Foley, Stuart Hamblen, Martha Carson, Jimmie Davis, or Tennessee Ernie Ford, who had built earlier identifications as country singers and then recorded religious songs that made the popularity charts. Thomas Dorsey's "Peace in the Valley," in fact, attained its greatest popularity through a Red Foley recording. At least one white quartet, the Jordanaires, gained an entree into Hollywood during the late 1950s and early '60s, as well as considerable recording success, through their work as backup singers for Elvis Presley. The Statesmen, especially their lead singer, Jake Hess, received great acclaim on their own and through admiration showered on them by Presley. It may not be too much to say that Presley revered Hess, though he was never able to emulate Hess's remarkable tenor style. The Statler Brothers, none of them actually named Statler, gained initial exposure for their classic gospel quartet performances as part of Johnny Cash's traveling show, but they soon left the gospel field altogether to win fame as country singers. They kept a gospel presence in their repertory, stayed with the four-part harmonies that made them famous, suffered minimal personnel change, and thus sustained a remarkable popularity with continued recordings, personal appearances, and, for a time, their own television program. No quartet, however, took gospel music farther afield from its traditional moorings or from its earlier image than the Oak Ridge Boys. Even before they left the gospel field to take a prominent place in country music, the "Oaks" tested the limits of tolerance of traditional gospel lovers. They wore long hair and mustaches and fancy costumes at a time when most other white gospel performers continued to dress and behave in a fairly traditional manner, and sang hard-charging, hand-clapping gospel songs to the accompaniment of electric, rock-style instrumentation. The Oaks carried their high-energy gospel music into the nightclubs of Las Vegas and profited from modern promotional techniques that seemed worldly to some other gospel performers. Although they might have been embarrassed when an overzealous adman asserted that they "sing the hell out of a gospel song," they seemed to enjoy the hip image that surrounded them. Like the Statler Brothers, the Oak Ridge Boys continued to rely on their gospel-based vocal harmonies as they moved into the country music mainstream, even on their crossover cover of Dallas Frazier's "Elvira."

Despite the exceptional success attained by the Oak Ridge Boys, white quartets, on the whole, stayed close to the one-night-stand regimen, playing in churches, courthouses, and school auditoriums, at all-night singing conventions, and on the increasing numbers of evangelistic television programs. Performing schedules were as grueling for the quartets as for the country and rhythm and blues singers, and big, customized buses with the names of gospel groups painted on their sides became as common on the nation's roads and highways as those of country and western singers. Quartets began making effective use of television during the 1960s, with several of the groups, such as the Florida Boys and the Happy Goodman Family, combining to present syndicated shows on Saturday afternoons or Sunday mornings. Connections with the old publishing houses faded. The legendary gospel name "Stamps," for example, became merely a registered name owned by bass singer J.D. Sumner, with no affiliation with either a business or any member of the Stamps family. The evolution of the gospel business increasingly has paralleled that of the country music industry, not only in the nature of the music performed, but also in the techniques used to advertise and merchandise the music. Although many amateur performers continued to buy sheet music and songbooks, gospel publishing companies waned in importance relative to the record companies. The Gospel Music Association (GMA), headquartered in Nashville, was formed to help build a popular image for the music while promoting its sale. A Hall of Fame, similar to the one that promotes country music, was started to celebrate noted figures in the music, and the GMA instituted the annual Dove awards to honor particularly successful gospel figures.

If any quartet can be said to have dominated the gospel world during the 1960s and 1970s, it would be the Blackwood Brothers. And if any one singer in white gospel music can be designated a superstar of that era, it would be James Blackwood, born in Choctaw County, Mississippi, on August 4, 1919. James Blackwood began singing with the Blackwood Brothers Quartet when it was organized in 1934, consistently won the Dove award as top male gospel singer, and became a member of the Gospel Music Hall of Fame in 1974. The

Blackwoods's music grew out of their Pentecostal church experience and reflected a sense that their concerts should be religious services in song. Although they had already gained considerable popularity both in the South and in the Midwest, where they spent the 1940s, their status as the top act in white gospel music came in 1954 when they won first place on the Arthur Godfrey Talent Show and subsequently saw their version of "Have You Talked to the Man Upstairs" climb into the top ten of the *Billboard* popular music charts. Tragedy followed soon thereafter when two of the quartet's members, R.W. Blackwood and Bill Lyles, lost their lives in the crash of their small plane near Clanton, Alabama. The Blackwood Brothers experienced numerous changes in personnel over the years, often pulling various male family members into the quartet, and long remained at the top of the gospel music business through the adroit fusion of innovation and tradition. The evangelical fervor and sincerity with which the Blackwood Brothers strove to infuse their performances evoked the old-time primitivism of the little country church, a quality their admirers appreciated as much as their consummate vocal musicianship.

One gospel group that challenged the Blackwoods's supremacy almost from the time of its founding in the mid-1960s was the Cathedral Quartet, named for Rex Humbard's church in Akron, Ohio. The Cathedrals, like the Blackwood Brothers, employed a mixture of veteran and younger singers and had an uncanny sense of how to mix the traditional and innovative without losing their audience in the process. As a group and as individuals, the Cathedrals won numerous Dove awards and pointed the way toward the future of gospel music. As the 1970s wound down, that future began to look increasingly as if it were going to bring some very dramatic changes in a musical form much beloved to southerners and to many people in other parts of the United States and the rest of the world.

If audience involvement was often an important factor in the performance of both white and black gospel music, it was positively indispensable in the soul music that became such a vital force in U.S. popular culture in the mid-1960s. Soul music was something of an extension of rhythm and blues in that it was first popularized by singers who had earlier gained identification in r&b, but its real power and distinctiveness came from the infusion within it of black gospel music and of the social and political ferment of the period out of which it arose. According to Peter Guralnick, "Southern soul music developed out of a time and a set of social circumstances that are unlikely to be repeated. . . . It was for a considerable length of time limited almost exclusively to a black audience which had grown up on the uninhibited emotionalism of the church and to a secret but growing legion of young white admirers who picked up on rhythm and blues on the radio and took it as the key to a mystery they were pledged never to reveal."[10] Soul was very much a partnership between black performers and composers who wanted to find a mixed-race audience for their music and for their freedom message and white musicians, composers, and recording company personnel who accepted the message and recognized the commercial potential of the music. References can be found using the word "soul" as a term for black music as early as the nineteenth century, but the term came into wide use in the mid-1960s, inspired in large part by the emergence of the Black Power movement. The word was susceptible to many definitions, but to most people at the time soul was clearly identifiable with and a product of the black experience in the United States. Many observers, black and white, assumed that soul was something only African Americans had, something that embodied the essence of their survival and grew out of their culture as a people who endured slavery, segregation, and rural poverty. The term came to be widely used, particularly after 1967–68 when the media seized upon it in the wake of riots and urban unrest, to describe a wide range of black musical styles. "Soul" was often linked to rhythm & blues experience, but usually soul singers pointed to some type of gospel music training or inspiration. In fact, much of the style associated with soul music had specific origins in churches or in church-derived music.

Soul music was associated largely with two groups of performers: second-generation northern African Americans, particularly some of those who recorded for the Motown label in Detroit; and, more importantly, southern-born blacks and whites, especially those associated with the independent recording labels and studios in Memphis, Macon, and Muscle Shoals. The Motown Sound, which arose at about the same time as soul music, had a heavily commercialized, somewhat formulaic pop sound that was palatable to the general white audience. Seldom has a recording studio produced such an instantly recognizable sound, almost without regard to artist or song selection. Such Motown stars as Diana Ross and the Supremes were sometimes disparaged for trying to de-emphasize their ethnicity to win the approval of white fans and critics. In addition, there was no small irony in the fact that Motown, a black-owned label, made its reputation largely by selling records to whites while the premier soul labels, which were white-owned, developed their success by appealing to African Americans and the black pride ideal. Motown artists nevertheless had a large following among blacks too, particularly among black youth who took great pride in the success of their peers, while soul music produced similarly large sales among whites.

Another Detroit singer, Memphis-born Aretha Franklin, many would argue, was the most popular African American performer in the late 1960s and early '70s and unquestionably a major force in the entire world of American popular music. Although she was not southern-reared, Franklin's style was clearly moored in the black church, and she freely admitted the influence of the gospel-singing Clara Ward. Her father was the Reverend C.L. Franklin, the prominent pastor of the New Bethel Baptist Church in Detroit, who successfully carried on a tradition introduced by the Reverend J.M. Gates in the 1920s, having recorded over fifty best-selling albums of sermons. Resistant to attempts made by occasional producers to change her style but continually adapting as she added decades to her success, Franklin became a soul icon. She transformed Otis Redding's song "Respect," as Peter Guralnick says, "from a demand for conjugal rights into a soaring cry of freedom,"[11] moving audiences with the incredible power and range of her voice and her determination to include women's perspectives in the call for black power and liberation.

Southern-born singers usually performed with styles that were considerably more earthy than those of northern performers. But this did not prevent some of the southern singers, such as Ray Charles, from winning wide acclaim among white listeners in areas other than the South. Born Ray Charles Robinson in Albany, Georgia, on September 23, 1930, and blinded by glaucoma at the age of six, Charles turned to music and began playing professionally in Florida as a teenager. In 1948 he moved to Seattle, where he organized a piano trio in the fashion of Nat "King" Cole's earlier popular group. Although his rough voice and limited range did not permit him to recreate the Nat Cole vocal sound, Charles had uncanny intuition about how to use his voice to great effect and exhibited a fascination with all kinds of popular music. In 1952 he signed with the Atlantic label as a blues and rhythm & blues singer, and he contributed mightily to the popularization of the r&b genre and to the mixing of categories that came in the mid-1950s. His influence went beyond the immediate realm of genres of vernacular music, however. In the early 1950s Charles recorded gospel songs along with his blues and r&b selections, then went on to become one of the first r&b entertainers to record secular remakes of gospel songs. "I Gotta Woman" had been "I Gotta God" in 1954, and "This Little Light of Mine" became "This Little Girl of Mine" in 1955. Charles's biographer Michael Lydon tells how Charles and musical companions were traveling through the Indiana countryside late one night: "Ray was always searching for good music on the radio, and when he found a gospel station, that's where he stopped the dial. One night near South Bend, [Renald] Richard remembered vividly, a gospel tune came on with a good groove, and they started singing along," adapting the words and beginning the process of applying gospel vocal techniques to quite a secular theme.[12] His use of gospel vocal techniques—falsetto shouts, groans, extended melisma, and call-and-response patterns, usually between Charles and his female backup singers, the Raelets—attracted mixed reactions, including a great deal of criticism from ministers. But gospel music was too important to him, as was the freedom to draw from any musical form. He had never sung in a gospel group; he simply had heard and absorbed the music all his life. But Charles never sang one type of music exclusively. He tried to revive traditional jazz and in 1955 recorded "A Bit of Soul" and in 1956, "Houseful of Soul," two of the first usages of the term in the post-World War II period.

In 1959 Charles's recording of "What'd I Say" made the pop charts, his first of many such experiences. In 1959 he joined ABC-Paramount and in 1960 recorded "Georgia on My Mind," which became number one on the pop music charts and, later, the state song of Georgia. Charles went on to record show tunes, pop standards, and some very successful albums of country and western songs. In his progress toward becoming one of the most successful musicians of all time, Ray Charles retained a very large following among African Americans, although some of his original fans, annoyed by his eclecticism, accused him of selling out to the lure of commercial success. However, Charles was an eclectic musician from the time he entered professional music in the mid-1940s. In discussing his country albums, for example, Charles noted that as a boy he had often listened to the Grand Ole Opry, and that one of his earliest professional stints was with a white country band called the Florida Playboys.[13] He was simply contributing to a southern music tradition of long standing.

Music coming out of Memphis had been fusing country and western music with rhythm & blues since the mid-1950s. Memphis's emergence as a recording center had begun about 1954 when Sam Phillips and his Sun label began recording white talent covering r&b tunes. The second stage in that evolution began in 1959 when a local banker and ex-country fiddler named Jim Stewart and his sister, Estelle Axton, opened a studio in a former vaudeville theater in the heart of the black ghetto. Their Stax label achieved national prominence in 1962 when a local band named Booker T. and the MGs recorded a million-seller, "Green Onions," an accomplishment followed by a string of hits made by Al Green, Otis Redding, Sam and Dave, and Wilson Pickett. Organist Booker T. Jones and the other MGs served as the session musicians for Stax. The label's success benefited from the easy-going ambience and biracial character of the people who owned and produced it. Stewart was white; his vice-president was black. The house band was racially mixed, and the company's two principal writers, Isaac Hayes and David Porter, were black men who freely borrowed from many musical sources, including country and western lyrics.

The Memphis Sound, as developed by Stax and several other small companies, was touted as a composite of two southern folk traditions, black r&b and white country. The contrast with Detroit's Motown was obvious. As Arnold Shaw said, "The Memphis Sound has more grit, gravel, and mud in it than the Detroit Sound."[14] By the early '70s, Memphis was the fourth-largest recording center in the nation, behind New York, Los Angeles, and Nashville, and some of the most exciting sounds in the soul genre were coming out of its studios.

Many fine musicians were associated with the Memphis soul scene, but Otis Redding was the acknowledged superstar of the Memphis Sound. Born the son of a minister in Dawson, Georgia, in 1941, Redding grew up in Macon in an active r&b environment that included Little Richard, the singer Redding most admired. Although he had recorded a few songs on small labels in Macon and on the West Coast, Redding's most fruitful recording affiliation came with Stax after November 1962. By 1966 he had taken his music to enthusiastic audiences in Britain and France, and a British music magazine, *Melody Maker,* called him the world's number-one male vocalist. Redding was always popular among African-American fans, but after a critically acclaimed performance at the Monterey Pop Festival in 1967 he seemed on the verge of winning large-scale white support as well. But on December 10, 1967, his private plane crashed into Lake Monona, in Madison, Wisconsin, killing him and four of his band members. The posthumously issued "Sitting on the Dock of the Bay" was an award-winning and best-selling record.

Many soul singers showed evidence of having absorbed nonblack musical influences or, as in the case of Ray Charles, of having consciously striven to win white support. But James Brown, the "King of Soul," never compromised his musical approach. Many fans and critics said his was the "blackest sound" in American popular music, and he never diluted it even when singing before white audiences. Brown's music, therefore, most closely conforms to the popular image of soul: black music performed for black audiences. Brown was born in Georgia near the South Carolina line in the early 1930s, but he grew up in Augusta where he essentially reared himself, dropping out of school in the seventh grade and working at everything from shoeshining and cotton picking to dancing in the streets for nickels and dimes. Orphaned, poor, and black, Brown was led by his frustrations into a short experience with juvenile delinquency, and he served almost four years in a reform school. After his release at the age of nineteen, he began singing in a church in Toccoa, Georgia, in order to support his early marriage. Soon thereafter he took his gospel-influenced style into the dives and honky-tonks of the Deep South, and in 1956 he recorded his first big hit, "Please, Please, Please," for the King label.

Until the mid-1960s, when the emphasis on Black Power encouraged a closer look at authentic black talent, Brown remained almost totally unknown to the white world, while consistently ranking at the top of the r&b list. Brown never tried to cross over into the pop field, either during the rock 'n' roll period, or during the Motown era, a resolution that endeared him all the more to militant black fans. His songs were never the type that white pop artists could easily cover, and he never modified his approach to make his music more accessible to whites. Brown's great reputation in the ghettos was enhanced in the mid-1960s when he began visiting them and communicating directly with the teenagers there. His first publicized trip of this sort was to San Francisco in 1966, where he advised black youngsters to remain in school. The visit was soon followed by a recording of "Don't Be a Drop-Out." After the assassination of Martin Luther King Jr. in April 1968, Brown responded to urgent pleas from the mayors of Boston and Washington, D.C., by appearing for hours on television in both cities pleading for ghetto-dwellers to remain orderly and stay off the streets.

Brown's prominence in quelling riots and his adulation in the black ghettos contributed to the larger public's discovery of him, and his sociopolitical identification was one of the major factors that generated the publicity he received at the time. Americans were acutely conscious of Black Power rhetoric and the ghettos in 1968. Brown definitely identified with Black Power, though he alienated some of the black radicals, such as H. Rap Brown and Amiri Baraka (formerly LeRoi Jones), when he opposed the violence of the riots and affirmed his commitment to the United States, as in "America Is My Home." Along with his emphasis on education, which was almost a religion to him, Brown promoted the idea of black economic self-help. Black capitalism, to Brown, seemed to be the essence of Black Power, and it was this aspect of his career, especially his fabulous commercial success, that most intrigued the media. Magazine accounts invariably stressed his wealth and material acquisitions, as they have always done when discussing any folk-derived musician who has made it big. Admittedly, Brown's earnings and investments were enough to attract anyone's notice. In 1968 his gross from one-nighters was about $2.5 million. He owned two radio stations, including one in Augusta where he had once shined shoes, a record production company, extensive real estate, a house that was essentially a castle, a wardrobe legendary for its size and flamboyance, numerous expensive automobiles, and his own Lear jet.

Musically, Brown was unique in that his was almost a totally black sound, and he succeeded with it as no other African-American performer ever had.

By 1968, after leading the r&b field for years, he was named *Cash Box*'s choice as the number-one male vocalist in all of popular music. He achieved this distinction with a style that seemed to come not only from the rural southern black churches but, with its heavy emphasis on beat and rhythm at the expense of lyrics, from African roots as well. At a time of musical amalgamation, when the leading Motown performers were reaching out toward the middle-class mainstream, Brown reached far back to the very sources of black music. Performance was everything in a James Brown appearance. Using grunts, moans, and unearthly screams, repeating words endlessly and bending them to unbelievable lengths, and interacting with his musicians, chorus, and audience in a hypnotic, often erotic call-and-response pattern, Brown communicated with his enormous audiences as few performers had ever done. These performances were also remarkable as choreographic experiences, for Brown had few peers as a dancer. His act was folk in its earthiness and in its indebtedness to older forms and styles, but it was also ultramodern in its organization, polish, and timing.

Though Martin Luther King Jr.'s assassination ended much of the interracial cooperation on which soul music was based in the 1960s, the political, emotional, and moral fervor of the times produced some powerful musical messages through the songwriting of Smokey Robinson and Curtis Mayfield. Gone were the days when the Muscle Shoals "Alabama peckerwoods" and "southern crackers," as Robert Palmer called them, backed up the leading black singers of the day. Gone also, by the mid-1970s, was Stax, as Palmer says, "its equipment sold at public auction." He notes that soul music suffered an attrition of its own as groups broke up and key figures died or left the field, culminating in the experience of Al Green. When "Green abandoned secular music to preach the gospel, in 1979, there could be no doubt that the soul era was over."[15]

Creative tension, however, between the poles of eclectic folk background and contemporary techniques continued to enliven southern music. The sort of tension that yielded Brown, Charles, Redding, Franklin, and the others such success, drawing from various streams of southern musical experience, was in very large part the same matter of balance that affected the other "soul" music of the South and of the United States, country music.

Chapter 8

THE NATIONAL RESURGENCE
OF COUNTRY MUSIC

Southern-derived grassroots music of various genres suffered from the rock 'n' roll onslaught of the 1950s. After that, various forms made comebacks, though none more spectacular than that of country music, which gained a stature in U.S. popular culture that had scarcely been dreamed of during its hillbilly beginnings. Indeed, the boast of the Country Music Association (CMA) that country was "best liked worldwide" seemed not far from accurate. Fiddles and steel guitars, the instrumental mainstays of World War II-era country bands, virtually disappeared from country recordings for a few years, to be replaced by rock 'n' roll-style electric guitars or by pop-style instrumentation. The accent was now clearly on youth, and record companies energetically searched for new and exciting successors to Elvis Presley. Almost all older country singers tried their hands at either rock 'n' roll or some upbeat style that might appeal to a youthful audience. Rock 'n' roll left its mark on country music in many ways. Several rockabillies, including Jerry Lee Lewis and Conway Twitty, carved out very successful careers as mainstream country singers. Other rock 'n' roll musicians joined country bands, taking their instrumental licks with them and thereby altering, perhaps permanently, the sound of country music. Country music as a whole moved into the '60s thoroughly committed to a heavy electronic sound, created by the increasingly centralized recording establishment dominated by producers and marketing executives. Country music was on its way to becoming middle-class. Only bluegrass musicians held against the tide.

Although tradition-minded country fans despaired at what seemed to be the disappearance, or betrayal, of old-time country styles, some trends of the period turned out to be less threatening than they first appeared or faded fairly quickly. Tradition-based styles still flourished away from the glare of the public limelight. Some of them resurfaced with a vengeance a few years hence, commanding national attention as neo-traditional styles. But in U.S. popular culture, some transitory phenomena seize the public imagination with such intensity that they sometimes seem as if they will last—indeed, have already lasted—a lifetime.

By the time country music began its comeback about 1958, the term "hillbilly" had been abandoned except by a few scholars who used it to describe music from the days before World War II and by a scattering of fans and performers who, at least privately, liked to refer to themselves and their music as "hillbilly." The word "country" was now almost universally employed to describe the music, and the acknowledged center of the "industry," also now a commonly used word, was Nashville.

Much of country music's commercial regeneration can be attributed to the efforts of the Country Music Association. Founded in 1958 as a trade organization, the CMA worked to elevate the image of the music and to demonstrate its commercial potential to advertisers. One of the CMA's main strategies was to encourage radio stations to play country music exclusively. The fact that many stations did exactly that contributed greatly to the national popularization of country music, but it also often prompted a blurring of identity within the music. Most country stations developed their own versions of the Top Forty formats pioneered by rock or youth-oriented stations. Listeners could turn their radio dials all day long and hear nothing but the same handful of songs, and no one could ever be sure how the tight play-list was determined in the first place. Because of the rapid multiplication of country radio stations, a large number of announcers with no earlier experience with country music became associated with it. Some of these young deejays had come of age musically during the rock 'n' roll era, and they carried many of the perceptions of those years into their new affiliations with country music. To be sure, veteran country disc jockeys, who had a folksy rapport with their listeners that extended the hayseed image projected by the music, also had their own biases and predilections that affected their selection of records, influencing music styles in the process. But by the 1960s, these deejays had almost totally disappeared, leaving a rare exception here and there such as Gordon Baxter of Beaumont, Texas, who uncompromisingly insisted on maintaining his unique "loose board," downhome style of friendly chatter and favorite records. Baxter and a few other country deejays in the 1960s ignored the constant risk of getting fired for maintaining an individualized style counter to the homogenized, market-driven dictates of the Top Forty format.

Led by Chet Atkins, the country music industry reacted to the rock 'n' roll threat by attempting to create a product that would appeal to the broadest possible spectrum of listeners, that is to say, a music shorn of most of its "rural" characteristics. Atkins, RCA's recording director in Nashville and one of the prime forces behind the innovations unfolding there, explained the changes as a "compromise" that made country music more popular while permitting all of its substyles to endure and flourish. The music that emerged from the recording studios of Nashville, called variously the "Nashville Sound," "country-pop," "countrypolitan," or "middle-of-the-road music," de-emphasized or omitted fiddles and steel guitars and introduced pop-styled background voices and sedate, multi-layered instrumentation designed to reach new listeners while holding on to the older ones. Atkins and other record producers who sought to emulate his successful techniques deliberately sought to create recordings with appeal in all markets. Country songs had been picked up by pop singers with great frequency since the early 1950s when those written by Hank Williams enjoyed great vogue, but country singers themselves almost never appeared on pop charts. Rock 'n' roll, however, had changed all the rules, and in the climate of the '60s crossover hits became a typical, and sought-after, aspect of the music business. In the early part of the decade those country singers with smooth voices and little rural identification had the best chance of gaining acceptance as pop singers. Eddy Arnold, despite his popular designation as the Tennessee Plowboy, had long anticipated the country-pop approach, but Jim Reeves, from Panola County, Texas, a singer with a very smooth voice, won the widest acclaim with such songs as "Four Walls" and "He'll Have to Go." In the 1970s, Mac Davis, from Lubbock, Texas, and Glen Campbell, from Delight, Arkansas, built on and surpassed in many ways the popularity enjoyed in the '60s by such singers as Arnold, Reeves, and Roger Miller. Both Davis and Campbell, an especially versatile instrumentalist, hosted very popular nationally syndicated television shows built on images only loosely related to country music.

Country-pop's emergence paralleled Nashville's rise to preeminence as a music center. Culturally aspiring Nashvillians, who had once termed their city the "Athens of the South" and boasted of its massive replica of the Parthenon, and who had been embarrassed by the presence there of the Grand Ole Opry, learned to swallow their pride as money rolled in to feed the burgeoning music industry. Publishing and licensing houses, booking offices, and recording studios hummed with such activity that Nashville came to be described on billboards and in city-sponsored promotional material as Music City, USA, a nickname that garnered Nashville far-greater fame than its Athenian aspirations ever produced. Country singers appeared on the pop music charts so frequently in the early '60s that a large number of singers from other genres began coming to Nashville by the end of the decade to use its recording facilities and versatile session musicians, leading to, if not culminating in, Bob Dylan's watershed albums *John Wesley Harding* and *Nashville Skyline.* Nashville became known far and wide as country music's capital, but the music recorded there actually encompassed much of the full spectrum of popular music.

Country music's commercial revival and national surge of popularity in the 1960s and '70s were marked by an accompanying identification with national purpose and definition. This phenomenon was demonstrated by the music's growing "respectability," by recurring White House endorsement, and by the use of the term "American" by some of its performers to describe their music. In its most extreme form, the equating of "country music" and "Americanism" was shown during the mainstream or "middle" American backlash against the upheaval of the 1960s in such country lyrics as "when you're running down my country . . . you're walking on the fighting side of me."[1] During the '60s and early '70s, when urban-born folksingers and rock performers subjected the government and its domestic and foreign policies to withering criticism, the appearance of a spate of unabashedly pro-America songs contributed to country music's reputation for 100-percent Americanism. It also helped explain why President Richard Nixon would travel to Nashville during the most troubled period of his administration to participate in the formal opening of the new Grand Ole Opry House and play the piano for the delighted fans.

Country music's emergence as an ultrapatriotic and even jingoistic genre during the late stages of the Vietnam War was not simply an extension of southern working-class values into a national setting. It also reflected the polarization of the period and the country industry's attempts to gain acceptance by identifying with national trends and attitudes and capitalizing on public fears and neuroses. Merle Haggard, the California-born son of Okie migrants, became the singer most often identified with the "reactionary" or backlash songs of the 1970s. With a past that included some trouble with the power structure of the day, including some fairly serious run-ins with the law, and similarities in background to Woody Guthrie, Haggard might have been expected to espouse something of an anti-establishment political viewpoint. Indeed, several of his songs from the '70s, such as "Working Man's Blues," carried a vaguely populist tint. But Haggard became identified, possibly forever, with the militant conservatism of two songs, "Okie from Muskogee" and "Fightin' Side of Me." The first was his rebuke of the hippie culture and a paean of praise to the people who came to be called in the 1970s "Middle America." Though "Okie from Muskogee" was apparently conceived as a joke or parody, its astonishing popularity brought Haggard national exposure and media coverage aspiring performers often only dream of. "Fightin' Side of Me," with its "love it or leave it" stance toward critics of U.S. military actions and social values, served to confirm Haggard's conservative credentials, though people of his acquaintance insisted that he was anything but a reactionary or a warmonger. His ascent to stardom and country music's rise to national recognition were clearly helped along by the national mood of emotional schizophrenia that accompanied the Vietnam War, the civil rights movement, and the rise of the counterculture, including a perceived link between rock music and youthful rebellion. Haggard's compositions struck a responsive chord, particularly among audiences far from the South, and he received warm welcomes in such cities as Philadelphia and Duluth. Partly because of its identification with "the silent majority," country music was "discovered" by the media, scholars of pop culture, and even the national political establishment. Presidents Johnson and Nixon both brought country entertainers into the White House, gestures that no doubt disgusted those who recalled the artistic soirees of the Kennedy years.

As in the chaotic 1920s, many people in the turbulent '60s seemed to find something in country music that projected a more stable image than that conveyed by youth music. In the '20s, the cultural disintegrator was jazz, in the '60s, it was rock. But country music allegedly represented pure Americanism, and some people on the left of the political spectrum no doubt found the country music world strangely fascinating if not downright terrifying. An article in *Harper's* blamed everything from working-class alienation to the truckers' strike of 1972 on country music, while in *Mademoiselle* the music was described as "the perfect musical extension of the Nixon administration" and a repository of values that "ought to frighten every longhaired progressive urbanite, and every black man who is not part of it."[2] As in the early days of its commercial history, country music evoked stereotypically opposed responses, the feeling that it was either a music of unthinking bigotry, or a music of genuine patriotism and morality, something that might help hold the line against the longhaired, dope-smoking rebels who seemed intent on ruining the country.

Country music's identification during the Nixon years with "establishment" values was remarkable in light of its origins and development. Some wondered how a music once contemptuously dismissed as "hillbilly" and presumed to be the province of cultural degenerates living in a "benighted" region got to be the exemplar and upholder of national norms. Also surprising was the fact that a region famous for resistance to nationalization, whether in the middle decades of the nineteenth century or those of the twentieth, came to be seen as the hotbed of unquestioning patriotism. The relationship between country music and "Americanism" has always been odd and tenuous, rooted in the South's ambivalent relationship to the nation at large. The sense of being both out of the mainstream and at the same time being more "American" than other regions of the nation was an attitude that many southerners had held well before the Civil War, often feeling that the majority northern culture had violated or marginalized "original" American ideals. Regardless of the degree of mythology inherent in the viewpoint, the country music of the 1970s especially reflected southern ambivalence toward the rest of the nation. Conscious of its "southernness," and therefore presumably of its uniqueness, the music also reflected a conviction that the South embodied the best in the American character as a whole.

Country music industry leaders had energetically endeavored since the 1950s to broaden the base of the music, to make it more "respectable" and therefore, they reasoned, more marketable. Much of the identification of country music with establishment culture, by which it actually came to seem bourgeois in the years of backlash against '60s-era rebelliousness, therefore, came from conscious efforts of music industry executives and entrepreneurs to pass the music off as the embodiment of middle-class propriety and respect for law and order. Those who grafted a respectable, conformist attitude onto country music played havoc with its history and traditions, for the music was always much more complex than either its devotees or detractors recognized. The rural South from which the music sprang had always been a multifaceted place, in its own way something of a counterculture.[3] The resurgence of country music in the 1960s and '70s, with its image of national conformity, seemed strange coming from a region long noted for intense individualism. The tradition of the drifter, the rounder, and even the lawless man, preceded the period of commercialization and constituted a thread in the music from Jimmie Rodgers in the 1920s and '30s to Waylon Jennings and Willie Nelson in the '70s. The "law" was never treated with particular reverence in the old country songs, and personal morality, while often preached as a virtue, was just as often violated in practice. Endorsement of the status quo in country music, often assuming bland, homogenized forms and directed as much toward the pocketbook of Middle America as toward its mind or heart, obscured the music's historic diversity. Despite the abundance of songs stressing domestic virtues and sense of place, country music, as much as anything, has been the music of an uprooted people with an acute consciousness of a world of shifting values. Country music is indeed "American," but its Americanism is broad rather than narrow, deriving from many sources and presumptions and hardly contained within the political or social agenda of one particular group.

Country music's quest for legitimacy was not without its innovative or "liberal" components. Indeed, to a great extent the industry attempted to be all things to all people. While on one hand projecting conservatism, it also

strove to be aware of the latest developments and trends, and at least to give
the impression of broadening its horizons. The music's image as the most
male-dominated white Protestant music in America began to undergo some
alterations in the 1960s and early '70s. The period saw the emergence, for
instance, of the first black country superstar, Charley Pride, from Sledge, Mississippi, and the first Chicano superstars, Johnny Rodriguez and Freddy Fender
(Baldemar Huerta), from Sabinal and Weslaco, Texas, respectively. It also gave
rise to the first Cajun superstar, Doug Kershaw, from Tiel Ridge, Louisiana,
and at least one Jewish country singer, Kinky Friedman, from Austin, Texas,
who, if not a superstar, certainly became one of the most colorful and outra-
geous of country singers.

Probably more significant, though, than the ethnic breakthrough in country music in the 1970s was the burgeoning activity of women singers. Until
the appearance of Kitty Wells in the early '50s, almost no women in country
music had attained independent identities apart from men, and they had seldom won the financial rewards gained by male singers. Virginia-born Patsy
Cline had become a powerful presence in country music in the late '50s and
early '60s as an extraordinarily gifted song interpreter whose searing style made
many leading songwriters want her to record their work. She also made moves
in the early stages of the rise of country-pop that foreshadowed her coming
leadership in that phase of country music. Then she was killed in a plane crash
in March 1963. In the period of country music's resurgence, however, and
partly inspired by Cline's example, women began competing with men on
more than even terms and won the kind of success that black women singers
commanded in previous years. Tanya Tucker, Tammy Wynette, Crystal Gayle,
Melba Montgomery, Emmylou Harris, Loretta Lynn, and Dolly Parton were
only a few of the women who achieved stardom in the 1970s. Of these, some
built eclectic styles that attracted followers from outside country music, such
as Gayle, Lynn's sister, who achieved success as a middle-of-the-road pop
singer, and Tucker, Harris, and Parton, who did so as folk-rock-tinged country
singers.

Loretta Lynn's style and personality remained purebred country, but she
reached fans outside country music's normal base and achieved a recognition
in American life in the 1970s that none of the other women singers, and few
of the men, attained. Lynn appeared frequently on television shows and in
commercials, graced the covers of several mainstream magazines, including
Newsweek in June 1973, and wrote, with George Vecsey, a best-selling autobiography titled *Coal Miner's Daughter,* which was made into a critically acclaimed film at the end of the decade. She became widely known as much for
her wit and open, country honesty and charm, as for her highly praised sing-

ing. Born in Butcher Hollow, Kentucky, to a coal mining family, she began trying her luck at singing in Custer, Washington, in 1961, where she and her husband Mooney Lynn had moved in the early '50s. When her first song, "Honky Tonk Girl," appeared on a small label in '61, she and her husband set out by automobile across the United States, sleeping in the car and dressing in service-station washrooms, pushing her record to deejays in radio stations all over the country. Her hope was to achieve something of the success of her mentor, Patsy Cline. For years she maintained a personal appearance schedule almost as rigorous, but traveling in a style befitting a superstar who now enjoyed the luxury of agreeing to interviews and meetings with deejays only as she saw fit. Throughout the period of her remarkable success, Lynn continued to impress and delight fans with her personal qualities and always remained very accessible to those fans. Women especially admired her for the successful ways she balanced professional and family life, something increasingly important in the 1970s as more women began to work outside the home. Lynn moved away from the poverty of her humble origins and the downhome sounds heard on her early records, but her clear, pure voice and old-fashioned diction continued to give testimony to her mountain beginnings.

Mountain roots clung tightly to Dolly Parton also, even as she moved farther than Loretta Lynn from the "hard country" repertory. Parton won the readers' poll in *Rolling Stone* as the top country singer of 1977, and by the end of that year was hosting her own television show and making a determined effort to carve out an identity appealing to rock/youth audiences. One of eleven children born into a mountain farm family near Sevierville, Tennessee, her first singing experience came in a Church of God congregation where her grandfather was pastor, but she began appearing on local barn dances and singing on the radio in Knoxville as a small child. No one was really surprised, therefore, when she set out by bus for Nashville the day after she graduated from high school. Parton's entree to stardom came through her work on Porter Wagoner's syndicated television show and through her very popular duet recordings with Wagoner. Fans of Wagoner's television and road shows soon became fans as well of the buxom young woman who managed to combine an arresting physical appearance, flamboyant outfits and wigs, and a personality that was at the same time fetching and innocent. Parton seemed to be acting out the fantasies of a poor mountain girl whose family had never been able to buy her the makeup, jewelry, or fine clothes she desired. Many critics were put off by what they saw as Parton's affectations and missed the opportunity to hear one of the great talents in American popular music.

Like Lynn, Parton excelled both as a singer and as a songwriter. With one of the most expressive voices in any field of American popular music, she moved easily and convincingly from the tenderest love songs to rousing novelty tunes and even yodels. Although considered preeminently an entertainer, she also became one of the best writers in country music. Her compositions run the gamut of themes and emotions commonly found in country music, but even the most personal of her songs have a convincing, charismatic integrity and appealing universality. Some of the best songs deal with her childhood, with bittersweet recollections of growing up a sensitive child in a large, poor, but loving family. No song more effectively describes the ambivalent feelings that she and many people with country origins have when they reflect upon their rural experiences than "In the Good Old Days When Times Were Bad." But her greatest song, and probably her most intimate, is "Coat of Many Colors," a personal childhood narrative that weaves a poignant verbal tapestry of poverty and maternal love.

Women made dramatic gains in country music in the post-World War II era. They came to hold positions of power as industry executives, and as performers they competed on increasingly favorable terms with men, often producing greater incomes than male performers. To a certain extent, the progress of women in country music paralleled the increasing consciousness of women in the United States and general awareness of their rights in the 1960s and '70s. It also constituted an especially dramatic shift in both the status and the image of southern women. Revolutions, however, always unfold slowly in country music, and many women singers continued to sing of values associated with an older world while leading lives as entertainers that often ran counter to those values. Like many women, they found themselves caught between age-old expectations that had kept their mothers and grandmothers locked in tightly constricted roles and the growing recognition that they should have the same opportunities as men. Many women in country music felt enormous pressure to preserve the veneer of domesticity while pursuing careers with an aggressiveness and singleness of purpose that left little time or energy for home and family. For the most part, too, the world described in their songs was a man's world, and their lyrics dealt often with women who were dependent on men or those whose terms of existence were largely dictated by men. Tammy Wynette, for example, had a significant career on her own in the mid-1960s. When she married the great country singer George Jones in 1968, they became known as "Mr. and Mrs. Country Music." From then on, despite her own significant talent and broad appeal, Wynette became identified to a great extent by her relationship with Jones, through the time of their turbulent marriage, widely publicized divorce, and eventual reunion duet appearances. Though she continued to have a solid solo career and large following until the end of her life, Wynette became a stereotype or a role model, depending on one's perspective, even a political symbol, if only for her most famous song, "Stand By Your Man." She was the long-suffering, faithful woman whose life was essentially defined by a troublesome man and who opened her story by saying, "Sometimes it's hard to be a woman."

Old attitudes persist, but new ones crept into country music along with a new breed of writers and musicians. Consequently, the audience for country music changed significantly after the 1960s. Since that decade, country music ceased to be thought of as solely an expression of Middle America and gained an audience that cut across generational, geographic, and socioeconomic lines. In part, the broadened interest in country music reflected a wave of nostalgia or an urge to explore the roots of American life not confined to old people, transplanted ruralites, or die-hard reactionaries. The mood was shared by many young people as well in the 1970s, many of whom might have been radicals or members of the counterculture back in the '60s. Anyone who attended a blue-grass festival or a "progressive country" concert at the Armadillo World Head-quarters in Austin, Texas, or one of Willie Nelson's giant picnics in the '70s saw a remarkable spectrum of humanity turned on to the music. Country became chic among many Americans who once ignored or despised it. While the reasons for these reversals of attitude are many and complex, one simple, but important, factor is that the music itself changed. A new generation of songwriters appeared in the '70s. In the strong tradition of southern music, they drew upon the resources of other musical forms for sustenance and upon the social currents of their own day for inspiration. But their music was largely attuned to youth. Further, though the music was preoccupied with romantic love, that everlasting staple of American popular music, it treated the subject with a candor and guiltless sensuality rare in earlier country music.

In the 1970s the writer who most consistently appealed to the widest spectrum of American listeners was Kris Kristofferson. A highly untypical hillbilly, Kristofferson was an army brat born in Brownsville, Texas, and reared in California who became a Rhodes scholar preparing for a career as a professor of English literature. After a stint in the army, Kristofferson turned down an opportunity to join the faculty at West Point and moved to Nashville. Inspired by an early love for Hank Williams's music, he began writing country songs. "Me and Bobby McGee," recorded in 1969 by Roger Miller and later by Janis Joplin, was the first of a long succession of very successful Kristofferson songs recorded by leading country entertainers including "For the Good Times" (Ray Price), "Come Sundown" (Bobby Bare), "Help Me Make It through the Night" (Sammi Smith), and the song that won him his first CMA award, in 1970, "Sunday Mornin' Comin' Down" (Johnny Cash). Kristofferson's own recording career began in 1969 for Monument, and in 1973 he hit a chord that resonated deeply with southern audiences but also with fans all over the U.S. when he recorded "Why Me, Lord," inspired by a religious experience he had one evening in a Pentecostal church in Nashville. Religious themes did not dominate his music, though. He became quite well known in the industry and in the public mind as the writer of songs about freedom, honest relationships, and sensual experience. But his songs' appeal derived from their musical quality as well as from their thematic bases. They featured pretty, singable melodies, economy of language, and memorable aphorisms. Kristofferson moved on to stardom as an entertainer and actor, and his production of hit songs declined substantially, but the enduring quality of his best songs not only opened other commercial doors for him, it also indicated that country music had enormous market potential across lines that traditionally separated groups of people in the United States, including the all-important demographic distinction between youthful and not-so-youthful record buyers.

One of the factors that bridged gaps in the music marketplace was a change in attitudes about subject matter in songs, something Kris Kristofferson and others of his generation helped bring about. The passing of the rebellious 1960s did not mean that middle-class sensibilities with their moderating influences were going to regain control of U.S. culture. One trend that continued through the '70s was the inclusion of sexually suggestive lyrics in country songs. Such lyrics appealed to younger audiences and helped make country music more profitable, though producers and publishers had to worry about alienating more mature or more conservative customers. The more explicit of the new breed of songs aroused the indignation of many people both inside and outside of the country music industry. Some radio stations refused to play them. Veteran country songwriter Cindy Walker called them "skin songs."[4] Old-time country fans no doubt had some difficulty adjusting to such songs as Freddy Weller's "Sexy Lady," Charlie Rich's "Behind Closed Doors," and Conway Twitty's "You've Never Been This Far Before," but each song became a hit. Old double-standards made it more difficult for fans to accept such songs from women songwriters, though Floridian Linda Hargrove, one of the most candid and sensitive of the new breed of songwriters, wrote such a song, "Just Get Up and Close the Door," and saw it emerge as a hit for Johnny Rodriguez. Her own recording of "Mexican Love Songs" was even more explicit, featuring a woman who picks up a man in a honky-tonk and regrets waking up the next morning with a cowboy who "takes up three-fourths of the bed."

While a fairly diverse group of new songwriters contributed to the broadening of perspectives within country music, an entire community of musicians arose who introduced alternative styles that offered a direct challenge to establishment values. Many of these singers became strongly identified with the musical scene in Austin, Texas, one of several southern cities that became important music centers.[5] Austin's rise to musical prominence was accompanied by a heightened interest in what came to be called during the 1970s "progressive country music," an ambiguous term first associated with the eclectic programming pioneered by station KOKE in Austin, a format then copied by several other stations. KOKE program directors announced an intention to play all kinds of country music, from the traditional to the modern, but their selections actually leaned heavily toward rock-influenced material, and particularly toward that produced by Austin-based entertainers. Progressive country music, therefore, became increasingly associated with youth-oriented music, particularly country-rock and other hybrid forms, including some that drew on folk music. KOKE's programming, like the music played in most of the clubs in Austin, was aimed at the city's youthful audience, a generation reared on rock music. As the site of a state university with an enrollment of over forty thousand, Austin had a large and annually self-replenishing young audience that craved musical entertainment.

Many progressive country musicians in Austin, like the deejays at KOKE, affected cowboy dress, as did many of the young people who constituted the audiences. The stereotype initially associated with Austin music was that of the hippie in a cowboy costume, the "cosmic cowboy," as Michael Murphey expressed it in one of his songs. The first major locus of activity for these people and their music was the Armadillo World Headquarters, founded in 1970 in an old national guard armory, and a direct outgrowth of the city's counterculture movement. Beginning as a haven for rock music, the Armadillo soon began to feature country entertainers too, particularly those who, like Waylon Jennings and Commander Cody and the Lost Planet Airmen, could attract both country and rock audiences. The Armadillo also booked performers who, like Murphey, had come to be known to young Texans from their appearances on the state's coffeehouse circuit in the late 1960s and '70s.

Austin was the undeniable headquarters of the movement, and musicians backing any number of artists who appeared at the Armadillo called themselves the "Austin interchangeable band." But many people recognized the roots of progressive country in the folk-oriented music that emerged in the coffeehouses in Dallas, Denton, and Houston, as well as Austin, performed by Murphey, Steve Fromholz, Nanci Griffith, Townes Van Zandt, Willis Alan Ramsey, Bill and Bonnie Hearne, and others who went on to gain fairly wide reputations or at least had strong influences on well-known artists. Fromholz, for instance, and his then-partner Dan McCrimmon, calling themselves the duo Frummox, crafted songs of farming, ranching, and lost opportunities, as in Fromholz' "Texas Trilogy," every bit as evocative of rural traditions as the work of any country songwriter/performer and performed with the acoustic instrumentation of the old-time string bands. Much the same could be said of Ramsey, though he, like Fromholz, also infused a wry sense of humor into his often droll, ironic lyrics that distanced him from more mainstream songwriting, as did his use of open guitar tunings, as on his oddly haunting tune "Satin Sheets." The Hearnes, a legally blind married couple, added a rousing combination of tight vocal harmonies and gospel-based piano playing that gave energy to the new music while also reminding its performers of the importance of strong melodies. Nanci Griffith, Tish Hinojosa, and Lyle Lovett were only a few of the younger musicians who came under the influence of the Hearnes. Dallas-native Murphey achieved perhaps the greatest acclaim of the Austin-based musicians from that period, particularly later when he moved closer to mainstream country, and protested when his picture appeared on the cover of Jan Reid's *The Improbable Rise of Redneck Rock,* saying, "I'm not a redneck, and I don't play rock music." But Murphey continued and solidified the use of western and cowboy imagery in his music and his stage presence, later becoming widely identified with the burgeoning cowboy poetry movement.

In the early '70s, the number of youth-oriented clubs multiplied in Austin and they, along with the older country and western clubs in the city, such as the Broken Spoke, the Split Rail, and Soap Creek Saloon, soon gave Austin the reputation of being a thriving center of live music. Much of the talent found in the city—Frieda and the Firedogs, for example, led by gifted Louisiana-born singer and piano player Marcia Ball—enjoyed only local or Texas recognition in the '70s. But a few musicians of national or growing repute, such as Jerry Jeff Walker, the New York urban folksinger who had written "Mr. Bojangles," and Doug Sahm, the versatile Texan who had been prominent in the 1960s rock scene, made Austin their base of operations. The city was already a burgeoning community of musicians when Willie Nelson moved there from Nashville in 1972.[6] Nelson, a major if long-neglected talent in country music, was both a supreme vocal stylist, whose blues-tinged voice was one of the most distinctive since Jimmie Rodgers, and a gifted songwriter whose finely crafted songs had placed him in the vanguard of Nashville's new breed of writers. After he moved to Austin, Nelson demonstrated that he was consummately skilled in still another art, that of image building.

Willie Nelson was born in 1933 in Abbott, Texas, where he absorbed a heavy diet of gospel, honky-tonk, pop, and western swing music, all of which later appeared in his own highly individualistic style. In Nashville, where he moved in the early 1960s, Nelson won immediate success as a songwriter, supplying hit songs for other entertainers: "Crazy," for Patsy Cline, "Funny

How Time Slips Away," for Billy Walker, "Hello Wall," for Faron Young, and "Night Life," for Ray Price. Nelson was far from being a failure in Nashville, and although he was at least on the periphery of a small group of musicians known as the "Nashville Rebels" (or "Outlaws"), he was really neither an iconoclast nor a nonconformist. His decision to move to Austin was primarily motivated by losing his home in a fire, but more generally by his desire to return to what he saw as the simpler and more familiar pace of his native state of Texas. Nelson deliberately set out to build an audience among the rock-oriented youth of Texas and beyond, and he succeeded in a way that was unprecedented for a country singer.

Nelson became a national phenomenon, landing roles in movies and appearances on the most prominent television programs, including those aimed at young audiences. The most intriguing facet of Nelson and his updated image, however, was that his singing remained emotive, even plaintive as often as it was mischievous, and his style and choice of songs became more traditional. Many of the listeners he attracted to gospel and earlier varieties of country music, including honky-tonk, probably would not have listened to such music without Nelson's endorsement. Nelson also introduced many country music fans, young and old, to the concept album, which he carried off to critical acclaim in the 1970s with *Red Headed Stranger* and with *Phases and Stages,* one side of which presents love lost through the eyes of a man and the other side through those of a woman. There was some irony in the fact that Waylon Jennings, a talented country writer/performer in his own right, became best known in the decade as Nelson's comrade and fellow "Outlaw," capitalizing on the Texas image of expansiveness and easy living in his songs, especially his number one hit of 1977, "Luckenbach, Texas," in which he urges his listeners to "get back to the basics of love." Nelson moved to Austin, established his own recording company, and maintained his original musical sound, adjusting his physical image to suit contemporary Texas youth tastes, while Waylon, also a native of Texas, remained in Nashville and aligned with the largest record company in America, RCA, while singing of being an outlaw, cut free from the constraints of the Nashville establishment. Jennings later recorded and appeared with Nelson, Kristofferson, and Johnny Cash in a group they called the Highwaymen, perpetuating an image of independence and just a touch of lawlessness. All four performers had fairly legitimate claims to nonconformity, but Nelson came the closest of the four to living what he sang and wrote about, both in his free-spirited lifestyle and unconventional approach to his work, both of which got him into considerable trouble from time to time.

The fusion of country and rock sounds and the consequent gravitation of a youth audience toward country music resulted as much from the experimentation of country-oriented rock musicians as from the innovativeness of country musicians. For some new fans, finding their way into the country music subculture seemed to be another way to rebel against the establishment. Furthermore, many young fans admitted an interest in country music only after the music was lent respectability through an endorsement by a rock singer such as Bob Dylan, Stephen Stills, or Neil Young. Dylan, for instance, probably did more than any other individual to break down prejudice against country music when he went to Nashville and hired local musicians to help him record an album of his own country-flavored songs, *Nashville Skyline,* including a duet with Johnny Cash, "Girl from the North Country," which became a hit single. About nine months before Dylan's album appeared, however, the folk-rock group the Byrds released *Sweetheart of the Rodeo,* the first album by a rock group to be composed exclusively of country songs. The Byrds were well known for their experimentation, having earlier pioneered in the performance of psychedelic rock and folk rock, but at least two of their members, Chris Hillman and Gram Parsons, had experience with and genuine love for country music. Together, they comprised the nucleus of a later and more consistently country group called the Flying Burrito Brothers, the prototype of most of the country-rock groups that emerged later.

Gram Parsons was born Cecil Ingram Connors in Waycross, Georgia, on November 5, 1946.[7] Though he came from the right side of the tracks and was the heir of a considerable fortune, Parsons brought to rock music a fascination with hard-core, honky-tonk country music. When he left the Burrito Brothers, he set out on a campaign, about three years before Willie Nelson's highly publicized Texas ventures, to fuse more closely the sounds of country and rock and to break down the mutual suspicion between the two audiences. Parsons ultimately failed in his efforts within his own lifetime, but after his death in 1973 he and his music became objects of cultic adulation. Unfortunately, Parsons's self-destructive behavior, like that of so many of his peers, undermined his potential and caused the waste of a talented artist and visionary, and the young rock audience to which he appealed never came to terms with country music to the extent that he hoped. But the whole country-rock movement, including such successful entertainers as the Eagles, the Marshall Tucker Band, Linda Ronstadt, and Uncle Tupelo, owed a great debt to Parsons because of the inroads he made for country music within the youth audience of America. It is not possible to calculate the number of musicians, obscure and otherwise, who, knowingly or unknowingly, were touched by Parsons.

Chris Hillman, for instance, who deserves much credit for the creation of country-rock, a term he did not care for, had played bluegrass and country before joining the Byrds. He tells how Parsons started playing a Buck Owens' song, "Under Your Spell Again," at a rehearsal shortly after Parsons joined the Byrds. "I stopped in my tracks and ran over and caught the tenor part. This was Heaven," according to Hillman. "I'd found an ally and quite possibly my future."[8] The genealogy of country-rock influences becomes virtually impossible to trace among many of the major groups of the 1960s and '70s, but musicians who played with Parsons and/or Hillman, or with those who did, keep showing up. The Byrds were a source of the music, as can be heard on "Mr. Spaceman," "Chestnut Mare," and the satirical "I Wanna Grow Up to Be a Politician." In addition to Hillman and Parsons, Byrds alumni also included David Crosby, who was most famous for his membership in the group named for him, Stephen Stills, Graham Nash, and Neil Young. Stills and Nash were both veterans of the rock group Buffalo Springfield, which had also experimented with country-sounding songs or motifs, as on "Kind Woman," "Go and Say Goodbye," and their biggest hit, "For What It's Worth," which featured guitar effects that prefigured the use Crosby, Stills, Nash, and Young made of the steel guitar in "Teach Your Children." When that group broke up, Stills and Young, whose bitter anti-segregation songs had angered many white southerners, both pursued solo careers featuring frequent use of country sounds. Stills went on to form Manassas, an eclectic group he fronted in the mid-1970s that featured rock-influenced country-sounding songs and country-influenced rock-sounding songs. The group traveled and recorded with a steel guitarist, Al Perkins, and a mandolin and guitar player and vocalist, Chris Hillman.

Surely Gram Parsons' most direct and important influence was on his protege Emmylou Harris. Though southern-born, in Birmingham, Alabama, and reared in Virginia, Harris was the daughter of a career military officer, so her background could hardly be called country. Her first musical experience came as an urban folksinger, but Parsons taught her country phrasing and introduced her to what she called "root country," and she began adding to her repertory songs from Merle Haggard, George Jones, the Louvin Brothers, and the early Everly Brothers. Her first solo album in 1975, *Pieces of the Sky,* was highly praised, and a single from the recording, an old Louvin Brothers song called "If I Could Only Win Your Love," was one of the most popular country songs of the year. Harris brought one of the purest and most refreshingly clear voices heard in country music in a long time, and she was immediately touted as a future superstar. One of the most remarkable aspects of her success was the fact that she built strong bases of support with both rock and country audiences by generally adhering to older styles of country music, foreshadowing and providing leadership in a trend of traditionalism among younger country performers.

Despite all the modernizing trends of the postwar period, and despite the almost irresistible pressures placed on country musicians to modify their performing styles, many of the older forms did persist. Much of the impetus behind the revival of tradition-based styles came from the urban folk revival of the late 1950s and early '60s in which nonfolk entertainers performed folk material or songs with a folk sound. From the 1958 popularity of the Kingston Trio's "Tom Dooley," an adaptation of a North Carolina murder ballad, to the coming in 1964 of the Beatles, there had been a strong flurry of interest in what was loosely termed "folk" music. Urban folk music, thus seen, may have prospered as a reaction against rock 'n' roll, but more likely it represented just one more flirtation with the exotic or novel. Although urban folk music drew much of its inspiration and repertory, at least indirectly, from the South, from the protest singing of such 1930s radicals as Aunt Molly Jackson and Woody Guthrie, and from the Library of Congress collection of southern field recordings, it was basically a facet of mainstream pop music and was supported by the widest possible spectrum of Americans, most of whom had no identifiable roots in the cultures from which the songs derived. Southern folk music had often featured anti-authoritarian, even protest, themes, but as many northerners, especially young people, embraced the music of the folk, they put their own stamp on the presentation and interpretation of the music. It took on an especially progressive political orientation as a result of the identification of many folk music figures with the ideals of President John F. Kennedy and the civil rights movement. But its tone became more strident and cynical after Kennedy's death and as the promise of reform dissipated in the wake of America's deepening involvement in Vietnam. Urban folk music became a vehicle for many young people to express themselves both musically and politically, and to get a start in the music business, especially after rock 'n' roll receded from its first delirious peak. Many a veteran of the urban folk movement, such as Janis Joplin and Bob Dylan, went on to a career in rock or other forms of pop music. As Robert Palmer says, "Once country rock reared its head, the neo-folkie harmonies of Crosby, Stills, and Nash and the early-seventies proliferation of introspective, folk-based singer-songwriters were sure to follow. The Eagles were just around the bend."[9]

On the other hand, the folk fad did contribute to an awakening of interest in real grassroots American music. Once their appetites for folk music were whetted, many young people reached back for the rural roots of such music: blues, cowboy, hillbilly, Cajun, and other related forms. This interest had important social and musical consequences. A few recording companies released material from the 1920s that had long been buried in their vaults, and devoted collectors produced longplaying recordings of music taken from their

own private collections of old 78s. Many urban enthusiasts had been introduced to rural music of various sorts through the invaluable *Anthology of American Folk Music,* an assemblage of hillbilly, blues, Cajun, and gospel recordings
taken from the collection of Harry Smith and released on the Folkways label
in 1952. Partly as a result of interest engendered by the urban folk revival,
Sam Charters came upon the concept of country blues, a matter of great importance for black-white musical interaction as white, urban, fairly affluent
young people, both in the U.S. and beyond, found themselves captivated by
the music of black, rural, older people, often of modest means.[10] Other collectors and scholars became interested in exploring the origins of current-day
popular music and found that they had to modify some of their preconcep-
tions and prejudices about plain folk. Most happily of all, several of the pioneer performers, such as bluesmen Mississippi John Hurt and Furry Lewis,
and hillbillies Dock Boggs, Clarence Ashley, and Buell Kazee, were rediscov-
ered and given chances to build second careers they never could have imagined. Furthermore, the urban folk audience was receptive to newer performers
with a traditional orientation, such as the Balfa Brothers, Cajun musicians
who received a hearing far beyond the borders of southwest Louisiana. Finally,
scholars for the first time began to recognize the relationship between folk
music and such commercial forms as blues, gospel, and country. The most
significant result of this interest was the publication in 1965 of the "hillbilly
issue" of the *Journal of American Folklore,* a collection of essays devoted solely
to various aspects of early commercial country music, something folklorists in
earlier times considered unworthy of study.[11]

Indeed, even within the evolutionary framework of 1960s and '70s commercialization, the distinctive musical sounds of the working-class South endured. Some country singers, such as Kentuckian Marshall Louis "Grandpa"
Jones made no compromises at all with the newer sounds. A few, such as the
immensely talented Arthel "Doc" Watson, a blind musician from Deep Gap,
North Carolina, were skillful enough to alternate convincingly between the
very oldest folk styles and the most modern innovations. Watson, a singer of
great subtlety and power with a repertory ranging from sixteenth-century ballads to modern blues tunes, made his greatest impact as a guitarist. Often
performing with his son Merle, Watson exhibited a precision and speed in
executing solo guitar "runs" seldom heard before from any guitarist, even one
with eyesight. Watson's playing set off a vogue for flat-picking, as opposed to
the use of a thumb pick or the fingers as so many guitarists did who were
influenced by the folk revival. His work touched scores of young musicians in
both country and rock music, most notably, Dan Crary, Norman Blake,
Clarence White, and Tony Rice. When the Nitty Gritty Dirt Band pulled a

number of country musicians into their plan to record an album of traditional country tunes, Watson joined them, performing blistering duets with master fiddler Vassar Clements, one of the true stars of the album, on such tunes as "Black Mountain Rag" and "Down Yonder." The album, *Will the Circle Be Unbroken,* featured cover art recalling the Union and the Confederacy and the statement, "Music makes a new circle." Grand Ole Opry mainstay Roy Acuff, country matriarch Maybelle Carter, vocalist Jimmy Martin, banjo legend Earl Scruggs, finger-picking guitarist and vocalist Merle Travis, and several noted Nashville sidemen joined the eclectic Dirt Band for a rousing marathon recording session that resulted in a three-disc album, a great deal of fine music, and a considerable amount of goodwill.

One musician who refused, quite famously, to accept the Dirt Band's invitation to join the *Circle* session was Bill Monroe. He was so committed to maintaining the purity of the bluegrass music he had done so much to create that he chose not to participate in whatever hybrid music might result from cooperation with a California band with such a strange name. For decades, Monroe had been creating sounds that were deeply grounded in tradition, though he himself was always innovative enough to survive and flourish in the modern period. Born in Rosine, Kentucky, in 1911, Monroe took his mandolin style, his high tenor singing, and his pioneering string band, the Blue Grass Boys, to the Grand Ole Opry in 1939, where they remained until Monroe's death in 1996. Through the long march of country music evolution, and during a period marked by the almost universal adoption of electric instruments, Monroe preserved acoustic instrumentation and the "high-lonesome" style of singing, and in so doing created a genre of tradition-based music that spread around the world. Scores of musicians served apprenticeships with Monroe and then moved on to form their own bands. Many others heard his broadcasts, bought his records, or attended his road shows, and subsequently began copying the sounds Monroe and the Blue Grass Boys popularized.

All of the original bluegrass bands resisted electrical amplification, sang in a high, strident style featuring two and three-part harmony, leaned toward old or old-fashioned songs, and generally performed them at breakneck tempos. Although other instruments have since been adopted by bluegrass musicians, the "classic" bands, those clinging most closely to the original Monroe pattern, featured guitar and string bass for back-up rhythm, and mandolin, fiddle, and five-string banjo as lead instruments. Monroe's chop-style of mandolin chording was crucial in setting the distinctive rhythmic surge of bluegrass music, but other talented musicians made important contributions that made the music both unique and popular. Preeminently, Earl Scruggs, born in Flint Hill, North Carolina, in 1924, played with the Blue Grass Boys from

1944 to 1948 and featured a style that revolutionized the sound of the banjo and did much to make bluegrass music popular throughout the United States and beyond. Building upon styles long heard in the hill country of the Carolinas, Scruggs perfected a highly syncopated, three-finger style that made the banjo a solo instrument of dazzling speed and versatility. Don Reno, from Spartanburg, South Carolina, also knew the style, having learned it from Dewitt "Snuffy" Jenkins, but Reno joined the Blue Grass Boys only after Scruggs had left the group to form, along with Lester Flatt, another very popular bluegrass organization. Otherwise, what is called "Scruggs style" picking might have been called "Reno style."

Initially, the bluegrass audience was concentrated in small towns and rural communities of the South among people who resented the pop trends of country and western music. By the early 1950s, however, bluegrass began to win adherents in the North, particularly on college campuses. In 1954 the patriarch of urban folk music, Pete Seeger, included a section on "Scruggs picking" in the second edition of his banjo instructor. Three years later the style won further sanction among urban folkies when Folkways Records issued an album edited by Mike Seeger called *American Banjo Scruggs Style*. Because bluegrass resisted electrical amplification and adhered to traditional songs and sounds, and because so many of its prominent musicians came from the southern hills, the music appealed to many young Americans as a form of mountain folk music, and it was certainly more folklike than the Nashville-dominated country music of the day. Bluegrass music clearly profited from its association with the urban folk boom of the late '50s and early '60s. Earl Scruggs appeared to rave reviews at the first Newport Folk Festival in the summer of 1959, and in that same year Alan Lomax, the best-known American folklorist, further popularized the music among academics and avant-gardists when he termed it in an *Esquire* article "folk music with overdrive."[12] As Flatt and Scruggs led the way with appearances all over the United States, they not only became the busiest of all country groups during those years, they also helped bluegrass music gain a respectability in U.S. popular culture that no other form of country music had ever attained.

Oddly, the country music industry was largely indifferent to the bluegrass phenomenon, particularly during the period of the greatest academic interest in it. Bluegrass groups, such as those led by Bill Monroe, Flatt and Scruggs, Bobby and Sonny Osborne, and Jim and Jesse McReynolds, appeared regularly on the Grand Ole Opry, and a few other bluegrass entertainers, such as Mac Wiseman, the Stanley Brothers, and Don Reno and Red Smiley, attained some commercial recognition during the 1950s. But bluegrass fans generally encountered little but frustration in the search for their favorite kind of music. The Top Forty country radio stations did not play bluegrass, juke-box vendors would not distribute it, and the major record labels essentially pretended that it did not exist. Although the reasons for the country music industry's neglect of bluegrass may never by known, mainstream country singers may have been jealous, or even contemptuous, of the acclaim received by bluegrass in the academic community, or industry people may have been cool to the rural image bluegrass continued to embody at a time when country music was trying to become more sophisticated.

Regardless of the neglect, bluegrass bands proliferated since the 1950s, and the genre spawned its own substylings, ranging from traditional to pro-gressive, and bluegrass generated its own methods of dissemination. Vast num-bers of communities all over the U.S., and many in other countries, came to have at least one bluegrass band, although the music performed was often only remotely related to the original Bill Monroe sound. Bluegrass developed a particularly strong following among southern migrants in the North, espe-cially in Detroit and in the southern portions of such states as Pennsylvania, Ohio, Indiana, and Illinois. In fact, few bluegrass singers had a more pro-nounced rural sound or stronger commitment to tradition than Larry Sparks, born in Ohio of Kentucky-born parents.

Since at least the mid-1950s, the Washington, D.C., area became home to the greatest concentration of bluegrass interest in the U.S. The city and surrounding metropolitan area had a large number of clubs catering to the mixed assortment of government workers, students, military personnel, and others from all over the United States. As a city with a large population of ex-southerners, many of them from contiguous areas where the music long thrived, Washington was peculiarly situated to be a bluegrass capital. Several bluegrass bands worked out of the area, the two most important being exemplars of the "progressive" sound, the Country Gentlemen and the Seldom Scene.

As demonstrated by the mixed audiences of devotees found in Washing-ton, bluegrass music had attained a merger of cultures long before Gram Par-sons and Willie Nelson attempted their respective experiments with country and rock. Lacking the media support that mainstream country or country rock enjoyed, bluegrass musicians effected this merger largely through appear-ances at festivals. The first bluegrass festival, organized by Bill Clifton and held near Luray, Virginia, in 1962, was sparsely attended, and festivals did not become annual events until after 1965 when Carlton Haney began sponsor-ing his popular affairs. By the 1970s, however, if bluegrass fans had enough time and money, they could attend a festival somewhere every week in the United States from May until November.

Even the larger festivals, attended by thousands of people, such as those at Bean Blossom, Indiana; Camp Springs, North Carolina; and Hugo, Oklahoma, still managed to retain the brush arbor feeling of the old-time camp meetings. People camped out for days, listened to the music of visiting professional bands, and stayed up all night jamming with each other on fiddles, guitars, banjos, and mandolins. The festivals became meeting grounds for young and old, liberals and conservatives, hippies and rednecks. Truck drivers, coal miners, and farmers shared benches with "freaks," college students, and white-collar workers, and stood by campers for hour after hour trading instrumental licks and harmonizing on "Salty Dog Blues" or "Roll in My Sweet Baby's Arms." Probably nowhere else in the polarized '60s and early '70s could one find a similar forum where such disparate groups communed so peacefully. McGovern and Wallace supporters attending the festivals may not have reconciled their political differences as a result of their similar musical preferences, but their shared passion for bluegrass suggested a common aesthetic based upon a genuine search for sources and a reaction against the plasticized offerings of pop culture.

Bluegrass music may have represented an impulse toward tradition, but its directions have often been shaped by people and forces outside the South, by the urban folk music movement and by folklorists and others who clung to the romantic myth of the southern mountains as the sole repository of American folk music. Honky-tonk music also experienced a revival in the 1960s, but it never gained the endorsement of intellectuals or folklorists, nor did it really ever become chic among the urban middle classes. Its evolution, therefore, could be said to reflect more honestly the organic changes in southern white working-class life than one might find in the development of any other form of music. Because honky-tonk music generally reflects no particular ideology, it has never been very interesting to academics and intellectuals. Because it rarely deals with mountain life or little country churches, but instead concentrates on people's private concerns and does so with a heavily electrified beat, it has never been very appealing to folklorists, with very few exceptions, or to those whose conceptions of folk music remain shaped by the vision of a pastoral and nontechnological society. Some writers, such as Nat Hentoff and Nicholas Dawidoff, have offered a reappraisal of honky-tonk music for its lyrical honesty about the lives of people on the edges of the American dream. Dawidoff says of George Jones's work, "[H]is recordings that will endure are about the permutations of sorrow; the ways people adjust their hopes as time grows shorter; how you get through a life that you never planned on; the way abiding misfortune feels and how you get used to it; what it's like to be left behind. This is not music for swinging teens. It's raw stuff for grown-up people who . . . know something about disappointment. And what he means when he says of record companies, 'They've taken the heart and soul out of country music,' is that they've removed the pain."[13]

During the heyday of rock 'n' roll interest, the honky-tonk style had been affected more adversely than any other form of country music. Only two major singers, Ray Price and George Jones, both from Texas, remained true to the honky-tonk sound. Price, in fact, gained great success with the form during the very peak years of the rock 'n' roll boom. Jones's rise as a singer in the early 1960s paralleled the general resurgence of the honky-tonk style. During these years Jones built his reputation as one of the supreme stylists of country music, singing about cheating and drinking to the accompaniment of a bluesy fiddle and wailing steel guitar. The honky-tonk revival was made possible partly by the revitalization of these two instruments, which had declined in use so drastically during the late '50s. They, like virtually all instruments in the honky-tonk bands, were now electrified, and pedals had been universally attached to the steel guitars, permitting the musicians to stretch and bend the strings in order to achieve a more sustained and flexible vibrato. By the end of the '60s innovative steel guitarists such as Pete Drake, Buddy Emmons, Ralph Mooney, and Lloyd Green were appearing regularly on Nashville recording sessions. Similarly, the fiddle regained much of the prominence it had once enjoyed. The CMA's choice as instrumentalist of the year in 1976 was Nashville's most popular session fiddler, Johnny Gimble, a native of Tyler, Texas.

Honky-tonk music withdrew from its encounter with rock 'n' roll bearing some of the characteristics of its adversary. Rock-derived instrumental licks showed up in every form of country music, especially as disco and punk rock drove many guitarists away from the rock field and into country music, and much of the energy of rock 'n' roll suffused the performances of some of the honky-tonk singers. Buck Owens, for instance, a native of Sherman, Texas, but identified with the Bakersfield, California, country music scene, became the top-rated male country singer of the mid-1960s with a style that ranged from rockabilly to honky-tonk. In the '70s Kentucky-born Gary Stewart won acclaim among country fans because of his pleading, husky vibrato and honky-tonk-style voice, but he also received critical praise in *Rolling Stone* for his rollicking rockabilly style. Several singers began their careers as rockabillies and later shifted with great effectiveness to the honky-tonk style. Gene Watson, Buck Owens, Darrell McCall, Johnny Bush, and Porter Wagoner were some of the singers people had in mind when they used the expression "hard" country to describe performers who seemed more "pure" country, not necessarily exclusively honky-tonk, but uncompromisingly devoted to the expressiveness of country music, as so many honky-tonk performers were.

Honky-tonk music has had almost as tenuous an existence in country music as bluegrass. After the early '60s, the industry as a whole was never hospitable toward the hard country sound because of perceived limits of its market, and singers were easily tempted into the financially more rewarding pop areas of country music where greater possibilities for crossover hits existed. Honky-tonk fans in the '70s continually hoped that Ray Price might return to his original sound, or that someone would restore the old George Jones style to country music. Consequently, singers or recordings were periodically seized upon by hopeful fans as the harbingers of genuine and full-scale honky-tonk revivals, such as Mel Street's "Borrowed Angel," Wayne Kemp's "Who'll Turn Out the Lights," Ronnie Milsap's "I Hate You," Johnny Rodriguez's "Pass Me By," John Conlee's "Rose Colored Glasses," and Norman Wade's "Close Every Honky Tonk." The promise usually remained unfulfilled. Rodriguez's first album was consistently honky-tonk in style and repertory, a worthy reflection of his Texas inheritance, but his succeeding albums persistently moved away from that original sound toward the more lucrative field of country-pop. In the 1970s, two proponents of the honky-tonk sound, though both preferred the term hard country, were Vernon Oxford and Moe Bandy, natives of Arkansas and Mississippi respectively. Oxford's pure country sound built a remarkable popularity among music devotees in Great Britain. Bandy conformed for a time to the classic mold of the honky-tonk musician: the singer with his guitar in front of a band with a fiddle, pedal steel guitar, and electric walking bass—the essence of the Texas shuffle beat—singing songs about cheating, hurting, and drinking to a noisy crowd sliding across a smoky dance floor. Honky-tonk and Moe Bandy seemed made for each other, particularly in songs such as "I Just Started Hating Cheating Songs Today," "Don't Anyone Make Love at Home Anymore?" and "Hank Williams, You Wrote My Life." But he moved away from his honky-tonk style and, for the most part, its enthusiasts remained disappointed for the rest of the decade, though the style became more popular as the twentieth century drew to a close.

Honky-tonk music's spirited cousin, western swing, declined but did not die after World War II, even though the large bands of the Bob Wills variety became rare. Hoyle Nix of Big Spring, Texas, and Waco native Hank Thompson kept the swing genre going during the 1950s and '60s, playing for dances all over the Southwest. Their bands were typically small, and Thompson was best known for his interpretation of such honky-tonk songs as "The Wild Side of Life." But the memory of Bob Wills's exciting bands was still vivid throughout the Southwest, and songs that he and the Texas Playboys introduced remained in the repertories even of musicians far removed from the western swing tradition. Long before Wills died in 1975, a western swing renaissance was under way, largely through the efforts of Merle Haggard, who

recorded a tribute album to Wills in 1970 using several former Texas Playboys, began including western swing numbers in his performance repertory,
and learned to play the fiddle in the Bob Wills style. A band of young musicians, Asleep at the Wheel, inspired in large part by Haggard's tribute, focused
their efforts on western swing and helped make Wills, admitted to the Country Music Hall of Fame in 1968, a cult figure in the southwest in the 1970s, as
he had been in that region in the 1930s and '40s.

Through the performances of Merle Haggard and Asleep at the Wheel,
and other longtime admirers such as Willie Nelson, a new generation of western swing enthusiasts came into existence who previously knew Wills, Milton
Brown, and other swing pioneers, if at all, only through their recordings. Asleep
at the Wheel and other young "revivalists" such as Cooder Browne and Alvin
Crow and His Pleasant Valley Boys made their headquarters in Austin, Texas,
and drew throngs of youthful, rock-oriented audiences who were already en-
thused by the burgeoning Austin music scene. They were so successful that
the Public Broadcasting System chose to create a long-running program, *Austin City Limits,* and taped its first program on the campus of the University of
Texas in September 1975. The program consisted of Asleep at the Wheel and
Bob Wills's Original Texas Playboys, who had gotten back together after the
death of their leader the previous spring. Youngsters were not the only members of the reinvigorated western swing audience. Red Steagall and the Coleman
County Cowboys worked more directly within the country music mainstream
and found their most loyal listeners among traditional country music fans. A
native of Gainesville, Texas, Steagall carried on the tradition of western swing.
He also became a leading performer of rodeo music in the United States, sang
for rodeo dances all over the country and, as an ex-bull rider, succeeded in
writing in a very sensitive way about the sport and the way of life it reflects.
With his performance of "Lone Star Beer and Bob Wills' Music," Steagall also
paid tribute to two institutions cherished by country music fans in the Southwest.[14] The popularity of such musicians as Steagall and Asleep at the Wheel
demonstrated western swing's continuing influence in American music and
added evidence that younger performers could win a new hearing among country and rock audiences.

Western swing's resurgence was in part a tribute to the mythmaking
quality of regionalism, something folklorist Nick Spitzer called "romantic regionalism,"[15] in this case the supposedly liberated and expansive Southwest,
and to the man, Bob Wills, who put this freedom to the service of music.
Western swing appealed both to an older audience appreciative of the past
and to those too young to have experienced the music's heyday but hungry
for something enduring, an original and rare prize in the midst of the ever-

shifting patterns of popular culture. But it also demonstrated something true of much of the story of country music in the 1970s. By making room for young people who were, of all things, traditionalists as well as innovators, country music exhibited one of the key factors that always characterized southern music, the ability to combine the quicksilver of adaptability with the touchstone of continuity with the past. By the mid-1970s, the longhairs Merle Haggard derided in "Okie from Muskogee" and the rednecks Charlie Daniels derided in "Ballad of the Easy Rider" were shocked to find that they liked much of the same music—hard country, bluegrass, western swing—and, before long, many country stars began wearing long hair themselves and dressing more like counterculture wanderers, or people who lived in the country, than like middle-class aspirants. A symbolic gap was bridged through music, something inconceivable as recently as the early part of the same decade. More change was to come, but nothing as dramatic as the changes of the 1970s.

Chapter 9

A FUTURE IN THE PAST

At the dawn of the twenty-first century, southern music had come to a cross-roads. Indeed, it seemed as if it might disappear altogether, as the "American-ization of Dixie" and musical homogenization came to fruition. The turbulent 1960s and '70s brought pressures and changes to U.S. culture as a whole, the kinds of upheaval always reflected in the popular music of any age. Some observers were left to wonder if anything traditional in the United States might survive, especially regional differences, most especially those in a region whose racial and political values had been so thoroughly denounced by many people in the news media and other institutions that shape public opinion. Partly because of the political resurgence of the South beginning in the 1980s and partly because of changes in the structure of the organizations that produce and market music, southern music adapted with the times, as the people of the South themselves had always done. Ironically, southern political resur-gence paralleled the departure from office of Jimmy Carter, the first president elected from a southern state other than Texas since before the Civil War (Vir-ginia-born Woodrow Wilson had been a longtime resident of New Jersey when he was elected). Though Carter had an identification with southern music, Ronald Reagan and George Bush both claimed to appreciate the old-time American values allegedly inherent in country music and appropriated politi-cally active country music fans fairly successfully. When ultra-patriotic coun-try artists such as Lee Greenwood began singing at Republican Party events, one could tell that the days of the Solid (Democratic) South were over. Far from disappearing, however, southern styles of music actually adapted to the future by reverting, in some surprising and also ironic ways, to methods and sensibilities deeply rooted in their past.

For one thing, southerners of all races remained actively involved in making music, and the musical landscape on which they operated became much more diverse. Southern musicians already familiar to the public were joined by musicians from immigrant groups not previously associated with the South. Cubans, Puerto Ricans, and other "Latin" people who had begun moving to southern cities in the years following World War II included musicians who began to make their mark in the musical life of the nation, Cuban-Floridian superstar Gloria Estevan among them. Asians, especially those displaced by the Vietnam War, added their presence, particularly in the coastal towns of Texas. Vietnamese and Hmong immigrants enriched the cultural fabric of the South and further confounded notions of the region as a bastion of cultural or musical "purity." Klezmer bands sprang up in Austin, Houston, New Orleans, and elsewhere in the South, reflecting the musical interests of Jewish communities in those places as well as the growing diversity of musical tastes of the general public in many cities in the region.

Two musical phenomena that illustrate the changes in southern music were the Cajun/Zydeco revolution and the explosion in various musical forms formerly lumped together under the term "Latin," including Tejano and Salsa. These forms challenged older ideas about southern distinctiveness, particularly the presumption that the region's uniqueness rests on Anglo-Saxon hegemony. These two broad groups actually reinforced two of southern music's preeminent characteristics, its diversity and its cultural rootedness, and encouraged people to abandon an always-faulty notion, that southern music flows from a uniform ethnic/racial past.

Tejano music's flowering was part of a larger public fascination with Hispanic or Latino music of all kinds, something that in turn reflected the spectacular growth of Spanish-speaking communities throughout the United States. The long migrations of farmworkers and other immigrant people seeking blue-collar jobs took elements of Tejano style to the Midwest, the North, and both coasts of the U.S. Texas-born Chris Plata, for example, became one of the most highly regarded participants of the vernacular, roots music scene in Madison, Wisconsin, with a style that flowed easily from Tex-Mex to rock 'n' roll. Other Hispanic musicians, such as Flaco Jimenez, continued to enjoy popularity as the twenty-first century dawned through his appearances at festivals and other venues and on the television program "Austin City Limits." Jimenez's conjunto accordion style was widely admired and imitated, and he worked in numerous acts with only a peripheral relationship to Tejano music. Along with Doug Sahm, Augie Meyer, and Freddy Fender, Jimenez performed with the Texas Tornadoes, mixing country, rock, and Tejano styles. Like the San Antonio-raised Sahm, Arizona native Linda Ronstadt grew up listening to traditional Mexican music. She contributed to the diversification of American popular music as a whole through her popular songs over several decades but also to the diversification of southern music through her recordings of two albums of canciones and corridos in the 1980s, including songs from her own Mexican ancestry. She thus encouraged singers in Texas and elsewhere to realize that the music of Hispanics could attract audiences from beyond their own ethnic communities. California native Ry Cooder exhibited a fascination for all kinds of ethnic music, especially Latin American and African, and, like Ronstadt, helped broaden and deepen the public's taste for different kinds of music and encouraged performers to make places for themselves in the musical marketplace.

Cooder, Ronstadt, and Sahm helped introduce the public to Santiago Jimenez, the father of Flaco Jimenez, Narciso Martinez, and other Tejano musical pioneers. Cooder almost single-handedly popularized a whole generation of aging Cuban musicians through his work on albums and television programs highlighting the Buena Vista Social Club, work that became immensely popular in Florida particularly. Such efforts were complemented by those of Chris Strachwitz, the legendary German immigrant who came to the U.S. as a teenager in 1947 and began reissuing the music of Tejano artists in the early 1960s on his Arhoolic label, which also kept before the public blues and other roots performances that might have been lost to memory. One of the high points in the rediscovery of Tejano music came in 1982 when the National Endowment for the Arts gave Lydia Mendoza a National Heritage Fellowship,[1] the reward for a career that spanned over fifty years and included at least fifty albums and more than two hundred songs.

Although burgeoning Tejano music drew much of its vitality from a sense of ethnic pride and cultural nationalism, it became much more than simply a force for nostalgia or musical conservatism highlighting only its oldest and most traditional performers. Its musicians moved freely between the Anglo and Hispanic cultures and benefited from the patronage of an audience that was increasingly urban and musically sophisticated. They also took advantage of a musical infrastructure of clubs, radio stations, record companies, and television programs that skillfully marketed their music. The musicians tended to dress like South Texans who had helped build the ranching empires of that area while also evincing great pride in their Mexican heritage. They generally spoke both English and Spanish and thus were able to deal more effectively with the people who managed the musical infrastructure and maintain greater control over their own careers. The first musicians who began making listeners conscious of the thriving Tejano culture in the 1960s, working-class youth who sang with the urgency and idioms of rock 'n' roll, Freddy Fender, Sunny Ozuna and the Sunliters, and Little Joe Hernandez y la Familia, achieved much success in the late twentieth century. They became role models for other Hispanics who hoped to achieve middle-class status in the U.S. without giving up their own heritage. Younger Hispanic artists followed in the footsteps of their forebears and proudly presented their music—usually in Spanish—with the full panoply of styles ranging from rock to blues, country, disco, and hip-hop.

Music created by San Antonio-born Rosie Flores, for instance, refutes many of the limitations people from the majority culture might like to place on artists of her ethnic background, and illustrates the interplay of musical forms that shape the styles of recent performers. She started singing professionally when she was a child and made recordings for major labels beginning in 1987 when she recorded *Rosie Flores* for Warner Brothers. She went on to record several albums for Hightone and Rounder that combine her love for old-time hillbilly music, honky-tonk, and rockabilly, as well as Tex-Mex, and impressed critics with her range and versatility and with the fact that she did her own lead guitar work. Her fourth album, *Rockabilly Filly,* which came out in 1995, features duets with the veteran rockabillies Wanda Jackson and Janis Martin. Flores's music rocks when she wants it to and evokes images of the barrio or the honky-tonk, again, as she sees fit, not as the strictures of other people might try to determine.

While most Hispanic performers played in small barrio clubs and cafes, mainly in the region of South Texas bounded by Corpus Christi, San Antonio, and Houston, some attained superstar status. La Mafia, Emilio Navaira, Laura Canales, and Selena Quintanilla presented their music in large arenas replete with all the trappings of huge stadium rock shows. They also extended the reach of Tejano music into northern Mexico, California, and other areas where large numbers of Spanish-speaking people lived, confounding earlier understandings of the wholly Texan nature of the music.

Selena began her career singing in her family's band when she was eight years old. Her father, Abraham, had been the leader of a '60s doo-wop group, Los Dinos, and became the driving force in his daughter's career, encouraging her to sing and insisting that she improve her Spanish. As her style matured, so did her own self-image and direction. Selena created a sensual persona modeled on the stage presence and provocative costuming of the pop singer Madonna. Like no one before her, Selena dominated the "Latin" music charts in the United States in the early '90s with such songs as "Bidi Bidi Bom Bom," "Como La Flor," and "Amor Prohibido." She became immensely popular in Mexico, an accomplishment not often enjoyed by Tejana musicians. At the peak of her popularity, she was shot to death by the president of her fan club after Selena and others accused her of embezzlement.[2] Selena's legacy may be difficult to ascertain because of the brevity of her career, but her immense success pointed to the huge potential of "ethnic" music to hold its own in a popular music marketplace not often eager to embrace departures from the mainstream and to the increasing diversity of the music of the southern United States.

Another example of this diversity in the late twentieth century was found in Cajun music. The music's popularity was accompanied by a fascination with all things Cajun: the humor, cuisine, and free-wheeling pursuit of a joyous life encapsulated in the expression *laissez les bon temps roulez*. The appearance of Dewey Balfa, Gladius Thibodeaux, and Louis Vinesse Lejeune at the Newport Folk Festival in 1964 may date the beginning of a revival of interest in traditional Cajun music. Even among many Cajuns, especially those aspiring to middle-class acceptance, Cajun music had been viewed as "nothing but chanky-chank," according to Barry Jean Ancelet, Jay Edwards, and Glen Pitre in *Cajun Country*. But appearing on the bill at Newport with such stars of the day as Peter, Paul, and Mary and Joan Baez, and receiving a standing ovation gave Cajun music a lift both at home and in the U.S. as a whole.[3] Balfa especially was impressed by the enthusiastic reception, and the veteran fiddler returned to Louisiana determined to revive interest in the music among his own people, many of whom had suffered humiliation, even violence, on account of their supposed cultural inferiority. Other Cajuns, such as folklorist Ancelet, followed Balfa's lead and re-established the teaching of Cajun French instruction in the schools, long forbidden in South Louisiana, and began teaching young people the methods of Cajun music.

Cajun and Zydeco music, and the cultures that surrounded them, won broader attention by various means. The disastrous World's Fair of 1984, for example, an economic nightmare for its host city of New Orleans, managed to introduce the rich musical resources of Louisiana, including the sounds of Cajun and Zydeco, to thousands of tourists. Most people, in fact, made their first acquaintance with Louisiana music either through periodic visits to New Orleans or through such movies as *The Big Easy*, which featured songs by Terrance Simien, Beausoleil, and Buckwheat Zydeco, or through participation in public spectacles such as the Summer Olympics in Atlanta in 1996. During the closing ceremonies of those Olympic games, Buckwheat Zydeco played for an international television audience that may have numbered in the billions. Long before the Cajun revival occurred, the music could be heard at Alan Fontenot's Club in the New Orleans suburb of Metairie, and it was showcased constantly at the Jazz and Heritage Festival in New Orleans and in such local clubs as Mulate's, Tipitina's, Michaul's, and the Maple Leaf Bar.

New Orleans, of course, is neither a Cajun nor a Zydeco town. Most connections between the city and these forms exist because entrepreneurs know tourists think Cajuns live in New Orleans and because many New Orleanians like Cajun and Zydeco music. To find these forms in their authentic social contexts, one could visit such towns as Thibodeaux, Lafayette, Breaux Bridge, and Rayne in Southwest Louisiana, or Port Arthur, Texas. Devotees also heard the many varieties of Louisiana French music at the annual Festivals Acadiens in Lafayette or the Zydeco Festival in Plaisance. Barry Jean Ancelet, one of the most articulate and tireless champions of Cajun culture, established another popular venue for the music in Eunice, Louisiana, a radio show held at a local theater each Saturday night with everything, including announcements, commercials, and entertainment, presented in Cajun French.

"French" revival styles did not always closely resemble the kind of music that Dewey Balfa and his brothers had played, but they did represent the diverse influences at work on the musicians of Louisiana. Above all, they reflected the fact that Cajun and Zydeco musicians, like all southern musicians, were Americans who grew up immersed in the sounds of a broadscale popular culture. "Traditional" Cajun music thrived, put forth by such bands as Balfa Toujours, headed by Dewey's daughter Christine, and Beausoleil, preserving the sound and ambiance of the old times even as musicians added modern songs and riffs to their presentation. In business since 1933, the Hackberry Ramblers continued to perform their infectious mixture of Cajun and country music in the twenty-first century for both American and European audiences. In 2002 accordionist Edwin Duhon (age ninety-two) and fiddler Luderin Darbone (age eighty-nine) were rewarded with National Heritage Fellowships. While the older styles remained popular, fans more often were likely to hear music that blended the rhythms and energy of rock and r&b with the traditional accordion and fiddle sounds so associated with Louisiana French music. Cajun music and Zydeco burst onto the national scene partly because of their infectious dances, conveyed by Zachary Richard (described as the Cajun Mick Jagger), Wayne Toups, Steve Riley, and Bruce Daigrepont.

Zydeco largely outstripped Cajun music in popularity by the turn of the century, largely because its heady components of blues, r&b, and even hip-hop, appealed to young fans. As Zydeco musicians were quick to point out, their style of Louisiana French music diverged pretty dramatically from Cajun style. Although they typically sang in French and used accordions and rhythm rubboards, pioneered by Clifton Chenier's brother Cleveland, such Zydeco stars as Chenier himself, Boo Zoo Chavis, Buckwheat Zydeco, Queen Ida Guillory, and Rockin' Dopsie also used saxophones, drums, and electric guitars and basses to produce their unique versions of African-American/Louisiana-French blues styles.

New Orleans and the exotic aura of Cajun culture may have been blended falsely in the popular imagination, but the city still had enough romance and charm of its own to reaffirm its image as the country's most musical city. Historically neglected by the city's power establishment, even once denounced as "whorehouse music" by local newspapers, New Orleans music nevertheless flourished in legendary proportions and began to gain the support of the city's leadership. In the last quarter of the twentieth century, local musical traditions and commercial opportunities came to be encouraged by the Orleans Parish school system, which established a vigorous Music in the Schools program encouraging the performance of jazz, helped in various ways by Ellis Marsalis and various members of his famous musical family. The city's political and business establishment learned to see the wisdom of supporting music and backed the maintenance of music parks, protecting musical venues in the French Quarter, and enhancing the annual Jazz and Heritage Festival.

Music continued to float from virtually every corner of New Orleans with styles still reflecting the character of local neighborhoods. As if to demonstrate the perennial importance families have in passing music on to their children, groups such as the Neville, Batiste, and Marsalis families dominated much of the musical life of New Orleans. The two most famous Marsalis offspring, saxophonist Branford and trumpeter Wynton, made national reputations in jazz. Wynton also earned considerable acclaim in the field of classical music and hosted a National Public Radio musical program broadcast from Lincoln Center. They and other members of their family, however, continued to appear in New Orleans, touching base with the culture that gave rise to their music with its distinctive r&b sound, Mardi Gras, festivals, and funerals with their "second line" tradition of accompanying musicians returning from depositing the departed at the cemetery. The marching brass bands persisted, though the bands added contemporary styles of music to their traditional jazz repertories. Preservation Hall continued to draw tourists, and locals and tourists also mixed at Tipitina's, the Maple Leaf Bar, Snug Harbor, and the Mid-City Bowling Lanes, known locally as "Rock and Bowl," a favorite stop-off of visiting musicians such as the Rolling Stones. New Orleans r&b and funk bands, the Meters, the Radiators, and the Neville Brothers, explored the edges of eclecticism, with the Nevilles adding a strong Caribbean influence, touching on the city's connections with that region. Irma Thomas, Charmaine Neville, Marcia Ball, and Dr. John established names for themselves and loyal followings among people in New Orleans and from other places who came to the city specifically to see these artists perform.

A culture unto itself, New Orleans can hardly be called a typical southern city. Even with its prominent monuments and street names celebrating its Confederate past, New Orleans is simply different from everyplace else, southern or otherwise, with its own dialects, its own terminology, and its own musical styles and rhythms. Country music, on the other hand, remained the most self-consciously southern style of music in the United States. Despite the prominence of a few Canadians and other outlanders, southern-born personalities continued to dominate the music. In fact, many fans and critics continued to gauge a song's authenticity by the degree of southern "twang" in its singer's style. For many devotees of country music, though, the identity of the form and its integrity came under threat of dissolution from various forces, including longstanding ones such as industrial/market pressures and some newer ones related in odd ways to the actual success of country music. Like many things southern, as country music entertainers became more successful, and more affluent, and as the people who performed and patronized country music became less rural, the character of the music, and of the people, changed in some dramatic ways.

Even with the arrival of new forms, and the perpetuation of longstanding traditions of southern musical diversity, old conceptions and perceptions of the South and its music survived the end of the twentieth century. The South continued to fascinate musicians in the United States and beyond, fueling the styles of performers and the lyrics of songwriters. Southerners themselves became more prominent in the making of these songs than in days gone by when "outsiders" dominated the field, but the outsiders hardly went away. Many of them made music dealing with or linked to the South, including John Fogerty, Robbie Robertson, Ry Cooder, Eric Clapton, Ray Benson, Bruce Springsteen, and Little Feat, among others. They created songs inspired by southern themes and often became promoters of southern styles, performers, and viewpoints. Some such figures, including those associated with the "insurgent" alternative country movement, gloried in the rowdier or seamier traditions of country music, affirming stereotypes many southerners would just as soon had disappeared. Some of the musicians, however, who affirmed and repopularized those aspects of the music included southerners, such as Steve Young; Jimmie Arnold, with his concept album *Southern Soul*; Tim O'Brien, with *Songs from the Mountain*; and Marty Stuart, with *The Pilgrim*. Hank Williams Jr. expressed an unabashed neo-Confederate stance in his country/rock/honky-tonk music, while Dale Watson, Wayne Hancock, and Hank Williams III explored the rough edges of honky-tonk and rockabilly.

West Virginia native O'Brien produced and performed on two albums in 1999 that employed traditional themes, *Songs from the Mountain,* inspired by Charles Frazier's popular Civil War novel, *Cold Mountain*, and *The Crossing*, a collection consisting mostly of original songs asserting a link between southern country music and Celtic roots. Marty Stuart, from deep in the heart of Dixie, produced and performed on *The Pilgrim*, based on a story he remembered from growing up in Philadelphia, Mississippi. Jimmie Arnold's *Southern Soul* was a musical tour-de-force on which he wrote or arranged all of the songs, sang all of them, and played most of the instruments heard on the recordings, so intense was his desire to link his own experience with the mythical South he was trying to represent.

Southern Soul was particularly remarkable, focusing on the myth of the Lost Cause and the ways the southern rebel spirit could be used to rationalize hedonism and social nonconformity. Virginia-born Arnold, who employed traditional and original songs to tell the story of *Southern Soul*, embodied much of the life he sang about. The son of Pentecostal cotton mill workers, he moved back and forth between drug and alcohol addiction and preaching the gospel, felt equally at home in Pentecostal and Baptist churches or among the denizens of the biker subculture, and hastened through a wanton lifestyle his death at age 40. He thus fused his own rebellious and self-destructive story with that of the Lost Cause.

Music was always a solid reality of the South, but the mythic South continued in a number of ways to attract a variety of songwriters and musicians. Although cable music video channels proliferated on television, digital technology revolutionized the recording industry, and Internet access redefined marketing strategies, huge numbers of southerners and others in the U.S. and from outside the country continued to throng to live-music festivals in the South. From the long-running old-time fiddle contests in Galax, Virginia, and Union Grove, North Carolina, and the Kerrville, Texas, Folk Festival to the Jazz and Heritage Festival in New Orleans, music lovers found their way to live music venues that demonstrated the exotic appeal of the South long after the music industry had gone high-tech. MerleFest, in Wilkesboro, North Carolina, became known as one of the best showplaces for acoustic musicians of all kinds in the United States. *A Prairie Home Companion,* a live public radio program, and *Austin City Limits,* the public television program recorded before a live audience, became mainstays in the presentation of many southern-born or -styled musicians who had little likelihood of being heard on Top 40 radio. Robin and Linda Williams, for instance, natives of North Carolina and Alabama, knew more country songs, and treated them with greater affection, than most performers who dominated the broadcasts of mainstream radio. Known for their touching original songs, close harmonies, and down-home sensibilities, the Williamses found their largest audiences through the broadcasts of "Prairie Home Companion."

Songwriters especially continued to be drawn to the names of southern places and to images that seemed rooted in the region's customs and traditions. John Fogerty and Robbie Robertson, for example, joined the ranks of musicians with concept albums, celebrating the sensuous abandon and rhythmic drive of southern music and culture, while acknowledging the danger and intrigue long associated with the region, in short, a mythical land of perpetual appeal to artists and musicians. Both Fogerty and Robertson used Louisiana as the setting for their albums, a state that always seemed especially exotic to outsiders, and to many insiders. Robertson's album, *Storyville* (1991), used some of New Orleans's best and best-known musicians, including members of the Neville Brothers, the Meters, the Zion Harmonizers, and Mardi Gras Indians, and focused on the legendary red-light district of early twentieth-century New Orleans.

Fogerty and Robertson illustrate the vital role played by non-southerners in the making and mythicization of the musical South. Eric Clapton and Bonnie Raitt, among many other non-southerners, performed that function in the blues, recording the songs of the great southern blues artists, putting their own interpretations especially on the Delta blues tradition, and sometimes appearing and recording with blues artists such as B.B. King, Buddy Guy, and John Lee Hooker. Bruce Springsteen drew passionately from varied musical traditions, but became especially compelling when paying tribute to the Dust Bowl-spawned radicalism of Woody Guthrie. Ray Benson and Asleep at the Wheel did not simply memorialize the music of Bob Wills and His Texas Playboys; they also evoked images of the expansive and liberated West, alongside those of the musically rich South. These and other artists simultaneously found sustenance in the cultural material of the South while also building on its image as a land occupied by musical people.

Northern or foreign-born musicians were not alone in playing upon romantic or stereotypical perceptions of the South, and white or country musicians were not the only ones who pursued dreams of reviving traditional southern sounds. The brass brands of New Orleans, for example, especially the Dirty Dozen and Rebirth, included many young players who had grown up hearing the stories of the old legendary brass and percussion masters of that city. As the older generation passed from the scene, many fans were delighted to find kids who wanted not just to take the place of the oldtimers but who also wanted to keep their music alive. The young bands even included musicians who had studied the musical styles that vary by neighborhood in New Orleans, hardly the sort of pursuit taken up by the stereotypical tough, young street kids in urban areas.

Older southerners continued to make highly appealing music without trying to capitalize on their southernness. Hazel Dickens and Doc Watson, for example, never moved away from their identities as southerners, which simply came out in their music. Other performers carried the South, with its diversity and its tendency to reach across cultural lines, in their styles and their personalities. Several used elements of their cultural origins very self-consciously without trying to adopt a southern "persona." Lucinda Williams, Iris DeMent, and Tish Hinojosa, for example, carried the traditions of the South in their music, drawing on southern experiences, places, and people for material without trying to identify themselves as overtly southern. They also linked their songs to a southern tradition of infusing music with social commentary.

Lucinda Williams's songs are often suffused with the imagery and atmosphere of the South. As the daughter of Miller Williams, the University of Arkansas literature professor who read one of his poems at President Bill Clinton's 1996 inauguration, she grew up in a series of university towns. She absorbed influences from her poet father and musician mother, but probably learned more from her experiences as a singer-songwriter on the folk and blues club circuits in the 1970s. The South appears as a backdrop and context for Williams's tales of loneliness, pain, and suicide in her award-winning album *Car Wheels on a Gravel Road* particularly. Referring constantly to places such as Baton Rouge, Jackson, West Memphis, Greenville, and Lafayette, Williams paints portraits of bittersweet relationships that bear close resemblance to the work of two famous southern namesakes, the simple clarity and economy of Hank Williams and the steamy and almost gothic atmospherics of Tennessee Williams. With her sensuous songs of personal angst and yearning, Williams became a strong force in U.S. popular music, prompting covers of her songs by Emmylou Harris, Steve Earle, Mary Chapin Carpenter, and others. Although her work generally defied stylistic classification, a quality that sometimes hampered Williams's commercial acceptance, no one could deny the powerful impact made by the South on the tone and subject matter found in her songs.

Iris DeMent grew up in California, but in a family and community made up of transplanted southerners. She was always aware that rural Arkansas remained a presence in the lives of her working-class parents, and she carried that influence in her diction, values, and music. Like Lucinda Williams, DeMent heard and absorbed the music of Bob Dylan, the Beatles, and others who were important to her generation, and she honed her performing skills and songwriting gifts on the coffeehouse circuits of the West Coast and Kansas City. She also borrowed heavily from the music, both religious and secular, bequeathed to her by her parents. Her affectionate song "Mama's Opry" is a loving tribute to her mother and the rural musical culture that did so much to shape her life.

DeMent did not set out to be a writer of protest songs, and wondered if she "was up for hate mail,"[4] but her honesty and sensitivity about the conditions in which many people live evoked from her some of the finest expressions of social comment heard since the days of Woody Guthrie. She explored child abuse in "Letter to Mom," the declining fortunes of Native Americans in "These Hills," the bitter legacy of the Vietnam War in "Wall in Washington," materialism and career-driven anxieties in "Quality Time," and a host of injustices such as the corporate control of American life and politics in "Wasteland of the Free."

Tish Hinojosa did not think of herself as a southerner, and when she described her move to Nashville in the title track to her album *Taos to Tennessee*, she declared that "Southern ways are new to me." Hinojosa's music instead carries the imprint of a dual heritage, the experience of growing up in a Mexican-American family in San Antonio. In "The West Side of Town," she simultaneously pays tribute to her parents and to the generations of Mexican immigrants who forged new lives in the land north of the Rio Grande. As a child, she heard the same kinds of pop music available to Williams and DeMent, but she also absorbed the Tejano rhythms beloved by her father and the Mexican love songs brought to Texas by her mother. Out of these varied sources, Hinojosa fashioned an eclectic repertory that speaks sensitively about personal experiences and social issues. In "Something in the Rain," for instance, a song dedicated to labor leader Cesar Chavez, she addresses the consequences of pesticides and other hazards that threaten the lives of migratory workers and their children.

Hinojosa, DeMent, and Williams illustrate qualities that have always been present in the music of the South: its diversity, its rootedness in tradition, and its ability to change without losing its identity. Like Nanci Griffith, Jimmie Dale Gilmore, Steve Earle, James McMurtry, Townes Van Zandt, Willie Nelson, Steve Young, and other southern-born musicians, they also reaffirm the importance of the singer-songwriter, a figure far removed from the tunesmiths of Tin Pan Alley or the slavish devotion to old forms simply for the sake of preserving them and denying the claims of all subsequent experience.

No musical genre embodied these qualities more strongly than country music, and no form has been more strongly torn between tradition and innovation. Consequently, country music underwent dramatic changes since the 1980s. Bruce Feiler argues in fact that the music most identified, whether accurately or romantically, with rural America had become suburbanized, something that happened as lower-middle-class and working-class southerners and other country music fans became more affluent and abandoned rural areas and cities alike and moved to the suburbs. Jack Temple Kirby went so far as to say that country music's middle-class homogenization represented a "betrayal" of its working-class roots.[5]

Someone who represented the suburbanization of country music was crossover star Mary Chapin Carpenter. In her 1992 hit single "He Thinks He'll Keep Her," for instance, many country music fans, male and female, identified with the woman whose increasingly lonely life was characterized in part by the scheduling demands of her busy children: "She drives all day." Such concerns, long the subject matter of essays and short stories on the lives of well-to-do suburbanites, made as much sense to many country fans as they did to fans of pop music. In the same way, Carpenter's appeal to both groups made sense because people in the two groups were coming increasingly to resemble one another, and in fact, were in some ways indistinguishable.

Perhaps it was appropriate that this particular trend in country music was illustrated in the post-'70s era by a New Jersey native who graduated from an Ivy League university. As Carpenter enjoyed a rush of popularity in the 1980s and '90s, it became apparent that Top Forty country voiced many of the feelings, values, and aspirations of people who did not grow up in working-class homes. Its sound, and often its message, was closer to '80s rock than to traditional country. Many country radio stations turned to a Top Forty format, tightening their playlists so greatly that they seemed only to push "safe" recordings that struck many critics and country music lovers as bland and homogenized. On the other hand, for every fan who felt betrayed by the crossover success of Carpenter and others and who longed for more country stars such as Dwight Yoakam and Marty Stuart, who openly embraced the name "hillbilly," there was probably another fan who was won over to country music by the energy and musicianship of the new country artists or one who felt that being southern or being interested in country music did not mean one should reject success.

Many people were attracted also to country music because of the infusion in the 1980s and '90s of female stars such as Carpenter, Reba McEntire, Kathy Mattea, K.T. Oslin, Patty Loveless, Leanne Rimes, Lee Ann Womack, and Roseanne Cash. Many new fans, especially women, were attracted by the incorporation of contemporary subject matter. Without abandoning the well-established themes of romantic difficulty, marital distress, and job dissatisfaction, country artists such as Carpenter, McEntire, and the Dixie Chicks spoke for many women who were tired of being powerless to change a society they felt they were holding together. McEntire's music, such as her song "Is There Life Out There?" spoke to the needs of women who were undereducated or otherwise disadvantaged. The Dixie Chicks inspired numerous contrasting responses, sometimes enraging traditionalists with their rock-based, show-band approach, but also impressing audiences with their musicianship and socially relevant songs. They certainly raised many eyebrows and the consciousness of many people with their hit "Goodbye Earl," in which an abusive husband gets what many women would have agreed he had coming to him.

Lyrics that dealt with up-to-date social concerns did not mean that country music abandoned its heritage. Indeed, social commentary was part of the heritage itself, and a sizable segment of the country music community placed a high value on nostalgia, another dimension of the form's background. Southern themes and metaphors continued to appear in country songs, even as country music videos became popular. The music video marketing innovation was something many people decried for its shortening of kids' attention spans and its ability to distract listeners from the shortcomings of some songs that might not have flourished simply as music on the radio.

Music videos seemed to many people to be something new that would lead to no good, but country music entertainers used videos to communicate their endorsement of age-old values just as frequently as they did to flout them. Randy Travis tugged on viewers' heartstrings with images of old couples still in love just as his lyrics promised his own undying affection in his 1987 hit "Forever and Ever, Amen." Travis and many others employed in music videos southern scenes, especially small towns, churches, football fields, and other locales not unique to the South but having iconic significance for many southerners, offering a reassuring message of continuity with the past. Alabama's video for "Song of the South" employed images of the Great Depression and the New Deal to reaffirm the spirit of perseverance in the face of desperate odds, inhospitable weather, and grim economic forces. Shania Twain, years later, offended many viewers with a video for her hit song "I Feel Like a Woman," in which she appears in increasing stages of undress. By then, however, most fans knew that she was just another expression of the eclectic country music marketplace. Twain's song and video could have dealt with the sexual exuberance of a free-spirited woman anywhere, but many other country stars still used the South as a reference point, sometimes because it simply made sense in the context of the song and in light of their own lives. Sometimes they were trying to tap into a sense of nostalgia that many people felt for a comforting past or a bygone South. The Nashville Network, which began broadcasting by cable in 1983, Country Music Television, and the Great American Country cable network all included programming that focused on the southern past, but they all also distributed and helped popularize virtually all of the most pop-flavored country music being produced. This kind of programming went far beyond anything previously seen on Dolly Parton's or Barbara Mandrell's network television shows, which featured music and comedy that downplayed the "countryness" of their stars in order to assure viewership. The cable networks simply put videos on the screen, usually without comment even from a "veejay." If a video on a country music cable network seemed not very country, the viewer had no context in which to make sense of the song, no host or hostess to interpret the ways the song might or might not seem country. The result was liberating or scandalous, depending on one's perspective.

Pop influences elicited strong reactions from neo-traditionalists in country music. As James Cobb points out in *Southern Cultures*, the clash, one might even say dialectic, between traditionalism and modernism, is a longstanding conflict in country music and in southern culture as a whole.[6] But a particularly telling example of the depth of feeling about the perceived captivity of country music by pop market forces arose in 1999 in the bluegrass hit "Murder on Music Row" by Larry Cordle and Larry Shell, covered by country superstars Alan Jackson and George Strait. The song spoke to the feelings many country lovers felt, hardly new but pressing nonetheless, about the commercial enslavement of their art. It also reflected, however, an effort to preserve the heart of country music that had been going on for quite some time.

Neo-traditionalists such as Strait, Emmylou Harris, John Anderson, and Ricky Skaggs had been trying since the late 1970s and early 1980s to pull country music back to its roots without simply being nostalgic or antiquarian. They showed that more "authentic" country music could sell, and they won numerous awards and salutations of people in the business, including many whose work the traditionalists were trying to overcome. Harris became president of the Country Music Association, the genre's promotional and educational organization, and managed to win many fans to older-styled music without alienating admirers of the newer forms. Randy Travis and Dwight Yoakam joined the traditionalists' ranks in the 1980s, and along with Gene Watson, Keith Whitley, Vern Gosdin, Alan Jackson, Marty Brown, and Brad Paisley added a commitment to country influences such as those of Lefty Frizzell and other forebears. All of these neo-traditionalists and others tried to convey at least the aura of earlier country music, if not its substance. If they did not succeed in stemming the tide of pop influences on country music, at least it could be said that they persisted, stayed on the scene, and remained largely popular at the turn of the century. Asleep at the Wheel continued to carry on the western swing tradition, enlisting numerous and sundry guest artists to record two tribute albums to Bob Wills and His Texas Playboys in the 1990s. Cowboy music stayed in the marketplace courtesy of Riders in the Sky, the Sons of the San Joaquin, Chris LeDoux, Michael Martin Murphey, Red Steagall, and Don Edwards. Murphey, Steagall, and Edwards also made reputations in the burgeoning cowboy poetry movement.

Other artists who seemed country but successfully mixed rock elements into their music included Marty Stuart, Travis Tritt, and Gary Stewart. Tritt's 1990 song "Put Some Drive in Your Country" spoke of how he loved "old country" but missed Duane Allman, and how he had a feeling that Hank Williams would be adding some (rock) drive to his music if he were still around, as, indeed, Hank Williams Jr. was prone to do. That several of these and other country artists contributed to a highly successful tribute album honoring the Eagles suggested how important rock music had been to them during the 1970s. The most phenomenally successful of such artists, also one of the most multi-faceted, was Garth Brooks, the Oklahoma native whose performances mixed very traditional-sounding tunes with those that had dramatically strong pop influences. That he was able to sell astronomically large numbers of albums and perform to huge crowds virtually everywhere, including New York's Central Park, seemed to be evidence that country music had indeed become a national phenomenon.

In the aftermath of the 1970s, rock music moved further away from its roots as dance music. As punk rock became ascendant, rock music also moved away from the kind of blues-based guitar styles that had formed the core of rock 'n' roll from the 1950s until well past its metamorphosis into rock. The place to find old-time rock guitar playing, whether country purists liked it or not, was in country music. In addition, one of the few places where people could go dancing, at least for those who could not stand disco music, was the local country dance hall or nightclub. Few old-time roadhouses remained, but owners of clubs and dance halls soon found their establishments all the rage. In one of those chicken-and-egg situations that occur so often in popular culture, the country dance craze inspired and was fueled in large part by *Urban Cowboy*, the John Travolta/Debra Winger film of 1980. The film was set in Pasadena, Texas, and largely filmed at Mickey Gilley's famed club. The fact that Travolta had starred in a disco-dance movie, *Saturday Night Fever*, in 1977 did not seem to bother country-dance fans, many of whom got their initiation to country music through *Urban Cowboy*. A general dance craze broke out in the United States in the 1980s and '90s, when ballroom dancing made something of a comeback, various forms of Latin and Cajun dance gained new adherents, and a resurgence of swing music occurred. By the '90s, line dancing became popular, phenomenally so in some places, a form of stylized group dancing adapted from African-American step-dancing such as the Harlem Shuffle, aided in its popularity by such music videos as Billy Ray Cyrus's "Achy Breaky Heart." To some, line dancing resembled a form of working out, and its aerobic dimensions no doubt contributed to its popularity in a country increasingly obsessed with trying to get in shape. It also had some democratic advantages in that one could participate with or without a partner in tow.

Bluegrass continued to thrive, and even vaulted to unexpected heights of popularity through its inclusion in the movie soundtrack *O Brother, Where*

Art Thou? After the death of patriarch Bill Monroe, Ralph Stanley was elevated to that honorific position. Ricky Skaggs returned to the exclusive performance of bluegrass. Del McCoury carried on the tradition with some modern
dimensions, as did the Nashville Bluegrass Band, Seldom Scene, James King,
Alison Krauss, Doyle Lawson, the New Grass Revival, Nickel Creek, and Bela
Fleck. Increasing numbers of women found their way into bluegrass bands.
Indeed, the feminization of bluegrass may have been one of the most important trends in southern music in the late twentieth and early twenty-first centuries, with Lynn Morris, Rhonda Vincent, Dale Bradley, Suzanne Thomas,
Linda Williams, Laurie Lewis, and Clair Lynch joining Alison Krauss in achieving bluegrass prominence. Even Dolly Parton had a hit album in the form,
The Grass Is Blue, in 1999. This seemingly old-fashioned musical genre ironically attracted a growing youthful component. Musicianship continued to be
staggering, with dizzying speed still one of the most common characteristics
of the music. Contemporary sounds found their place in bluegrass, but the
old cabin home still attracted musicians and fans, and the form remained
overwhelmingly the province of white musicians, despite its deep debt to
African-American culture.

Artists who reached across the lines of musical categories abounded in
the South in the closing years of the twentieth century. Because hard-to-classify usually equals hard-to-market in the music business, the popularity of
such musicians was remarkable in some cases and downright surprising in
others. In the 1980s Alejandro Escovedo combined Mexican musical influences from his family experience, a love of rock music, and the iconoclasm of
the punk movement, defying stereotypes about the kind of music someone of
his background might play. He worked with the cowpunk group Rank and
File, then created an excited following as a solo performer based out of Austin.
Texan Chris Duarte also surprised many listeners who thought he might in-
cline toward something more "Hispanic," but he exploded onto the blues-
rock scene in the 1990s, blending jazz, hip-hop, and funk sounds held together
by his Stevie Ray Vaughan-inspired guitar playing. The Indigo Girls likewise
challenged categories throughout the '90s, drawing on a rich songwriting ability
infused with traditional southern concerns for theological integrity and community with lesbian sensibilities and employing folk, rock, gospel, country,
and other motifs. REM, like the Indigo Girls, a group with Georgia roots,
established a reputation for writing and performing rock music with literate,
"intelligent" lyrics and became a particular favorite of film producers, who
included their songs on soundtracks as far back as the mid-1980s. Hootie and
the Blowfish, a pop band with South Carolina roots, achieved acclaim for lead
singer Darius Rucker and the group's romantic moodiness, though the band

exhibited little southern identity. Widespread Panic and Southern Culture on the Skids had somewhat more modest success with multilayered music evoking southern themes and attracting admiration among singer-songwriters who invited various members of the two bands to record with them and among film producers who used their music in movies.

Because one of the clearest realities of southern music in the late twentieth and early twenty-first centuries was the difficulty of trying to categorize artists and their songs, independent radio stations became a precious source of support for those artists. A fairly extensive number of disc jockeys played older country music on college and other independent stations with Americana or roots-music formats, stations such as WWOZ in New Orleans, KABF in Little Rock, and WORT in Madison. Realizing the connections among country music and the broad folk traditions of the United States, programmers at such stations cycled hard-to-classify contemporary artists into their playlists. They helped tremendously to keep such artists afloat by creating followings for them. Such disc jockeys also contributed to the success of another musical form that drew heavily on southern roots, alternative country.

Alternative country singers and groups carved out a place among young fans especially, who liked their southern themes drenched in an edgy iconoclasm. Alternative country music often defied clear definition, ranging from rock-flavored to neo-honky tonk to various other forms of fusion, but its main unifying element was its opposition to Nashville's industrial approach to music making and the homogenized predictability of Top Forty radio programming. Some alternative musicians such as Marty Brown, Dale Watson, Wayne Hancock, Hank Williams III, Iris DeMent, Tish Hinojosa, Buddy and Julie Miller, Nanci Griffith, and Gillian Welch were drawn to country music by way of rockabilly, punk country, gospel, or music from the urban folk revival and its later offshoots. Watson and Hancock explored the honky-tonk form with abandon, emerging as unabashed apologists for a hard country sound. Some alternative artists, even those with non-southern roots, were viewed as traditionalists, such as Jimmie Dale Gilmore, Joe Ely, BR5–49, Big Sandy and the Fly-Right Boys, the Derailers, and the Carpetbaggers, but seemed more at home in the rockabilly mode. Consequently, many alternative country performers seemed too traditional, or too folky, to be played on mainstream country radio stations. Others, however, were drawn not only to older styles of country music and to such older artists as Hazel Dickens and Ralph Stanley, but they also embraced country music's raunchier traditions, illustrating the continuing appeal of its darker romantic side. Steve Earle, Robbie Fulks, Uncle Tupelo, and others found enough of a fan base to stay in business despite refusing to play the games required by the music industry. They persisted partly because their superb songwriting meant that their work got recorded frequently by more mainstream artists who were bold enough to record songs written by alternative country musicians but not bold enough to break away from Nashville's corporate culture. Many alternative musicians were northerners or were from the West Coast. They brought their romantic visions of what country music and its culture should be, and they and their southern-born compatriots alike judged Nashville to a great extent on how it conformed to such visions.

Some alternative country acts earned the name "insurgent," a term coined by Bloodshot Records in Chicago. They tended to have strong country-rock dimensions and often looked to Gram Parsons for inspiration; others alluded to traditional sources. Some seemed to have been pushed toward country music by producers and record company executives. The rise of alternative or insurgent country began when Uncle Tupelo made its first recordings in 1990, including a Carter Family song called "No Depression in Heaven." By 1994 the band dissolved and re-emerged as two other country-rock bands called Wilco, led by Jeff Tweedy, and Son Volt, led by Jay Farrar. Some called the genre No Depression music, and it spawned a website and a magazine with the same name. Other groups followed the lead of Tweedy and Farrar and of Jason and the Scorchers, including the Old 97s, Whiskeytown, Freakwater, the Bottle Rockets, Hazeldine, and the Waco Brothers.

Once a linchpin of southern music, jazz settled into a pattern of being largely a northern form, except for the vibrant jazz scene in New Orleans and the work of a few southerners who blended traditional and progressive forms of the music. In the years after the eclipse of the cool jazz of the 1950s and the toning down to some extent of the more often frenetic experimental jazz of the 1960s and '70s, a fusion movement followed in which jazz was often combined with rock, as in the music of Pat Metheney. Always an urban phenomenon, live jazz music was presented in few southern cities as the twentieth century came to a close, though San Antonio, of all places, supported it, largely through the efforts of Jim Cullum, longtime host of a National Public Radio program on traditional jazz. The music was more often identified with New York, Chicago, or Kansas City, reflecting, however, one of the constant features of southern music, its migration and evolution. The northernness of jazz was made possible by the black diaspora, the vast migrations of African Americans throughout the first two-thirds of the twentieth century.[8] With the swing craze of the 1990s, some southern bands with jazz connections came to the fore, especially including the Squirrel Nut Zippers from North Carolina, whose song "Got My Own Thing Now" showed an excitement about the swing form as pure as if the band had discovered it itself.

Squirrel Nut Zippers vocalist Katherine Whalen, a Billie Holiday devotee, also recorded in North Carolina with a group called the Jazz Project. She and two Mississippi natives added further to the recognition that jazz could provide a creative setting for mixing the avant-garde and the traditional and could flourish around vocalists. Cassandra Wilson combined traditional southern jazz with elements of the New York and Chicago progressive movements, folk, rock, and blues. Olu Dara, a fixture on the New York avant-garde loft scene, combined cornet, trumpet, and guitar with his sensuous vocal styles and created a captivating sound that "fused" and "crossed over" without seeming commercially self-conscious.

Although hip-hop culture was broadly associated with urban life in the North and on the West Coast, a southern stream of rap music emerged in the late 1980s, especially in Miami, Atlanta, and New Orleans. The most important performers in southern rap were 2 Live Crew, featuring Luther Campbell's sexually explicit lyrics, and Arrested Development, which offered material more intellectually complicated. In the 1970s gospel music entered a period dominated by a phenomenon known as "Contemporary Christian." Growing largely out of the publishing and recording companies associated with WORD, Inc., which began in Waco, Texas, Contemporary Christian represented a philosophical and commercial stance bent on capturing customers, or saving wayward souls, depending on one's perspective, away from sinful music and toward that of the gospel. But it was far from the old-time gospel music associated with the South. One measure of the popularity of Contemporary Christian music, somewhat ironically, was that it helped inspire the creation of a new category of music, "Southern Gospel," to distinguish the older-styled music from the more modern, pop-styled forms. Amy Grant, who became the wife of country star Vince Gill, Sandi Patti, and hosts of young pop-influenced artists appeared, singing what sounded very much like ordinary love songs, until the listener realized the loved one being addressed was most often Jesus. Grant became the queen of Contemporary Christian, though she alienated many fans by occasionally performing and recording with secular artists such as Chicago's Peter Cetera.

Gospel music in some ways illustrated the notion that the future of southern music was in its past. Shirley Caesar, for instance, incorporated soul and r&b elements into her music, managing to update it without losing the feeling fans saw and heard in her work, gaining ten Grammys, seventeen Doves, and numerous other awards for her almost forty albums. She continued to bill herself as "Pastor" Shirley Caesar and the Queen of Gospel and appeared in such diverse locales as Disney World, VH1, the first Bush White House, and the second Clinton inauguration, while another gospel singer-songwriter, Bill

Gaither, also bridged the past and the future. Gaither produced a series of popular old-fashioned "gospel sing" videos, using new formats to recreate old forms of expression for audiences that had never gotten to partake of them, bringing J.D. Sumner and the Stamps, Jake Hess, Howard and Vestal Goodman, and other gospel legends before old fans as well as new ones. Still, the driving market forces meant that fans of Contemporary Christian music dominated the world of gospel music. They wanted updated styles and recording techniques borrowed from the pop world. When they asked the old question "Why should the devil have all the good tunes?" they had little interest in seeing the crossover phenomenon head the other direction.

In the last decades of the twentieth century, southern music renewed its diversity, not ignorant of market forces and pressures, but more assertive of its own identity. New forms, new alliances, combinations, and discoveries ensued, and a great deal of interesting music emerged. Fans and analysts were left wondering if southern traits still discernible in the various styles of music associated with the region at the dawn of the twenty-first century were "authentic" or "natural" or whether "southernness" was largely a pose or a bow to tradition. If southern music was still American music, they also wondered, was it America's music?

CONCLUSION

For many who made and loved southern music, the South of imagery endured even as its performers and musical forms gradually became absorbed into the national mainstream. The lure of the South for American musicians remained as strong as it was in the days of Stephen Foster and his cohorts, who did so much to create public conceptions of the South. Though a long procession of northern poets contributed to the mythologizing of Dixie and its inhabitants, southern musicians played active roles in keeping their own special versions of the southern myth alive. They also reminded observers that there is not one South but many.

For over a century and a half the South has left its imprint on American music, not only as a source of images, but as an exporter of musicians and styles. Beginning with the spirituals in the late nineteenth century and exploding into the national consciousness after World War II, southern music forms did more than merely contribute to the revitalization of American popular music; they virtually became popular music itself. Forms born in cotton fields, textile mills, and other work places and in the shacks, honky-tonks, and churches of the South moved on to national outlets, northern concert halls, and the lounges of Las Vegas. Music became one dramatic avenue through which poor southern boys and girls could attain glamor and wealth and escape the ghettos, coal camps, textile villages, and tenant farms that had long held their forebears in bondage.

But in a sense, at the hour of its victory southern-born music also suffered defeat. Commercial acclaim, general popularity, and international recognition were won at the price of the loss of distinctiveness and individuality. The world was enriched by the periodic infusions of southern-derived music, but southern musicians have absorbed much from that wider world to which they were introduced. Southern styles became so enmeshed in American popular culture, in fact, that it became impossible to determine where their southern-ness ended and their American-ness began. Gospel and secular styles were so closely intertwined that often only their lyrics differentiated them; black and white musicians borrowed freely from each other; country and pop moved closer to each other; and musicians in all genres strove to find the key to universal popularity. The result was not exclusively a homogenization of American popular music, for the various genres remained somewhat distinct even as they borrowed from each other. But certainly one could wonder which force had been stronger, the southernization of U.S. music or the nationalization of the South.

Breaking down barriers between the races, between income groups, even regions of the country was a worthy, one might say essential, goal of U.S. and southern society. But the diminishing of musical distinctiveness represented more than the loss of cherished traditional styles. It also meant, potentially, the loss of an important dimension of the cultural identity of large numbers of people in the U.S., especially those in the ranks of the less affluent and the less powerful in the South.

All was not lost, however. Away from the beaten and jaded paths of professional entertainment, older expressions of the folk South persisted and found an expanding audience, one much too large to be dismissed as simply old people engaged in a quaint pursuit of nostalgia. In fact, that audience was basically an audience of the young. The enthusiasm for folk music is no more vividly demonstrated than by the immense throngs who attend the fiddlers contest each year in Union Grove, North Carolina, or who seek out other such meets in such places as Huntsville, Alabama, or Athens, Texas. The proliferating bluegrass festivals provide further evidence of the back-to-the-roots urge that always seems to run so strong in the history of U.S. culture. The folklife festivals, such as those in Kerrville, Texas, in New Orleans, and on the Mall in Washington, D.C., provide samplings of the wide range of southern music, food, crafts, and customs to ever-increasing audiences. The large-scale appeal of the music was still only part of the story, however, with long-running jam sessions and recurring picking parties taking place in people's homes, American Legion halls, and countless public places around the country.

All one would have to do to know that folk music, for instance, was far from being solely a spectator sport would be to visit the Stone County Courthouse square in Mountain View, Arkansas, on virtually any evening when the weather is nice. Though people in the United States embraced processed, prefabricated, franchised culture, a great hunger for the homemade and the genuine endured, an impulse that led people to the folk resources of the South. The immense popularity of the guitar was inspired primarily by the example of rock musicians, but increasing numbers of young people took up such folky instruments as the fiddle, banjo, autoharp, and dobro steel guitar. Bluegrass music, which long drew upon the resources of tradition, became a haven for young musicians, and the performances of musicians not yet teenagers thrilled festival audiences. The old forms of music showed a tremendous amount of vitality, captivating listeners at such non-traditional venues as world's fairs in Knoxville and New Orleans, the 1996 Summer Olympics in Atlanta, various presidential inauguration events, and vast numbers of music theaters and blues clubs in amusement parks, tourist meccas such as Branson, Missouri, and ordinary towns and cities. The *Old-Time Herald* flourished, becoming the clearinghouse for the modern folk-music movement, and the year 1997 saw the reissuance of the historic *Folkways Anthology* by the Smithsonian Institution.

Strange and wondrous things occurred, even within the context of commercialization. The homogenization of styles encouraged by the pop music world sometimes bred rebellion. The repetition and uniformity of the Top Forty concept could and did inspire a search for the novel and fresh. Dissatisfaction with mainstream pop music encouraged experimentation with new forms and occasionally led to a reaching back for the old. To young listeners who never heard the music during its first appearance, the old seemed new and innovative, as did rhythm and blues, urban folk music, bluegrass, and western swing during their respective "revivals" since World War II. The interest in the older forms of music was often fueled by "outsiders" who made use of southern materials, as seen with Joan Baez and Gillian Welch and Appalachian ballads, Tony Glover and blues, Asleep at the Wheel and western swing, the Red Clay Ramblers and old-timey fiddle band music, Si Kahn and John McCutcheon and protest music. Furthermore, much patronage came from northern audiences. But native southerners were responsible for much of the utilization of older southern music. Some of these southern musicians were conscious revivalists who merely recreated what they heard. Others, such as Steve Earle, were eclectic artists who built new forms out of the varied ingredients of the music, both traditional and contemporary, that surrounded them. These musicians became living testaments to the possibilities inherent in the fusion of tradition and modernity in southern music.

Some musicians, such as Lucinda Williams, Tim O'Brien, Katherine Whalen, Nanci Griffith, Cassandra Wilson, and Olu Dara, managed to combine both the oldest and newest strains in the music of the South, suggesting that a vigorous and organic regional music could still be produced through the absorption and transmission of a variety of styles and an earnest investment of sincere feeling. They and others also showed that commercialization, ever the blessing as well as the curse of all popular music, need not rob music of its soul. Even though teams of hired songwriters in Nashville and elsewhere produced quotas of material for country singers and marketing specialists decided what music should be produced and sold to the public, some musicians still created their art because they loved southern music, American music.

Southern music/American music is more than just the sum of southern styles, and certainly more than the music of national white culture. While much of it has been appropriated by upper-class interventionists,[1] it also has appropriated U.S. culture, with the help of a great deal of marketing and hard work by artists and business people associated with southern music. Southern music has been a hugely important part of momentous social changes, helping create a youth culture that altered enormous segments of modern western society, the mass media, and broad approaches to marketing products, serving various purposes in the Cold War and in other cultural and political struggles within the U.S. and beyond.

British- and African-American blendings continue to shape the musical culture of the U.S. as they have done since the inception of southern and American history. These fusions speak especially to youth. American youth culture became a worldwide phenomenon, one largely borne by music rooted in the South, whether it was ragtime at the turn of the nineteenth century, jazz in the 1920s, swing in the 1930s, bebop in the 1940s, rock 'n' roll in the 1950s, rock in the 1960s, their derivatives punk in the 1970s and '80s and hip-hop in the 1980s and '90s, or blues and country all the way through.

In the twenty-first century, the power and joy inherent in the South's musical diversity should encourage people to abandon an idea that dominated the thinking of too many people in the early twentieth century, that southern music flows from a pure, uniform racial and ethnic past. That presumption has been challenged persistently by the arrival, and the popularity, of the new musical styles of racially diverse southerners. These phenomena, however, actually represent something enduring indeed, qualities that can still be described as distinctive, that the South is a diverse and musical culture, regardless of how that diversity was underestimated, ignored, and denied by people with a racial or cultural/political agenda reliant on ideas about purity. That power and joy should also encourage people to understand that the South, the United States, and southern music/American music are better than they would have been without this cultural diversity.

NOTES

Introduction

1. George B. Tindall, "Mythology: A New Frontier in Southern History," in Patrick Gerster and Nicholas Cords, eds., *Myth and Southern History* (Chicago: Rand McNally, 1974), 1:1–15.

2. David Potter, "The Enigma of the South," in *The South and the Sectional Conflict* (Baton Rouge: Louisiana State University Press, 1968), 15.

Chapter 1. Folk Origins of Southern Music

1. Alan Lomax, *The Folk Songs of North America* (Garden City, N.Y.: Doubleday, 1960), 155; John Storm Roberts, *The Latin Tinge: The Impact of Latin American Music on the United States*, 2d ed. (New York: Oxford University Press, 1999), 38–39. See Alan Lomax, *Mister Jelly Roll: The Fortunes of Jelly Roll Morton, New Orleans Creole and "Inventor of Jazz"* (New York: Pantheon, 1993).

2. Lawrence Levine, *Black Culture and Black Consciousness: Afro-American Folk Thought from Slavery to Freedom* (New York: Oxford University Press, 1977), 6.

3. Dena J. Epstein, *Sinful Tunes and Spirituals: Black Folk Music to the Civil War* (Urbana: University of Illinois Press, 1977), 22, 80–100. See also Charles Joyner, *Shared Traditions: Southern History and Folk Culture* (Urbana: University of Illinois Press, 1999).

4. Levine, *Black Culture and Black Consciousness*, 194.

5. Paul Oliver, *Songsters and Saints: Vocal Traditions on Race Records* (Cambridge: Cambridge University Press, 1984), 22. See also the WPA Slave Narratives on the broad-ranging nature of black musical preferences, especially George Rawick, *The American Slave Narratives* (New York: Greenwood, 1972), part 4: 1430, 1505, 1650.

6. This is a central concern, for example, of both Eugene Genovese, *Roll Jordan Roll: The World the Slaves Made* (New York: Random House, 1972), and Lawrence Levine, *Black Culture and Black Consciousness*.

7. Dickson D. Bruce Jr., *And They All Sang Hallelujah: Plain-Folk Camp-Meeting Religion, 1800–45* (Knoxville: University of Tennessee Press, 1974), 96–122.

8. George Pullen Jackson, *White Spirituals in the Southern Uplands* (Chapel Hill: University of North Carolina Press, 1933), 31–34, 408–9; Joe Dan Boyd, "Judge Jackson: Black Giant of White Spirituals," *Journal of American Folklore* 83 (October-

December 1970): 446–51; and Boyd, "Negro Sacred Harp Songsters in Mississippi," *Mississippi Folklore Register* 5 (Fall 1971): 60–83.

9. David Evans, "Afro-American One-Stringed Instruments," *Western Folklore* 29 (October 1970): 229–45.

10. Epstein, *Sinful Tunes and Spirituals,* 36. Epstein has written a more complete study of the instrument in "The Folk Banjo: A Documentary History," *Ethnomusicology* 19 (September 1975): 347–71. The principal challenge to the Sweeney legend is Jay Bailey, "Historical Origin and Stylistic Development of the Five-String Banjo," *Journal of American Folklore* 85 (January-March 1972): 58–65. It is quite probable that the banjo attained national popularity through the performances of the touring white minstrel bands. Presumably these players adopted the instrument from black sources, but how greatly their styles of performance reflected black instrumental patterns is open to question. According to Robert Winans, the so-called Appalachian styles—"frailing" and "clawhammer"—"undoubtedly reflect[ed] preexisting black performance." White blackface minstrels ventured by riverboat and other means into the southern hills, whose residents absorbed the minstrel style of playing. Winans also contends that "southern rural whites . . . probably learned from both black musicians and minstrel players who toured the South with minstrel shows, circuses, and medicine shows." Winans, "Banjo," in Charles Reagan Wilson and William Ferris, eds., *Encyclopedia of Southern Culture* (Chapel Hill: University of North Carolina Press, 1989), 1042–43. Cecilia Conway contends that African Americans introduced the banjo and styles of playing it directly to white Appalachian dwellers in *African Banjo Echoes in Appalachia: A Study of Folk Traditions* (Knoxville: University of Tennessee Press, 1995). See also Philip Gura and James Bollman, *America's Instrument: The Banjo in the Nineteenth Century* (Chapel Hill: University of North Carolina Press, 1999).

11. David C. Morton with Charles K. Wolfe, *DeFord Bailey: A Black Star in Early Country Music* (Knoxville: University of Tennessee Press, 1991), 17.

12. D.K. Wilgus, *Anglo-American Folksong Scholarship since 1898* (New Brunswick, N.J.: Rutgers University Press, 1959), 3–123.

13. Paul Oliver argues that cakewalks and two-steps may not have originated on plantations, but that they were common in the large minstrel shows, *Songsters and Saints,* 33.

14. See the pioneering work on square dancing by S. Foster Damon, "History of Square Dancing," American Antiquarian Society, *Proceedings* (April 1952): 63–98.

15. The popularity of Shakespeare among the largely uneducated populace of the western frontier is depicted in Lawrence Levine, *Highbrow/Lowbrow: The Emergence of Cultural Hierarchy in America* (Cambridge: Harvard University Press, 1990).

16. Ronald L. Davis, *A History of Opera in the American West* (Englewood Cliffs, N.J.: Prentice-Hall, 1965), 6, 20–21; Henry A. Kmen, *Music in New Orleans: The Formative Years, 1791–1841* (Baton Rouge: Louisiana State University Press, 1966), 229, 232–33, 245.

17. Vernon Loggins, *Where the Word Ends: The Life of Louis Moreau Gottschalk* (Baton Rouge: Louisiana State University Press, 1958).

18. S. Frederick Starr, *Bamboula: The Life and Times of Louis Moreau Gottschalk* (New York: Oxford University Press, 1995), 42.

19. Loggins, *Where the Word Ends,* 141

20. Starr, *Bamboula,* 15–16, 43. See Carl Bode, *Antebellum Culture* (Carbondale, Ill.: Southern Illinois University Press, 1959).

Chapter 2. National Discovery

1. See Earl F. Bargainneer, "Tin Pan Alley and Dixie: The South in Popular Song," *Mississippi Quarterly* 30 (Fall 1977): 527–65.

2. Howard L. Sachs and Judith Rose Sachs, *Way Up North in Dixie: A Black Family's Claim to the Confederate Anthem,* provides an intriguing, and ironic, dimension to the story of the song "Dixie," proposing the possibility that Emmett picked up the song from black performers in Ohio.

3. Kmen, *Music in New Orleans,* 237–45; Sharon A. Sharp, "Dance, Black," *Encyclopedia of Southern Culture,* 149, 150.

4. Robert C. Toll, *Blacking Up: The Minstrel Show in Nineteenth-Century America* (New York: Oxford University Press, 1974), 40–48.

5. Ibid., 57.

6. William W. Austin, *Susanna, Jeanie, and the Old Folks at Home: The Songs of Stephen C. Foster from His Time to Ours* (New York: Macmillan, 1975), xx, 18, 123–35, 279–80. See also Ken Emerson, *Doo-Dah! Stephen Foster and the Rise of American Popular Culture* (New York: Simon and Schuster, 1997).

7. Austin, *Susanna, Jeanie, and the Old Folks at Home,* xi, 293.

8. Bill C. Malone, "William S. Hays: The Bard of Kentucky," *The Register of the Kentucky Historical Society* 93 (Summer 1995): 286–307.

9. Norm Cohen produced for the John Edwards Memorial Foundation an important recording called *Minstrels and Tunesmiths: The Commercial Roots of Early Country Music* (JEMF 109) that illustrated the nineteenth-century origins of folk and country music. The collection, in fact, includes some recordings of minstrel units.

10. Epstein, *Sinful Tunes and Spirituals,* 290.

11. *An Introduction to Gospel Song* (RBF Records RFS), compiled and edited by Samuel B. Charters.

12. Dvořák, for instance, stressed the importance of "plantation melodies" in an 1895 issue of *Harper's New Monthly Magazine* and called them "the most striking and appealing melodies that have yet been found on this side of the water." Reprinted in Bruce Jackson, ed., *The Negro and His Folklore in Nineteenth-Century Periodicals* (Austin: University of Texas Press, 1967), 428–34.

13. Jackson, *White Spirituals,* 242–302.

14. Another scholarly view of more recent vintage, the "Celtic thesis" of Grady McWhiney and Forrest McDonald, offers a different interpretation of white southern purity. They seek to explain the South's unique culture through its derivation from Scots, Scots-Irish, Irish, and Welsh foes of the English. Their thesis is interesting, though their use of evidence somewhat selective. They appeal to the abiding antago-

nism of their subjects toward the Anglo-Saxon power structure of Britain, which they say the "Celts" brought with them to the ante-bellum South. Southern purists and nationalists have to choose between the Anglo-Saxon South or the Celtic South. They cannot have it both ways, according to McWhiney and McDonald, although they might want to see the same traits in southerners of Anglo-Saxon and those of Celtic descent. See especially McWhiney's *Cracker Culture: Celtic Ways in the Old South* (Tuscaloosa: University of Alabama Press, 1988).

15. Nolan Porterfield, *Last Cavalier: The Life and Times of John A. Lomax* (Urbana: University of Illinois Press, 1996), 152, 234. See also Michael Lee Masterson, "Sounds of the Frontier: Music in Buffalo Bill's Wild West," Ph.D. dissertation, University of New Mexico, 1990.

16. See Wilgus, *Anglo-American Folksong Scholarship;* David Whisnant, *All That Is Native and Fine: The Politics of Culture in an American Region* (Chapel Hill: University of North Carolina Press, 1983), 93.

17. Lunsford, who was also a lawyer, had academic as well as personal interests in the folk songs of the southern mountains and was associated with Cecil Sharp's secretary and partner, Maud Karpeles. Loyal Jones, *Minstrel of the Appalachians: The Story of Bascom Lamar Lunsford* (1984; reprint, Lexington: University Press of Kentucky, 2002), 21.

18. Henry D. Shapiro, *Appalachia on Our Mind: The Southern Mountains and Mountaineers in the American Consciousness, 1870–1920* (Chapel Hill: University of North Carolina Press, 1978), 260, 261.

19. Romantics also contributed a good deal of confusion about what was indigenous to the mountains, promoting such things as morris dances, which were not native to the mountains, or dulcimers, which were very rare. David E. Whisnant calls the dulcimer "a romanticized feature of Appalachian music and culture," in "Festivals, Folk Music," *Encyclopedia of Southern Culture,* 1011. But see Charles Joyner, who in the same encyclopedia refers to the dulcimer as "a southern mountain folk instrument . . . used . . . for generations," "Dulcimer," 1055.

20. John Powell, "In the Lowlands Low," *Southern Folklore Quarterly* 1 (March 1937): 1–12.

21. Annabel Morris Buchanan, "The Function of a Folk Festival," ibid., 29–34; Whisnant, *All That Is Native and Fine,* 13, 187, 240–43. Buchanan's racial views were not as extreme as Powell's, by a considerable margin. Ibid., 319 n. 136.

22. The railroads, timber interests, and textile, coal, and petroleum industries were only a few of the phenomena that were already transforming the lives and culture of the plain people of the South in the 1930s. Archie Green has investigated some of the music inspired by industrial innovation in "Born on Picketlines, Textile Workers' Songs Are Woven into History," *Textile Labor* 22 (April 1961): 3–5; and in *Only a Miner: Studies in Recorded Coal-Mining Songs* (Urbana: University of Illinois Press, 1972).

Chapter 3. Early Commercialization: Ragtime, Blues, Jazz

1. Eileen Southern, *The Music of Black Americans* (New York: W.W. Norton, 1971), 312.

2. William J. Schafer and Johannes Riedel, *The Art of Ragtime* (Baton Rouge: Louisiana State University Press, 1973), 5; Edward A. Berlin, *King of Ragtime: Scott Joplin and His Era* (New York: Oxford University Press, 1994), 7–9.

3. Ragtime tempo has been a source of debate and controversy at least since Joplin's day. He continually fretted, for instance, over the speed with which some pianists played his and other ragtime pieces, presumably to demonstrate their ability to get through the often-intricate melodies, and on the sheet music of some of his compositions wrote such warnings as, "Notice! Don't play this piece fast. It is never right to play 'rag-time' fast." Berlin, *King of Ragtime,* 152. Other ragtime greats reveled in speed. Eubie Blake titled one of his compositions "Tricky Fingers," which featured a dizzying left-hand part and served him in his rivalry with another ragtime pianist noted for the speed of his playing.

4. Schafer and Riedel, *The Art of Ragtime,* 19.

5. Levine, *Black Culture and Black Consciousness,* 221.

6. Ibid., 237.

7. Samuel Charters, *The Legacy of the Blues: Lives of Twelve Great Bluesmen* (New York: Da Capo, 1977), 85.

8. Samuel Charters, *The Bluesmen* (New York: Oak Publications, 1967), 32; Alan Lomax, *The Land Where the Blues Began* (New York: Pantheon, 1993), ix. James C. Cobb, *The Most Southern Place on Earth: The Mississippi Delta and the Roots of Regional Identity* (New York: Oxford University Press, 1992), vii, 3–5, gives an excellent description of the Delta, an area running from just south of Memphis to just north of Vicksburg and bounded on the west by the Mississippi River and on the east by a line of bluffs running south from Tunica County to Greenwood and southwesterly to Vicksburg. Cobb points out that the Delta actually is the flood plain of the Mississippi and Yazoo Rivers. The region is bisected by U.S. Highway 61.

9. Jeff Todd Titon, *Early Downhome Blues: A Musical and Cultural Analysis* (Urbana: University of Illinois Press, 1977), 29. Legendary blues researcher Mack McCormick proposes a near-simultaneous development of the form in the Delta, the Atlanta area, and a triangle bounded by Dallas, Houston, and San Antonio, but blues students have been frustrated for years, waiting for his work to be published.

10. Charters, *The Bluesmen,* 32.

11. Titon, *Early Downhome Blues,* 47.

12. Lomax, *Land Where the Blues Began,* 13.

13. See "Enigmatic Folksongs of the Southern Underworld," *Current Opinion* 67 (September 1919): 165–66.

14. William C. Handy, *Father of the Blues* (New York: Macmillan, 1944).

15. Ibid., 67, 72, 120–22; Oliver, *Songsters and Saints,* 67.

16. Chris Albertson, *Bessie* (New York: Stein and Day, 1972), 34.

17. Perry Bradford, *Born with the Blues* (New York: Oak Publications, 1965), 117.

18. Albertson, *Bessie,* 34–36.

19. Titon, *Early Downhome Blues,* 23; Oliver, *Songsters and Saints,* 1, 8, 264, 269, 273–74.

20. Ibid., 264.

21. Ted Gioia, *The History of Jazz* (New York: Oxford University Press, 1997), 18.

22. Titon, *Early Downhome Blues,* xiii, xiv.

23. William J. Schafer, with the assistance of Richard B. Allen, *Brass Bands and New Orleans Jazz* (Baton Rouge: Louisiana State University Press, 1977), 94.

24. Rudi Blesh, *Shining Trumpets: A History of Jazz,* 2d rev. ed. (New York: Da Capo, 1976), 183–84.

25. Donald M. Marquis, *In Search of Buddy Bolden* (Baton Rouge: Louisiana State University Press, 1978).

26. Kathy J. Ogren, *The Jazz Revolution: Twenties America and the Meaning of Jazz* (New York: Oxford University Press, 1989), 47.

27. Al Rose, *Storyville, New Orleans* (Tuscaloosa: University of Alabama Press, 1974), 106, 123; Linda Dahl, *Stormy Weather: The Music and Lives of a Century of Jazzwomen* (New York: Pantheon, 1984), 13–14.

28. Burton W. Peretti, *The Creation of Jazz: Music, Race, and Culture in Urban America* (Urbana: University of Illinois Press, 1992), 39–42.

29. Blesh, *Shining Trumpets,* 212.

30. Marquis, *Buddy Bolden,* 2; James Lincoln Collier, *Jazz: The American Theme Song* (New York: Oxford University Press, 1993), 4, 277. Collier found the *Times-Picayune* clippings in the scrapbook of pioneer jazz musician Nick LaRocca.

31. *Dearborn Independent,* 6, 13 August 1921.

32. Blesh, *Shining Trumpets,* 225.

Chapter 4. Expanding Markets: Tejano, Cajun, Hillbilly, Gospel

1. Charles K. Wolfe, *Tennessee Strings: The Story of Country Music in Tennessee* (Knoxville: University of Tennessee Press, 1977), 27–54. See also Wolfe, *Grand Ole Opry: The Early Years, 1925–1935* (London: Old Time Music, 1975).

2. Joe Nick Patoski, "Little Joe," *Texas Monthly,* May 1978, 135.

3. Independent film and record producers Les Blank and Chris Strachwitz collaborated on a number of ventures dealing with folk and ethnic musicians. Strachwitz's Tejano reissues are on his own Folklyric label.

4. Barry Jean Ancelet, Jay D. Edwards, and Glen Pitre, *Cajun Country* (Jackson: University Press of Mississippi, 1991), 150.

5. Lauren C. Post, *Cajun Sketches* (Baton Rouge: Louisiana State University Press, 1962), 36.

6. Houston folklorist Mack McCormick is credited with the coining of the term Zydeco. Accordionist Clifton Chenier, from Opelousas, Louisiana, became the most famous of all the Zydeco musicians. The best discussion of this style is Ben Sandmel, *Zydeco!* (Jackson: University Press of Mississippi, 1999).

7. Barry Jean Ancelet, *Cajun and Creole Folktales: The French Oral Tradition of South Louisiana* (New York: Garland, 1994), xxii. See also Ancelet and Elemore Morgan Jr., *The Makers of Cajun Music/Musiciens cadiens et créoles* (Austin: University of Texas Press, 1984).

8. George B. Tindall, *The Emergence of the New South, 1913–1945* (Baton

Rouge: Louisiana State University Press, 1967), 184–218, and "The Benighted South: Origins of a Modern Image," *Virginia Quarterly Review* 40 (Spring 1964): 281–94.

9. There are challenges to the theory that hillbilly music was solely a southern phenomenon. See Roderick J. Roberts, "An Introduction to the Study of Northern Country Music," *Journal of Country Music* 6 (January 1978): 22–29, and Simon J. Bronner, "The Country Music Tradition in Western New York State," ibid., 29–60.

10. A.P. and Sara's son and daughter continued to perform for years at the Carter Fold near the old homeplace. Carlene Carter, June's daughter through her marriage to Carl Smith, became a well-respected country singer, as did Rosanne Cash, Johnny's daughter from a previous marriage.

11. Wolfe, *Tennessee Strings*, 52.

Chapter 5. The Great Depression and New Technologies

1. See Walker's discography in Helen Oakley Dance, *Stormy Monday: The T-Bone Walker Story* (Baton Rouge: Louisiana State University Press, 1987), 253–55.

2. Ibid., xi.

3. Oliver, *Songsters and Saints*, 189.

4. Scott DeVeaux, *The Birth of Bebop: A Social and Musical History* (Berkeley: University of California Press, 1997), 26.

5. The phrase is inspired by Thomas Tippett, *When Southern Labor Stirs* (New York: Cape and Smith, 1931). See also Tindall, *Emergence of the New South*, 318–54.

6. Archie Green, notes to *Sarah Ogan Gunning, Girl of Constant Sorrow*, Folk-Legacy Records, FSA-26. This phenomenon is also discussed in R. Serge Denisoff, *Great Day Coming: Folk Music and the American Left* (Urbana: University of Illinois Press, 1971), 15–37.

7. Cary Ginell, *Milton Brown and the Founding of Western Swing* (Urbana: University of Illinois Press, 1994), 227.

8. Charles R. Townsend, *San Antonio Rose: The Life and Music of Bob Wills* (Urbana: University of Illinois Press, 1976).

9. Ginell, *Milton Brown*, 68.

10. Hear, for instance, his opening chorus on "Right or Wrong," from September 1936, three months after Milton Brown's fine recording of the tune, and his work on "Bob Wills Special," recorded in April 1940.

11. See James Gregory, *American Exodus: The Dust Bowl Migration and Okie Culture in California* (New York: Oxford University Press, 1991).

Chapter 6. The Nationalization of Southern Music

1. An interesting study could be done of the Jews, Armenians, and other "minority" individuals who have contributed so vitally to the emergence of country, rhythm and blues, and other grassroots musical forms after World War II. The ways they threw themselves into the musical expressions of cultures not their own, often with

more enthusiasm, and even awareness, than the people who were members of the groups that produced the music, are truly fascinating.

2. Ginell, *Milton Brown,* xxviii.

3. Charles Keil, *Urban Blues* (Chicago: University of Chicago Press, 1966), 20.

4. Ibid., 102.

5. John Broven, *Walking to New Orleans: The Story of New Orleans Rhythm and Blues* (Sussex, England: Blues Unlimited, 1974), 13–17, 64–72.

6. Dewey Phillips is mentioned so often in connection with Sam Phillips, as is the fact that they were not related, that "no relation to Sam" is practically part of his last name.

7. Peter Guralnick, *Last Train to Memphis: The Rise of Elvis Presley* (Boston: Little, Brown, 1994) and *Careless Love: The Unmaking of Elvis Presley* (Boston: Little, Brown, 2000).

8. Immediately after his death, several books appeared which purported to have the "inside" and "hidden" story of Elvis's life. One of the most sensational is a book by three of his ex-bodyguards—Red West, Sonny West, and Dave Hebler—as told to Steve Dunleavy, *Elvis, What Happened?* (New York: Ballantine Books, 1977). For a review essay of this and four other such early books on Elvis, see Mark Crispin Miller, "The King," *New York Review of Books,* 8 December 1977, 38–42.

Chapter 7. The 1960s and 1970s: Rock, Gospel, Soul

1. Robert Palmer, *Rock & Roll: An Unruly History* (New York: Harmony Books, 1995), 32–33, 42.

2. Craig Morrison, *Go Cat Go! Rockabilly Music and Its Makers* (Urbana: University of Illinois Press, 1996), 255. Morrison points out that in one 1964 publication the Beatles were referred to as "redcoat rockabillies." Ibid., 183.

3. The best biography of Joplin, and one that contains a wide assortment of photographs, is Myra Friedman, *Buried Alive* (New York: William Morrow, 1973).

4. Stephen R. Tucker, "Rock, Southern," *Encyclopedia of Southern Culture,* 1027–28.

5. Michael Bane, "Hillbilly Band," *Country Music,* March 1977, 51.

6. Martha Hume, "Marshall Tucker at Home," *Rolling Stone,* 28 July 1977, 20.

7. Chet Flippo, "Getting By without the Allmans," *Creem,* November 1974, 34–37, 75.

8. See Stephen Ray Tucker, "The Western Image in Country Music," M.A. thesis, Southern Methodist University, 1976.

9. Tony Heilbut, *The Gospel Sound: Good News and Bad Times* (New York: Simon and Schuster, 1971), 94.

10. Peter Guralnick, *Sweet Soul Music: Rhythm and Blues and the Southern Dream of Freedom* (New York: Harper Perennial, 1986), 1–2.

11. Ibid., 332.

12. Michael Lydon, *Ray Charles: Man and Music* (New York: Riverhead Books, 1998), 112–13; Guralnick, *Sweet Soul Music,* 50.

13. Don Rhodes, "Lest We Forget: Ray Charles Reflects," *Country Music,* January 1975, 19.

14. Arnold Shaw, *The World of Soul* (New York: Paperback Library Edition, 1971), 219.

15. Palmer, *Rock & Roll*, 81, 94, 97.

Chapter 8. The National Resurgence of Country Music

1. Much of this material was discussed earlier in Bill C. Malone, "Country Music, The South, and Americanism," *Mississippi Folklore Register* 10 (Spring 1976): 54–66.

2. Florence King, "Red Necks, White Socks, and Blue Ribbon Fear," *Harper's*, July 1974, 30–34; Richard Goldstein, "My Country Music Problem—and Yours," *Mademoiselle*, June 1973, 114–15, 185.

3. Sheldon Hackney, "The South as a Counterculture," *American Scholar* 42 (Spring 1973): 283–93.

4. The term is also attributed to Grandpa Jones, but Cindy Walker says he got the phrase from her. Bill C. Malone, interview with Cindy Walker, Mexia, Texas, 12 August 12 1976.

5. These include Muscle Shoals, Alabama; Macon, Georgia; Bogalusa, Louisiana; Atlanta, Georgia; New Orleans, Louisiana; and Memphis, Tennessee. The Austin story was told in Jan Reid, *The Improbable Rise of Redneck Rock* (Austin, Texas: Heidelberg Publishers, 1974).

6. It was Townsend Miller, country music columnist for the *Austin American-Statesman*, who first gave Austin the sobriquet "colony of musicians."

7. See Judson Klinger and Greg Mitchell, "Gram Finale," *Crawdaddy*, October 1976, 43–58.

8. Chris Hillman, liner notes for *Farther Along: The Best of the Flying Burrito Brothers*, A&M Records, 1988.

9. Palmer, *Rock & Roll*, 171.

10. See Sam Charters, *The Country Blues* (New York: Rinehart, 1959).

11. *Journal of American Folklore* 78 (July-September 1965).

12. Alan Lomax, "Bluegrass Background: Folk Music with Overdrive," *Esquire*, October 1959, 108.

13. Nicholas Dawidoff, *In the Country of Country: People and Places in American Music* (New York: Pantheon Books, 1997), 212. See also Nat Hentoff, *Listen to the Stories: Nat Hentoff on Jazz and Country Music* (New York: HarperCollins, 1995).

14. Waylon Jennings had a hit song in 1974, "Bob Wills Is Still the King," which, oddly enough, was not done in western swing style. Though it contributed to the mystique surrounding Wills and his legendary band, the only hint of Texas Playboy influence is heard in a brief passage where Jennings imitates the singing of Wills's great vocalist, Tommy Duncan, while mentioning how much he would like to be able to hear Duncan sing again.

15. Nicholas Spitzer, "Bob Wills Is Still the King: Romantic Regionalism and Convergent Culture in Central Texas," *John Edwards Memorial Foundation Quarterly* 2 (Winter 1975): 191–97.

Chapter 9. A Future in the Past

1. See Chris Strachwitz with James Nicolopulos, *Lydia Mendoza: A Family Autobiography* (Houston: Arte Publico Press, 1993).

2. See Joe Nick Patoski, *Selena: Como La Flor* (New York: Little, Brown, 1996).

3. Ancelet, Edwards, and Pitre, *Cajun Country*, 161.

4. David Cantwell, "Homespun of the Brave," *No Depression*, Nov./Dec. 1996.

5. See Bruce Feiler, *Dreaming Out Loud*. See also Feiler, "Gone Country: The Voice of Suburban America," *The New Republic*, February 1996, 19–24, which argued that country music was bigger than rock and that it had become the music of the suburban U.S.; Jack Temple Kirby, *The Countercultural South* (Athens: University of Georgia Press, 1995), 71–73.

6. James C. Cobb, "Rednecks, White Socks, and Pina Coladas? Country Music Ain't What It Used to Be . . . and It Really Never Was," *Southern Cultures*, (Winter 1999), 41–48.

7. See the newsletter *Women in Bluegrass*, edited by Murphy Henry, one of a growing number of women banjo players. See also "Banjo Women," by Geoff and Susan Eaker, which includes, but is not limited to, women bluegrass artists.

8. The 2001 broadcast of the Ken Burns film series *Jazz* and accompanying book and soundtrack recording reintroduced the public to what is often called America's "classical" music and acquainted listeners with the southern roots of the form.

Conclusion

1. Such as David Whisnant describes in *All That Is Native and Fine*.

BIBLIOGRAPHICAL NOTES

Chapter 1. Folk Origins of Southern Music

Our interpretation of southern folk music has been much influenced by Alan Lomax. His *Folk Songs of North America* (New York: Doubleday, 1960) remains the best one-volume collection of American folk songs and is a repository of provocative theories about the conservatism of folk styles and their relationship to culture. A more concentrated exposition of his theories is "Folk Song Style," *American Anthropologist* 61 (December 1959): 927–55. The most useful study limited exclusively to white style is Roger Abrahams and George Foss, *Anglo-American Folksong Style* (Englewood Cliffs, N.J.: Prentice-Hall, 1968).

The numerous studies of black folk styles generally concentrate on African origins. Melville Herskovits stresses African survivals among black people throughout the Western Hemisphere in his *Myth of the Negro Past* (Boston: Beacon Press, 1958). Richard Waterman limits his study to music but makes the same general point as Herskovits in "African Influence on the Music of the Americas," in Sol Tax, ed., *Acculturation in the Americas* (Chicago: University of Chicago Press, 1952). Works that are more appealing to the general reader include Marshall Stearns, *The Story of Jazz* (New York: Oxford University Press, 1970) and Paul Oliver, *Savannah Syncopators: African Retentions in the Blues* (New York: Stein and Day, 1970). Both writers argue that all American black music shares traits that were retained from the African experience. John Storm Roberts reminds us, however, as Jelly Roll Morton did long ago, that American music has also been profoundly influenced by "Spanish" styles: *The Latin Tinge: The Impact of Latin American Music on the United States* (1979; reprint, New York: Oxford University Press, 1999).

Students wishing to explore a serious scholarly interest in black music should begin with the important collection edited by Roger Abrahams and John F. Szwed, *Afro-American Folk Culture: An Annotated Bibliography of Materials from North, Central, and South America and the West Indies*, 2 vols. (Philadelphia: Institute for the Study of Human Issues, 1977). The complicated question of black-white folk interaction, and the degree of cultural borrowing on either side, has inspired some of the finest American scholarship of the last two decades. Much of this work was presented at a symposium at the University of Mississippi, and was anthologized in a volume edited by Ted Ownby: *Black and White: Cultural Interaction in the Antebellum South* (Jackson: University Press of Mississippi, 1993). Bill C. Malone contributed an essay to the volume called "Blacks and Whites and the Music of the Old South," 149–70.

Neither John Blassingame nor Eugene Genovese, to cite only two examples of a large group of historians who have grappled with the problems of a slave society, has concerned himself with music as such, but both have perceptively discussed the mechanisms by which black slaves preserved a sense of community: Blassingame, *The Slave Community* (New York: Oxford University Press, 1972); and Genovese, *Roll Jordan Roll* (New York: Pantheon Books, 1974). Mechal Sobel takes on a much smaller time period, but makes a fine contribution with *The World They Made Together: Black and White Values in Eighteenth-Century Virginia* (Princeton, N.J.: Princeton University Press, 1987). Charles Joyner has devoted a lifetime of scholarship to the thesis of a shared culture among southern whites and blacks and can be best appreciated through his *Shared Traditions: Southern History and Folk Culture* (Urbana: University of Illinois Press, 1999). Dena Epstein's focus, on the other hand, is totally on music in her impressively researched *Sinful Tunes and Spirituals: Black Folk Music to the Civil War* (Urbana: University of Illinois Press, 1977). Lawrence Levine, *Black Culture and Black Consciousness* (New York: Oxford University Press, 1977), one of the indispensable books in black history, uses folklore and oral history as tools for perceiving black consciousness. Levine demonstrates the continuity in black music from the slave songs to rhythm and blues.

Although Frank Owsley and his students attempted to delineate the lives of southern rural whites in the antebellum era (see *Plain Folk of the Old South* [Baton Rouge: Louisiana State University Press, 1949]), no studies of poor whites are comparable to what Genovese, Levine, and others have done for blacks. Readers will profit, though, from J. Wayne Flynt, *Dixie's Forgotten People: The South's Poor Whites* (Bloomington: Indiana University Press, 1979); Edward L. Ayers, *The Promise of the New South: Life After Reconstruction* (New York: Oxford, 1992), which has a fine chapter on the role played by music in the lives of rural southerners after the Civil War; Grady McWhiney, *Cracker Culture: Celtic Ways in the Old South* (Tuscaloosa: University of Alabama Press, 1988), which provides a good social history of plain whites despite its belabored thesis; Ted Ownby, *Subduing Satan: Religion, Recreation, and Manhood in the Rural South, 1865–1920* (Chapel Hill: University of North Carolina Press, 1990); and David Hackett Fischer, *Albion's Seed: Four British Folkways in America* (New York: Oxford, 1989), which includes a provocative discussion of the Old World origins of southern white culture. Unfortunately, one finds nothing comparable to the interviews with ex-slaves collected during the Great Depression by the Federal Writers Project: George Rawick has edited nineteen volumes under the title *The American Slave: A Composite Autobiography* (Westport, Conn.: Greenwood, 1972). The Federal Writers Project, however, did compile a massive amount of material about white farmers and workers, but it has been used only rarely, as in *These Are Our Lives* (Chapel Hill: University of North Carolina Press, 1939) and *Such As Us: Southern Voices of the Thirties* (New York: W.W. Norton, 1978). When historians explore "white culture and white consciousness," they will find a large number of ballads and folk songs already collected and published, as well as a storehouse of field recordings in the Library of Congress Archive of Folk Song and in other repositories.

D.K. Wilgus discusses folk song collections and collectors in *Anglo-American*

Folksong Scholarship since 1898 (New Brunswick, N.J.: Rutgers University Press, 1959). Serious researchers should familiarize themselves with Francis James Child, *The English and Scottish Popular Ballads*, 5 vols. (Boston: Houghton, Mifflin, 1882–98) because, for good or ill, Child left his imprint on virtually all collectors who came after him. Tristram P. Coffin surveys and describes the Child ballads that have survived in America in *The British Traditional Ballad in North America*, rev. ed. (Philadelphia: American Folklore Society, 1963), while G. Malcolm Laws Jr., concentrates on other types of British survivals in *American Balladry from British Broadsides* (Philadelphia: American Folklore Society, 1957) and on indigenous American products in *Native American Balladry* (Philadelphia: American Folklore Society, 1964). Of course, the indispensable introductions to folksong collecting in the Southern Appalachians are Olive Dame Campbell and Cecil J. Sharp, *English Folksongs from the Southern Appalachians* (New York: G.P. Putnam's Sons, 1917) and Emma Bell Miles, *Spirit of the Mountains* (1905; reprint, Knoxville: University of Tennessee Press, 1975).

Sociocultural studies of southern rural whites (yeomen and nonslaveholders) may be lacking, but religious investigations are not. Two of the great nineteenth century molders of musical repertoire and style, the camp meeting and the shape-note singing school, have inspired extensive scholarship. Charles A. Johnson, *The Frontier Camp Meeting: Religious Harvest Time* (Dallas: Southern Methodist University Press, 1955), and Bernard Weisberger, *They Gathered at the River: The Story of the Great Revivalists and Their Impact upon Religion in America* (Boston: Little, Brown, 1958), can still be read with great profit, but the most significant study of the early-nineteenth century revivals in the South is John Boles, *The Great Revival, 1787–1805: The Origins of the Southern Evangelical Mind* (Lexington: University Press of Kentucky, 1972). Both Boles and Dickson Bruce Jr., in his *And They All Sang Hallelujah: Plain-Folk Camp Meeting Religion, 1800–1845* (Knoxville: University of Tennessee Press, 1974), see the revivals as appealing essentially to the poorer classes of the South. Bruce's book describes the camp meeting songs as important sources for understanding the world-rejection philosophy of the "plain people." His conclusions should be compared with those of James C. Downey, "The Music of American Revivalism" (Ph.D. diss., Tulane University, 1968), a study that deserves to be better known.

All works on southern shape-note music have drawn from George Pullen Jackson's ground-breaking study *White Spirituals in the Southern Uplands* (Chapel Hill: University of North Carolina Press, 1933). Although Jackson was indifferent if not hostile to secular rural music, and even to other types of religious folk music, he made many acute observations about urban-rural antagonisms that are still relevant to an understanding of southern music. Jackson's conclusions about shape-note singers, writers, and publishers have been amplified and extended by several scholars. Joe Dan Boyd found the tradition alive in some black communities, as he reports in "Judge Jackson: Black Giant of White Spirituals," *Journal of American Folklore* 83 (October-December 1970): 446–51; and in "Negro Sacred Harp Songsters in Mississippi," *Mississippi Folklore Register* 5 (Fall 1971): 60–83. Harry Eskew concentrates on the area of first shape-note activity in the South in "Shape-Note Hymnody in the Shenandoah Valley, 1816–1860" (Ph.D. diss., Tulane University, 1966); Rachel Augusta Harley writes about the first southern shape-note publisher in "Ananias Davisson: Southern Tunebook Compiler" (Ph.D. diss., University of Michigan, 1972); and Charles Linwood Ellington discusses the most famous songbook to emerge from the shape-note movement in "The Sacred Harp Tradition of the South: Its Origin and Evolution" (Ph.D. diss., Florida State University, 1969). Buell Cobb takes a much more extensive look, though, in *The Sacred Harp and Its Music* (Athens: University of Georgia Press, 1978).

The most neglected area of southern religious music is that dealing with the Holiness-Pentecostal-Sanctified movement. As a folk phenomenon of itinerant preachers and musicians who left few written or published recollections of their work, the movement is difficult to document through conventional historical methods. It will require researchers skilled in oral history and folklore to recreate this important musical tradition. Studies of both white and black music make constant allusions to its influence, but no scholar has made a major effort to document the relationship. A good beginning that makes a few suggestive comments about music is Robert Mapes Anderson, *Vision of the Disinherited: The Making of American Pentecostalism* (New York: Oxford University Press, 1979). Paul Oliver talks about some of the black Sanctified singers who appeared on commercial recordings in *Songsters and Saints: Vocal Traditions on Race Records* (Cambridge: Cambridge University Press, 1984).

Folk interchanges among art and popular music in the nineteenth century and earlier have not been much studied. The presence in folklore of popular-derived forms, as well as of songs and dances from cultivated sources, is well recognized, but just how such music moved into the possession of the folk is not quite so clear. The roles played in this process by itinerant musicians and traveling shows in the nineteenth century will be discussed in the bibliographic notes for the next chapter. Here we will only suggest that the phenomenon is very old (see Carl Bridenbaugh, *Vexed and Troubled Englishmen, 1590–1642* [New York: Oxford University Press, 1968]), and evidence of it can be found in studies of dance masters and concert musicians, traveling actors, equestrian shows, circuses, and puppet shows.

For the purposes of this book, we have found O.G. Sonneck, *Early Concert-Life in America* (Leipzig: Breitkopf and Hartel, 1907), to be the indispensable source for high-art music in the early period. For a study of the music of an individual city no work has surpassed that of Henry Kmen, *Music in New Orleans: The Formative Years, 1791–1841* (Baton Rouge: Louisiana State University Press, 1966). Both he and Ronald Davis, who included New Orleans in his purview in *A History of Opera in the American West* (Englewood Cliffs, N.J.: Prentice-Hall, 1965), allude to the pervasive interest in opera among all the social classes in the city. The most celebrated product of the New Orleans antebellum musical scene, Louis Moreau Gottschalk, recorded his observations of the United States during his concert tours: *Notes of a Pianist* (Philadelphia: J.B. Lippincott, 1881). His principal biography, however, is S. Frederick Starr, *Bamboula: The Life and Times of Louis Moreau Gottschalk* (New York: Oxford University Press, 1995). Much can still be learned from Vernon Loggins, *Where the Word Ends: The Life of Louis M. Gottschalk* (Baton Rouge: Louisiana State University Press, 1958), which shows Gottschalk's indebtedness to the folk resources around him. Although Loggins does not stress it, Gottschalk may also have absorbed material from the popular traveling shows that came to the city, or from people who heard the music of the shows. Carl Bode, in *Antebellum Culture* (Carbondale: Southern Illinois University Press, 1959), and Lawrence Levine, *Highbrow/Lowbrow: The Emergence of Cultural Hierarchy in America* (Cambridge: Harvard University Press, 1990), show that the boundaries between folk and popular culture were very thin.

Chapter 2. National Discovery

The literature of black-face minstrelsy is extensive, although little of it deals with the phenomenon's effects on southern musicians. Carl Wittke, *Tambo and Bones* (Durham, N.C.: Duke University Press, 1930), remains a solid factual history of minstrelsy. Edward LeRoy Rice, *Monarchs of Minstrelsy* (New York: Kenny, 1911), is a mine of biographical information by an ex-minstrel entertainer. Constance Rourke, *American Humor* (New York: Harcourt, Brace, 1931), is the best analysis of the kind of comedy projected by the minstrel shows. The standard interpretation of minstrelsy is Robert C. Toll, *Blacking Up: The Minstrel Show in Nineteenth Century America* (New York: Oxford University Press, 1974), which comments perceptively on the folk origins of minstrel material and shows how the form contributed to racial stereotyping in the United States. Toll's *On with the Show: The First Century of Show Business in America* (New York: Oxford University Press, 1976) also treats minstrelsy but within the framework of a larger survey of American entertainment. Eric Lott, *Love and Theft: Blackface Minstrelsy and the American Working Class* (New York: Oxford University Press, 1993), explores the minstrel show as a setting in which white feelings about African Americans, both fascination and aversion, were played out.

Very few biographies of nineteenth-century popular musicians exist, but Hans Nathan, *Dan Emmett and the Rise of Early Negro Minstrelsy* (Norman: University of Oklahoma Press, 1962), is a fine study of the supposed composer of "Dixie" and other enduring songs. Howard L. Sacks and Judith Rose Sacks, however, have cast doubt on Emmett's authorship of the famous southern song in *Way Up North in Dixie: A Black Family's Claim to the Confederate Anthem* (Washington: Smithsonian Institution Press, 1993). Considerable attention has been devoted to Stephen Foster. John Tasker Howard, *Stephen Foster, America's Troubadour*, rev. ed. (New York: Crowell, 1962), is an admiring biography written by a man with a high-art perspective. Of major importance are William W. Austin, *Susanna, Jeanie, and the Old Folks at Home: The Songs of Stephen C. Foster from His Time to Ours* (New York: Macmillan, 1975), and Ken Emerson, *Doo-Dah! Stephen Foster and the Rise of American Popular Culture* (New York: Simon and Schuster, 1997), which strip much of the romantic claptrap away from Foster and place his music in the context of Anglo-American popular song and hymnody. While the New York popular music scene in the Gay Nineties is the central concern of Edward B. Marks, *They All Sang* (New York: Viking Press, 1934), Marks saw some of his songs, such as "Mother Was a Lady," become standards in the repertories of southern singers. This is a delightful memoir that deserves to be reissued.

Bill C. Malone's short account of William S. Hays, in *The Register of the Kentucky Historical Society*, "William S. Hays: The Bard of Kentucky," 93 (Summer 1995):

286–307, is the only available study of this important songwriter, but his songs still endure in the popular culture of the South. Folklorists have seldom mentioned his name, even while printing his songs. Pop music historian Sigmund Spaeth made a few comments about Hays in *A History of Popular Music in America* (New York: Random House, 1948) and quotes some of his songs there and in his witty *Read 'em and Weep* (New York: Doubleday, Page, 1926) and *Weep Some More My Lady* (New York: Doubleday, Page, 1927), two of the few collections of nineteenth-century sentimental songs available. Nicholas E. Tawa writes extensively on the popular music of the nineteenth century, but has not delved into the music's survival in folk culture: *Sweet Songs for Gentle Americans: The Parlor Song in America, 1790–1860* (Bowling Green, Ohio: Popular Press, 1980), and *The Way to Tin Pan Alley: American Popular Song, 1866–1910* (New York: Schirmer Books, 1991).

The study of the popular song as both a reflector and shaper of public attitudes is still in its infancy. Earl Bargainneer, "Tin Pan Alley: The South in Popular Song," *Mississippi Quarterly* 30 (Fall 1977): 527–65, has discussed the fascination that songwriters have felt for the South. His essay, however, provides only a listing of songs. Now someone needs to seize upon Bargainneer's insights and explore more deeply the effects that pop songwriters have exerted on the shaping of popular conceptions of the South. Jack Temple Kirby, in *Media-Made Dixie* (Baton Rouge: Louisiana State University Press, 1978), comments on country music's South-molding role but neglects the larger and crucial pop music scene.

Many writers have commented on the presence of nineteenth-century pop songs in the repertories of twentieth-century folk and country musicians. Norman Cohen has centered directly on the subject in "Tin Pan Alley's Contributions to Folk Music," *Western Folklore* 29 (1970): 9–20. An indication that at least some folklorists are beginning to overcome the prejudice against the parlor songs is Bill Ellis, "The Blind Girl and the Rhetoric of Sentimental Heroism," *Journal of American Folklore* 91 (April-June 1978): 657–74, one of the first studies to treat such material without scorn or condescension.

Future students who are interested in pre-radio popular music and the complex manner in which it moved into the possession of the southern folk should be aware of the vast copyright holdings of the Library of Congress and of the collections of sheet music, pocket songsters, and related material in the New York Public Library, at Brown University, and in other repositories. Magazines and newspapers often contained song pages. The *Dallas Semi-Weekly Farm News,* for instance, contained a "young people's page" that printed song lyrics at the request of correspondents. With piano rolls, cylinder recordings, and the various kinds of printed musical material available, rural and small-town southerners had ample exposure to the nation's popular music.

Books about minstrelsy demonstrate one important way that popular music forms ventured even into some of the more remote backcountry regions of the South. Studies of other traveling shows will provide additional hints. Carl Bode, *The American Lyceum* (New York: Oxford University Press, 1956), and Joseph E. Gould, *The Chautauqua Movement* (New York: State University of New York Press, 1961), discuss two of the more high-toned purveyors of culture, while Gilbert Douglas, *American*

Vaudeville (New York: Dover Publications, 1963), and Albert F. McLean Jr., *American Vaudeville as Ritual* (Lexington: University of Kentucky Press, 1965), discuss the most popular form of organized show business in the early twentieth century. Country people saw vaudeville routines when they went to the city, but a type of vaudeville came to the villages in the form of the tent repertoire shows. At least two published studies survey the world of the tent-rep shows. One was written by a man who played a prominent role in their dissemination: Neil E. Schaffner, with Vance Johnson, *The Fabulous Toby and Me* (Englewood Cliffs, N.J.: Prentice-Hall, 1968). The other is William Lawrence Slout, *Theatre in a Tent* (Bowling Green, Ohio: Bowling Green Popular Press, 1972). Other studies of the phenomenon include: Larry Clark, "Toby Shows: A Form of American Popular Theatre" (Ph.D. diss., University of Illinois Press, 1963); Robert Dean Klassen, "The Tent-Repertoire Theatre: A Rural American Institution" (Ph.D. diss., Michigan State University, 1979); and Sherwood Snyder III, "The Toby Shows" (Ph.D. diss., University of Minnesota, 1966). Despite the ubiquity of the medicine show in rural America, surprisingly little has been written about it. The best study thus far is Brooks McNamara, *Step Right Up: An Illustrated History of the Medicine Show* (Garden City, N.Y.: Doubleday, 1976). McNamara found much material in issues of *Billboard* magazine, a source that other scholars have insufficiently utilized.

To investigate the discovery of black music in the late nineteenth century one should go directly to the publications that introduced the material to the literate northern public. Bruce Jackson, ed., *The Negro and His Folklore in Nineteenth-Century Periodicals* (Austin: University of Texas Press, 1967), contains reprints of the most relevant journal articles dealing with the subject. Of course, the real awakening of interest in the spirituals began with William Francis Allen, Charles P. Ware, and Lucy M. Garrison, *Slave Songs of the United States* (New York: A. Simpson, 1867). Dena Epstein, in *Sinful Tunes and Spirituals,* has commented on the book's reception and on its formative influence on folk scholarship. J.B.T. Marsh, *The Story of the Jubilee Singers with Their Songs* (Boston: Houghton, Osgood, 1880), is an old study of the pioneering black group, but it has been joined by Andrew Ward, *Dark Midnight When I Rise: The Story of the Fisk Jubilee Singers* (New York: Amistad, 2000). The vogue for the spirituals that followed the tours of the Jubilee Singers is discussed by several writers, most notably Eileen Southern in *The Music of Black Americans: A History* (New York: W.W. Norton, 1971) and Gilbert Chase in *America's Music from the Pilgrims to the Present,* 2d rev. ed. (New York: McGraw-Hill, 1966). Our own information has come principally from such music journals as *Etude, Musical Quarterly,* and *Musical Observer.*

There has been no adequate study of the turn-of-the-century vogue for musical nationalism or of its relationship to folk music. The interested student would be well advised to explore the "high-art" music journals mentioned above in addition to other contemporary popular and scholarly journals where people such as John Powell sometimes expressed their opinions. D.K. Wilgus, *Anglo-American Folksong Scholarship since 1898,* provides the best discussion of the motivations that underlay the collecting exploits of American folklorists, Anglo-Saxonist or otherwise. John A. Lomax, *Cow-*

boy Songs and Other Frontier Ballads (New York: Sturgis and Walton, 1910), is still the indispensable introduction to that genre, but the conclusions of this book should be balanced with those of John White, *Git Along, Little Dogies: Songs and Songmakers of the American West* (Urbana: University of Illinois Press, 1975), which has done much to divest cowboy song scholarship of the myths of anonymous or communal origins. Nolan Porterfield has given us the best biography of John Lomax: *Last Cavalier: The Life and Times of John A. Lomax* (Urbana: University of Illinois Press, 1996). Benjamin Filene delves into the cultural and ideological underpinnings of the search for folk music in *Romancing the Folk: Public Memory and American Roots Music* (Chapel Hill: University of North Carolina Press, 2000).

Sources of the preoccupation with the southern mountains are discussed most perceptively in Henry Shapiro, *Appalachia on Our Mind: The Southern Mountains and Mountaineers in the American Consciousness, 1890–1920* (Chapel Hill: University of North Carolina Press, 1978). David E. Whisnant explores the roles played by "cultural interventionists" (ballad collectors, settlement school teachers, and festival entrepreneurs) in shaping public perceptions of Appalachia in *All That Is Native and Fine: The Politics of Culture in an American Region* (Chapel Hill: University of North Carolina Press, 1984). These discussions can be supplemented by material delineated in Robert F. Munn, *The Southern Appalachians: A Bibliography and Guide to Studies* (Morgantown: West Virginia University Library, 1961).

Very little attention has been devoted to the first urban folk movement, the vogue for the concert singing of folk songs that flourished in the World War I period and in the early 1920s. Jon G. Smith contributed a very fine essay on his grandmother, Ethel Park Richardson, in the *JEMF Quarterly,* "She Kept On a-Goin': Ethel Park Richardson," 13 (Autumn 1977):105–15, but very few scholars have dug extensively into the music journals and other periodical literature to track down information on the singers of folk songs and costume recitalists.

Chapter 3. Early Commercialization: Ragtime, Blues, Jazz

Eileen Southern, *The Music of Black Americans,* is the only general survey of African-American music in all its ramifications and is richly detailed and documented. Comprehensive accounts of ragtime include William J. Schaefer and Johannes Riedel, *The Art of Ragtime* (Baton Rouge: Louisiana State University Press, 1973), Rudi Blesh and Harriet Janis, *They All Played Ragtime,* 4th ed. (New York: Oak Publications, 1971), and Edward A. Berlin, *King of Ragtime: Scott Joplin and His Era* (New York: Oxford University Press, 1994). The transition made by African Americans from black-face minstrelsy to an independent expression of show business is discussed in Tom Fletcher, *100 Years of the Negro in Show Business* (New York: Burdge, 1954), a detailed but undisciplined account. James Weldon Johnson, in *Black Manhattan* (New York: Knopf, 1930), discusses the black show-business scene in New York in the 1890s and tells the story of some southern musicians, such as himself and his brother J. Rosamond.

The American people's awakening consciousness of the blues in the early years of the twentieth century is discussed by the man who was largely responsible for it:

William C. Handy, *Father of the Blues: An Autobiography* (New York: Macmillan, 1941). In *Born with the Blues* (Westport, Conn.: Hyperion Press, 1973), Perry Bradford discusses his role in the discovery of Mamie Smith and in the recording industry's decision to exploit the blues.

Blues has attracted a great wealth of scholarship, much of the best by English fans and collectors. Derrick Stewart-Baxter, for example, in *Ma Rainey and the Classic Blues Singers* (New York: Stein and Day, 1970), provides a good introduction to the style of blues first presented to the American public. At least three biographies of Bessie Smith are available: Paul Oliver, *Bessie Smith* (London: Cassell, 1959); Carman Moore, *Somebody's Angel Child: The Story of Bessie Smith* (New York: Crowell, 1969); and Chris Albertson, *Bessie* (New York: Stein and Day, 1972). We have found the Albertson book the most helpful.

Samuel Charters's fine work *The Country Blues* (New York: Rinehart, 1959) was not only the first study of that genre; it virtually defined it. In that book and in *The Bluesmen* (New York: Oak Publications, 1967) Charters relates the musicians to their sociocultural contexts, a method that regrettably is not always followed by other music historians. Paul Oliver's studies of the blues, from the African roots through the era of recording, have been of generally high quality; *Blues Fell This Morning* (London: Cassell, 1960) and *The Story of the Blues* (New York: Barrie, 1969) are excellent analyses as are Oliver's notes to the Columbia anthology, *The Story of the Blues,* Columbia G30008 (intended as a supplement to the book of the same name). Jeff Titon, *Early Downhome Blues: A Musical and Cultural Analysis* (Urbana: University of Illinois Press, 1977), is an impressive multidisciplinary treatment of the blues. William Ferris Jr., *Blues from the Delta* (Garden City, N.Y.: Doubleday, 1978), is an excellent study of the formative Mississippi blues scene that also has a useful annotated bibliography and discography that are relevant to the larger blues picture. The overall context of blues development in the Mississippi Delta is discussed in two excellent books: Alan Lomax, *The Land Where the Blues Began* (New York: Pantheon, 1993) and James C. Cobb, *The Most Southern Place on Earth: The Mississippi Delta and the Roots of Regional Identity* (New York: Oxford University Press, 1992).

Among the small number of biographies of early country bluesmen, two are of high quality: David Evans, *Tommy Johnson* (London: Studio Vista, 1971), and John Fahey, *Charley Patton* (London: Studio Vista, 1970). Unfortunately, there is no biography of Blind Lemon Jefferson and no full-scale study of the important Texas blues scene. Mack McCormick, one of the most knowledgeable of all the blues scholars and a folklorist of the highest competence, has long been conducting research on Texas blues music. But until his research assumes the form of a book, we will have to be content with the occasional record liner notes that carry a McCormick byline. Allan Turner provided an assessment of McCormick's work in "History As Close As a Turntable," Jim Harris, ed., *Features and Fillers: Texas Journalists on Texas Folklore* (Denton: University of North Texas Press, 1999), 124–36.

Blues music is susceptible to varying interpretations. Lawrence Levine, for example, in *Black Culture and Black Consciousness,* sees in blues singing a simultaneous expression of a personalized, individualistic ethos and an urge to retain the old communal roots. LeRoi Jones (Amiri Baraka), in *Blues People: Negro Music in White America* (New York: Morrow, 1963), interprets the music in the context of black nationalism. Tony Russell, on the other hand, sees a vigorous cultural interchange between African Americans and whites in *Blacks, Whites, and Blues* (New York: Stein and Day, 1970).

The literature on jazz is voluminous. No definitive bibliography is available, but Alan P. Merriam and Robert J. Branford made a good start in *A Bibliography of Jazz* (Philadelphia: American Folklore Society, 1954) as did Robert George Reisner, *The Literature of Jazz: A Selective Bibliography* (New York: New York Public Library, 1959). These accounts have been updated and superseded by Geoffrey C. Ward and Ken Burns, *Jazz: A History of America's Music* (New York: Alfred A. Knopf, 2000), the comprehensive compendium to Burns's television documentary of the art form. The bibliography compiled by Frank Tirro in *Jazz: A History* (New York: W.W. Norton, 1977), can also be consulted with great profit. There are several good book-length studies of jazz, including Rudi Blesh, *Shining Trumpets: A History of Jazz*, 4th ed. (London: Cassell, 1958); Barry Ulanov, *A History of Jazz in America* (New York: Viking Press, 1955); Rex Harris, *Jazz*, 5th ed. (Harmondsworth, England: Penguin Books, 1957); Marshall Stearns, *The Story of Jazz* (New York: Oxford University Press, 1970); Ted Gioia, *The History of Jazz* (New York: Oxford University Press, 1997); Kathy J. Ogren, *The Jazz Revolution: Twenties America and the Meaning of Jazz* (New York: Oxford University Press, 1989); Burton W. Peretti, *The Creation of Jazz: Music, Race, and Culture in Urban America* (Urbana: University of Illinois Press, 1992); James Lincoln Collier, *Jazz: The American Theme Song* (New York: Oxford University Press, 1993); and Gary Giddens, *Visions of Jazz: The First Century* (New York: Oxford University Press, 1998).

Among the biographies and autobiographies of jazz personalities the most important are Alan Lomax, *Mister Jelly Roll: The Fortunes of Jelly Roll Morton* (Berkeley and Los Angeles: University of California Press, 1973); Louis Armstrong's own story, *Satchmo: My Life in New Orleans* (New York: Prentice-Hall, 1954); Larry Gara, *The Baby Dodds Story* (Los Angeles: Contemporary, 1959); James Lincoln Collier, *Louis Armstrong: An American Genius* (New York: Oxford University Press, 1983); John Chilton, *Sidney Bechet: The Wizard of Jazz* (New York: Oxford University Press, 1987); and Don Marquis's superb piece of detective work on "the first man of jazz," *In Search of Buddy Bolden* (Baton Rouge: Louisiana State University Press, 1978) .

Despite endless speculation, the era of New Orleans music that preceded the first jazz recordings in 1917 is a murky period bathed in romance. No one has really done the kind of digging necessary to document the pre-1900 origins of jazz in the city. Henry Kmen told the story down to 1841 in *Music in New Orleans,* but his death in 1978 cut short the efforts that he had begun for the later period. William J. Schaefer has made a significant contribution to our knowledge of early jazz history in *Brass Bands and New Orleans Jazz* (Baton Rouge: Louisiana State University Press, 1977). Schaefer was assisted in his efforts by Richard B. Allen, the learned former curator of the William Ransom Hogan Jazz Archive at Tulane University, one of the most impressive repositories of jazz lore in the United States. Al Rose, in *Storyville, New Orleans* (Tuscaloosa: University of Alabama Press, 1974), provides an illuminating account of early ragtime and jazz musicians in the city and puts the relationship between the emerging music and the red-light district in the proper perspective. As previously noted, Marquis's book on Buddy Bolden fills in some of the missing gaps between the marching bands and the early recordings, and Harry O. Brunn, *The Story of the Original Dixieland Jazz Band* (Baton Rouge: Louisiana State University Press, 1960), comments on the oft-neglected contributions of white musicians to the developing art form while discussing the band of young white musicians who put the first jazz sounds on records. The inquiring reader would find it instructive to compare Brunn's white-oriented interpretation of jazz origins with the black perspective of someone such as Rudi Blesh.

Chapter 4. Expanding Markets: Tejano, Cajun, Hillbilly, Gospel

Compared to the abundant material available on blues and jazz, the publications devoted to country and other rural-derived white musical forms are recent and sparse. No bibliographies of country music, for example, are analogous to those available for blues and jazz, but Bill C. Malone, *Country Music, USA*, rev. ed. (Austin: University of Texas Press, 2002), and *Don't Get Above Your Raisin': Country Music and the Southern Working Class* (Urbana: University of Illinois Press, 2002) are good places to begin.

Two important repositories for country and other grass-roots forms of music have come into existence since the 1950s: the Southern Folk Life Collection at the University of North Carolina, Chapel Hill, built around the archives of the Australian collector John Edwards, and the Country Music Hall of Fame and Museum in Nashville. The Southern Folk Life Collection no longer publishes the *JEMF Quarterly*, but the Country Music Foundation issues a magazine called the *Journal of Country Music*. This journal, along with *Old Time Music*, published by Tony Russell in England, *Devil's Box*, a fiddle-oriented journal edited by Bill Harrison in Huntsville, Alabama, and *Old-Time Herald*, published and edited by Alice Gerrard in Durham, North Carolina, offer students of early country music ample outlets for scholarly or popular inquiries.

Before the dawning of academic interest, research and writing on country music were generally confined to dedicated fans and collectors who wrote for fan club journals, song magazines, or collectors' newsletters. Occasionally, an in-house publication appeared, such as George D. Hay, *A Story of the Grand Ole Opry* (Nashville: George D. Hay, 1953), or, even more rarely, a relative's loving memoir of a musician such as Carrie Rodgers, *My Husband, Jimmie Rodgers* (1935; reprint, with an introduction by Nolan Porterfield, Nashville: Vanderbilt University Press, 1995). The first book-length work devoted to country music came from a fan in 1961. Linnell Gentry, *A History and Encyclopedia of Country, Western, and Gospel Music* (Nashville: McQuiddy Press, 1961), is an anthology of essays on country music extracted from magazines and a collection of biographical sketches compiled from questionnaires. It was republished by the Clairmont Corporation in Nashville in 1969 and is still a useful and oft-quoted compendium of material.

The earliest scholarly interest in country music was inspired by the urban folk revival of the late 1950s and early '60s. One of the stimulating sparks actually occurred a few years earlier, in 1952, with the issuance of the Folkways recording, *Anthology of American Folk Music,* FA 2951–2953. The six long-playing records included hillbilly, Cajun, gospel, and country blues recordings made between 1927 and 1933 taken from the private collection of Harry Smith. Packaged under the respectable label of "folk music," the anthology introduced grass-roots music to an urban audience that had never heard it before. Happily for contemporary listeners, the collection has been re-released on CDs by the Smithsonian Institution.

In 1965 the *Journal of American Folklore,* after decades of neglect, devoted an entire issue, 78 (July-September 1965) to early country music. The "Hillbilly Issue," as it was called, contained important essays on the history of country music and pointed the way toward further research. A few years later *Western Folklore* published an issue, 30 (July 1971), called the JEMF issue, on the sources and resources of country music.

Robert Shelton was not an academician, but as folk music editor of the *New York Times* during the urban folk enthusiasm he became quite aware of the relationship between commercial country music and folk music. The result was *The Country Music Story* (New York: Bobbs-Merrill, 1966), an entertaining survey of country music history marked by a vast array of photographs gathered by Burt Goldblatt.

Bill C. Malone's *Country Music, USA* was based on his doctoral dissertation written at the University of Texas in 1965. The book was the first full-scale scholarly treatment of the subject and was, in fact, the basis for much of Shelton's work. Like Gentry's book, Malone's was the product of a southern country boy who wrote from within the culture that he discussed.

Archie Green, in contrast, came to country music from a preoccupation with labor lore. His search for labor-related materials led him naturally to phonograph recordings, and that in turn led to an exhaustive interest in all types of grass-roots music found on commercial recordings, radio transcriptions, song folios, and so forth. Green, *Only a Miner: Studies in Recorded Coal-Mining Songs* (Urbana: University of Illinois Press, 1972), is distinguished not only by its coverage of coal-mining songs, but also by the exhaustive knowledge it reflects of early hillbilly music. Like all of Green's work, it is indispensable.

The 1970s saw a proliferation of works on country music. Of special relevance to the early period of recording history are Douglas B. Green, *Country Roots: The Origins of Country Music* (New York: Hawthorn, 1976), an informal but fact-filled survey of country music history, and Charles Wolfe, *Grand Ole Opry: The Early Years, 1925–1935* (London: Old Time Music, 1975), and *Tennessee Strings: The Story of Country Music in Tennessee* (Knoxville: University of Tennessee Press, 1977). Wolfe's history of the Opry has been revised and enlarged as *A Good-Natured Riot: The Birth of the Grand Ole Opry* (Nashville: The Country Music Foundation Press and Vanderbilt University Press, 1999). Wolfe's work can also be found in numerous journals and on liner notes of phonograph recordings and CDs; he is easily the best scholar now working in the field of early commercial country music.

Biographies of early country performers are not plentiful, but a few are quite good. Regrettably, nothing in country music is comparable to the series of blues-oriented books edited by Paul Oliver for Studio Vista in London, but the University of Illinois Press with its Music in American Life Series is rapidly filling much of the gap. One of the University of Illinois publications, *Stars of Country Music,* contains essays on some of the early performers: Walter Haden on Vernon Dalhart, Charles Wolfe on Uncle Dave Macon, John Atkins on the Carter Family, D.K. Wilgus on Bradley Kincaid, Chris Comber and Mike Paris on Jimmie Rodgers, and Norman Cohen on an assemblage of performers he calls "early pioneers." The Comber and Paris essay was extracted from their subsequently published book on the life and career of Jimmie Rodgers: *Jimmie the Kid* (London: Eddison Press, 1976). All work on Rodgers, however, has been surpassed by Nolan Porterfield, *Jimmie Rodgers* (Urbana: University of Illinois Press, 1979), the definitive work on the Singing Brakeman and an invaluable interpretation of the early commercial period of country music. Rodgers's fellow pioneers the Carter Family are chronicled in Mark Zwonitzer and Charles Hirshberg's *Will You Miss Me When I'm Gone? The Carter Family and Their Legacy in American Music* (New York: Simon & Schuster, 2002).

The literature on white gospel music is much sparser than that on country music, and the gospel "industry" has been much slower than the country industry to recognize the need for historical documentation. Ottis J. Knippers, *Who's Who among Southern Singers and Composers* (Lawrenceburg, Tenn.: J.D. Vaughan, 1937), is a good introduction to the gospel personnel of the early commercial period, but it is rare and out of print. Mrs. J.R. Baxter and Videt Polk produced a similar work, *Gospel Song Writers Biography* (Dallas: Stamps-Baxter Music Company, 1971), but it contains little information on the quartets. Jo Lee Fleming, "James D. Vaughan, Music Publisher" (S.M.D. diss., Union Theological Seminary, 1972) is a first-rate work that deserves to be better known and is almost the only scholarly piece available on the post-1920 gospel period. Lois Blackwell, *The Wings of the Dove: The Story of Gospel Music in America* (Norfolk, Va.: Donning Co., 1978), was the first real attempt at a historical overview of the music, but it had only 154 pages of text, about 30 of which are devoted to the 1920s. James Goff's *Close Harmony: A History of Southern Gospel* (Chapel Hill: University of North Carolina Press, 2002) is the source that all music students should consult.

Cajun and Chicano styles of music have been similarly neglected by writers and researchers. The preservation and documentation of Cajun culture were given a decided boost, though, with the establishment in 1974 of the Center for Acadian and Creole Folklore at the University of Southwestern Louisiana in Lafayette. A number of academic theses have shed some light on Cajun culture, but say little about the music. Nicholas Spitzer contributed an impressive essay, "Cajuns and Creoles: The French Gulf Coast," in Allen Tullos, ed., *Long Journey Home: Folklife in the South* (Chapel Hill, N.C.: Southern Exposure, 1977), 140–55. Lauren C. Post's *Cajun Sketches* (Baton Rouge: Louisiana State University Press, 1962) was a valuable introduction to Cajun history and culture, but it can be supplemented by Pierre Daigle, *Tears, Love, and Laughter: The Story of the Acadians* (Church Point, La.: Acadian Publishing Enterprise, 1972), which contains a number of good biographical sketches and vignettes of

Cajun musicians, and by William Faulkner Rushton, *The Cajuns: From Acadia to Louisiana* (New York: Farrar, Straus & Giroux, 1979). Another useful, short introduction to Cajun music can be found in *Acadiana Profile*, 4 (October-November 1974): 4–7, written by Revon Reed, a leading authority on Cajun music. The best academic studies of Cajun culture and music are Barry Jean Ancelet and Elemore Morgan Jr., *The Makers of Cajun Music/Musiciens cadiens et créoles* (Austin: University of Texas Press, 1984); Ancelet, Jay D. Edwards, and Glen Pitre, *Cajun Country* (Jackson: University Press of Mississippi, 1991); Ancelet, *Cajun and Creole Folktales: The French Oral Tradition of South Louisiana* (New York: Garland, 1994); and Ann Savoy, *Cajun Music: A Reflection of a People* (Eunice, La.: Bluebird Press, 1984). Pre-commercial Cajun music can be sampled on an album produced for the Louisiana Folklore Society, *Folksongs of the Louisiana Acadians,* collected, edited, and annotated by Harry Oster. The best aural introductions to early recorded Cajun music are found on a series of records produced and edited by Chris Strachwitz on the Old-Timey label (especially vol. 1, *First Recordings, the 1920s,* and vol. 5, *The Early Years, 1928–1938*).

Tejano music is as old as any other form of American folk music, and its recording came about as early (i.e., in the mid-1920s) as any Anglo genre. Nevertheless, few published discussions or academic treatises of the genre exist. Two good discussions of its folk roots, however, are Americo Paredes, *A Texas-Mexican Cancionero: Folksongs of the Lower Border* (Urbana: University of Illinois Press, 1975) and Paredes, *With His Pistol in His Hand: A Border Ballad and Its Hero* (Austin: University of Texas Press, 1958). The best academic study of the commercial extensions of Texas-Mexican music is Manuel Peña, *Texas-Mexican Conjunto: History of a Working-Class Music* (Austin: University of Texas Press, 1985). Beginning students or devotees of Chicano music should listen to a series of albums produced by Chris Strachwitz on his Folklyric label, reviewed in the *JEMF Quarterly* issue mentioned above. These volumes, entitled *Texas-Mexican Border Music* and accompanied by brochures and discographies, are the products of Strachwitz's own indefatigable collecting of old 78-rpm records in the Chicano communities of the Southwest. Without his labors, students of American folk music would be infinitely poorer.

Chapter 5. The Great Depression and New Technologies

The Great Depression was a crucial period for American music, when folk simplicity began to give way to greater commercial awareness, but little has been done to treat the era's music in a comprehensive manner. Bob Coltman, in "Across the Chasm: How the Depression Changed Country Music," *Old Time Music* 23 (Winter 1976–1977): 6–12, follows a line of inquiry that should be instructive for students of other types of music.

The history of Mexican border broadcasting has been well told by Gene Fowler and Bill Crawford in *Border Radio* (Austin: Texas Monthly Press, 1987). Two books discuss the man who inaugurated border radio programming: Gerald Carson, *The Roguish World of Dr. Brinkley* (New York: Rinehart, 1960), and R. Alton Lee, *The Bizarre Careers of John R. Brinkley* (Lexington: University Press of Kentucky, 2002).

Ed Kahn analyzes the roles the X-stations played in the dissemination of folk music in "International Relations, Dr. Brinkley, and Hillbilly Music," *JEMF Quarterly* 9, pt. 2 (Summer 1973): 47–55. Another great purveyor of country music in the 1930s is discussed by Pat Ahrens in "The Role of the Crazy Water Crystals Company in Promoting Hillbilly Music," *JEMF Quarterly* 6 (Autumn 1970): 107–9.

Students of both country music and the blues often focus on one end or the other of the historical period of their subjects, concentrating on the early quasi-folk period of the 1920s or on the modern era of commercial growth, thereby neglecting the important interim period. Ivan M. Tribe, however, is an exception. His area of concentration has been the 1930s and '40s, and his prolific research, based principally on interviews, has borne fruit in many articles in such magazines as *Bluegrass Unlimited* and *Old Time Music* and in his books *Mountaineer Jamboree: Country Music in West Virginia* (Lexington: University Press of Kentucky, 1984) and *The Stonemans: An Appalachian Family and the Music That Shaped Their Lives* (Urbana: University of Illinois Press, 1993).

A few publications convey the feeling of what it was like to be a country musician during a period of hard times. *My Husband, Jimmie Rodgers* and a very rare account of Bob Wills, Ruth Sheldon, *Hubbin' It: The Life of Bob Wills* (1938; reprint, Nashville: Country Music Foundation Press, 1995), both treat their subjects during the Depression years. In 1977 the Country Music Foundation Press published the posthumous autobiography of Alton Delmore of the influential Delmore Brothers duet: Alton Delmore, *Truth Is Stranger than Publicity* (Nashville: Country Music Foundation Press, 1977). Edited by Charles K. Wolfe, the book recreates the atmosphere of hillbilly barnstorming during the 1930s and subsequent decades, as the Delmore Brothers became one of the most popular acts in country music.

The best account of black gospel music during the 1930s is Tony Heilbut's pioneering *The Gospel Sound: Good News and Bad Times* (New York: Simon and Schuster, 1971). It is actually a general survey of the total black gospel scene and is marked by the enthusiasm and affection of a devoted fan. Heilbut's discussion of Georgia Tom Dorsey is perceptive, but it has been superseded by Michael W. Harris, *Rise of Gospel Blues: The Music of Thomas Andrew Dorsey in the Urban Church* (New York: Oxford University Press, 1992). Bernice Johnson Reagon edited a collection of vignettes and analyses of Dorsey and five other black gospel composers, *We'll Understand It Better By and By* (Washington: Smithsonian Institution Press, 1992). James Goff's book, *Close Harmony,* has good material on white gospel music activities during the 1930s. The previously mentioned books by Ottis Knippers and Mrs. J.R. Baxter make useful references to musicians who performed during the Depression years, and two books on the Blackwood Brothers discuss the experiences of struggling quartets during that era: Kree Jack Racine, *Above All: The Blackwood Brothers Quartet* (Memphis: Jarodoce Publications, 1967), and James Blackwood, with Dan Martin, *The James Blackwood Story* (Monroeville, Pa.: Whitaker House, 1975). Scattered articles on Albert Brumley have appeared, including Bill C. Malone, "Albert E. Brumley: Folk Composer," *Bluegrass Unlimited,* 21 (July 1986): 69–77.

Books have been written on the various cultural projects of the Works Progress

Administration, and some scholars have used the material collected by the government-sponsored researchers. But no one has attempted to draw together in one study the disparate ventures in the folk music field undertaken by the W.P.A. or by other agencies such as the Resettlement Administration. One can envision a doctoral dissertation assaying "folk music and the federal government."

Samplings of songs about the Depression can be found in several good sources. The New Lost City Ramblers recorded an influential album, *Songs of the Depression,* Folkways FH5264, which contained selections taken mainly from commercial hillbilly recordings. No similar utilization of commercial blues or gospel music has been undertaken, but Lawrence Levine includes a valuable discussion of black Depression material in *Black Culture and Black Consciousness,* and Lawrence Gellert collected a vast amount of noncommercial folk material in the 1930s, much of the best of which is recorded on *Negro Songs of Protest,* Rounder 4004.

The awakening of southern labor is discussed by Thomas Tippett, *When Southern Labor Stirs* (New York: Jonathan Cape and Harrison Smith, 1931); George B. Tindall, *The Emergence of the New South, 1913–1945* (Baton Rouge: Louisiana State University Press, 1967); and most vividly by Irving Bernstein, *The Lean Years: A History of the American Worker, 1920–33* (Boston: Houghton, Mifflin, 1960). Liston Pope, *Millhands and Preachers: A Study of Gastonia* (New Haven, Conn.: Yale University Press, 1942), provides a cultural explanation of the floundering of radical unionism in the South, but the best analysis of the difficulties encountered by unions in the region is found in Jacquelyn Dowd Hall and others, *Like a Family: The Making of a Southern Cotton Mill World* (Chapel Hill: University of North Carolina Press, 1987). Archie Green concentrates more directly on the music of the textile workers in "Born on Picketlines, Textile Workers' Songs Are Woven into History," *Textile Labor* 21 (April 1961): 3–5; in his notes to the Dorsey Dixon record album *Babies in the Mill,* Testament T-3301; and in "Dorsey Dixon: Minstrel of the Mills," *Sing Out: The Folk Song Magazine,* July 1966, 10–13. John Greenway has a short section on the minstrel of Gastonia, Ella May Wiggins, in *American Folksongs of Protest* (Philadelphia: University of Pennsylvania Press, 1953), but the reader can get a better inkling of Wiggins's emergence as a labor martyr in articles contemporaneous with her death: Jessie Lloyd, "Ella May, Murdered, Lives in Her Songs of Class Strife," *Daily Worker,* 20 September 1929; and Margaret Larkin, "Story of Ella May," *New Masses,* November 1929.

Coal-mining songs that wound up on commercial hillbilly recordings are the subjects of Archie Green's *Only a Miner: Studies in Recorded Coal-Mining Songs,* but in the notes to Sara Ogan Gunning, *Girl of Constant Sorrow,* Folk-Legacy FSA-26, Green takes as his topic the songs of a woman who was an active participant in the labor conflicts of eastern Kentucky. His remarks about the mating of northern radical rhetoric and southern conservative balladry have often been quoted. Gunning's half-sister, Aunt Molly Jackson, one of the most famous of the southern protest singers, has been memorialized in an entire issue of *Kentucky Folklore Record* 7 (October-December 1961), and in Shelly Romalis, *Pistol Packin' Mama: Aunt Molly Jackson and the Politics of Folksong* (Urbana: University of Illinois Press, 1999). Samples of her singing style can be heard on *Aunt Molly Jackson,* Rounder 1002, a collection of songs originally recorded for the Library of Congress in 1939. Her story, as well as that of the other balladeers who struggled for economic justice in the eastern Kentucky coal fields, is discussed by John Hevener in *Which Side Are You On? The Harlan County Coal Miners, 1931–1939* (Urbana: University of Illinois Press, 2002).

Other regions of southern economic turmoil have also interested scholars, but few writers have concentrated on the music that arose from them. The Southern Tenant Farmers Union Papers in the Southern Historical Collection at the University of North Carolina have been explored by several writers, but no one has really dug through them to determine the role that music played in the union's organizing efforts. Likewise, insufficient effort has been expended to interview surviving union members who may have some recollections of musical activities, although John Greenway did discuss John Handcox, a leading STFU poet, in *American Folksongs of Protest*.

Sound analyses of the Dust Bowl migration and of its effects on California society include Walter S. Stein, *California and the Dust Bowl Migration* (Westport, Conn · Greenwood Press, 1973); Jacqueline Gordon Sherman, "The Oklahomans in California during the Depression Decade, 1931–1941" (Ph.D. diss., University of California, Los Angeles, 1970), and James N. Gregory, *American Exodus: The Dust Bowl Migration and Okie Culture in California* (New York: Oxford University Press, 1989). All students of Okie music should draw, like Stein, Sherman, and Gregory did, upon the music collection of Charles Todd and Robert Sonkin, now deposited in the Library of Congress Archive of Folk Song. Todd and Sonkin wrote a short account of their field research in "Ballads of the Okies," *New York Times Magazine* (17 November 1940), 6–7, 18. The important California country music scene has found its best chronicler in Gerald W. Haslam, *Workin' Man Blues: Country Music in California* (Berkeley: University of California Press, 1999).

The poet of the Okies, Woody Guthrie, has been much written about, but often from a romanticized, polemical, or distorted perspective. John Greenway's writings on Guthrie, in *American Folksongs of Protest* and in both popular and academic publications such as the obituary in the *Journal of American Folklore* 81 (January-March 1969): 62–64, are generally both admiring and sensible. Joe Klein wrote the most complete account of the Okie balladeer, *Woody Guthrie: A Life* (New York: Knopf, 1980), but the most accurate and unbiased Guthrie scholar, though in sympathy with his subject, was Richard A. Reuss, who compiled *A Woody Guthrie Bibliography* (New York: Guthrie Children's Trust Fund, 1968) and has written the most balanced assessment of the man in "Woody Guthrie and His Folk Tradition," *Journal of American Folklore* 83 (July-September 1970): 273–304. R. Serge Denisoff has done most to explain the relationship between southern protest singers and northern radical activists, as well as the urban folk music movement that resulted from this fusion, in "The Proletarian Renascence: The Folkness of the Ideological Folk," *Journal of American Folklore* 82 (January-March 1969): 51–65, and in more extended fashion in *Great Day Coming: Folk Music and the American Left* (Urbana: University of Illinois Press, 1971). Jerome L. Rodnitzky's purview is even larger in *Minstrels of the Dawn: The Folk-Protest Singer as a Cultural Hero* (Chicago: Nelson-Hall, 1971). Huddie "Leadbelly"

Ledbetter was more than a protest singer, but he played a crucial role in bringing folk music to the East Coast during the Depression years. His story has been well told by Charles Wolfe and Kip Lornell, *The Life and Legend of Leadbelly* (New York: HarperCollins, 1992).

Despite the revival of western swing in the 1970s, little published material, scholarly or otherwise, has been expended on the genre. In fact, Ruth Sheldon's 1938 biography of Bob Wills, *Hubbin' It,* was about the only kind of work outside of collectors's and fan club journals available until 1976 when Wills's piano player, Al Stricklin, along with Jon McConal, contributed *My Years with Bob Wills* (San Antonio: Naylor Company, 1976), and Charles Townsend completed his biography of Wills. Townsend's *San Antonio Rose: The Life and Music of Bob Wills* (Urbana: University of Illinois Press, 1976) is a fascinating account of the man who dominated the country music of the Southwest during the 1930s and who has left his imprint on thousands of musicians who came after him. His companion in the making of Western Swing has been ably discussed by Cary Ginell, *Milton Brown and the Founding of Western Swing* (Urbana: University of Illinois Press, 1994). No substantial study of W. Lee O'Daniel has yet appeared, although Seth McKay's outdated *W. Lee O'Daniel and Texas Politics, 1938–1942* (Lubbock: Texas Tech Press, 1944) is a useful source of information.

Those other dynamic forms of "western" country music—honky-tonk and singing cowboy—have also had few chroniclers. Except for scattered references to the music in popular magazines, Malone's doctoral dissertation of 1965 and the book that proceeded from it, *Country Music, USA,* and his essay in *The Encyclopedia of Country Music* (New York: Oxford University Press, 1998) contain the only extended discussions of the honky-tonk style.

The music of the singing cowboys has received a much fuller literary treatment than that extended to honky-tonk musicians. Douglas B. Green has written the definitive history of the genre, *Singing in the Saddle: The History of the Singing Cowboy* (Nashville: Vanderbilt University Press, 2002). His essay on Gene Autry in *Stars of Country Music* is a competent assessment of the first great singing cowboy's career by someone who later embarked on his own career singing western music, as "Ranger Doug" with Riders in the Sky. Autry was stingy with interviews, and, therefore, much of his story was always out of the reach of researchers. An indication that he may have been waiting to tell his own story came in 1978 when Autry, with the assistance of Mickey Herskowitz, published an autobiography called *Back in the Saddle Again* (Garden City, N.Y.: Doubleday, 1978).

Another great singing cowboy, Tex Ritter, is the subject of an affectionate biography by country singer and cowboy actor Johnny Bond: *The Tex Ritter Story* (New York: Chappell, 1976). Despite his very close personal and business associations with Ritter, Bond writes a reasonably objective, and always entertaining, account of "America's Most Beloved Cowboy." Until the appearance of Douglas B. Green's general study, the best account of the singing cowboy's effect on American popular culture and country music was Stephen Ray Tucker, "The Western Image in Country Music" (M.A. thesis, Southern Methodist University, 1976).

Chapter 6. The Nationalization of Southern Music

Although World War II was a watershed in the social history of the United States, writers on American music have devoted little attention specifically to the period from 1941 to 1945. Malone's *Country Music, USA,* however, explores the relationship between the war and the music's international expansion. All writers on rhythm and blues comment on the black migration northward, but few make references to the changed consciousness that the war promoted among African Americans. The one writer who has explored the full ramifications of the black exodus to the North is Nicholas Lemann, in his brilliant *The Promised Land: The Great Black Migration and How It Changed America* (New York: Knopf, 1991).

The best discussions of southern white migration to the North are Lewis Killian, *White Southerners* (New York: Random House, 1970), and Chad Berry, *Southern Migrants, Northern Exiles* (Urbana: University of Illinois Press, 2001). These studies explore the total social ramifications of the move made by white southerners to places such as Chicago, Detroit, Akron, Cincinnati, and Dayton. Now someone needs to explore the consequences of the migrations made by rural southerners into the cities of their own region. Pete Daniel has provided an excellent exposition of this demographic transformation in *Lost Revolutions: The South in the 1950s* (Chapel Hill: University of North Carolina Press, 2000).

The national burgeoning of country music spawned new "stars," some of whom have inspired biographical accounts. Townsend's biography of Bob Wills recreates much of the atmosphere of wartime America, and Elizabeth Schlappi, in *Roy Acuff, the Smoky Mountain Boy* (Gretna, La.: Pelican Publishing, 1978), explains how Acuff managed to become the symbol of American country music around the world. Ernest Tubb, the man who took the Texas honky-tonk style to the Grand Ole Opry, receives a full, sympathetic biographical treatment in Ronnie Pugh, *Ernest Tubb: The Texas Troubadour* (Durham: Duke University Press, 1996). Hank Williams, another singer whose career began during the war years but who did not attain superstardom until the early 1950s, has inspired four competent biographies: Roger M. Williams, *Sing a Sad Song: The Life of Hank Williams* (1970; reprint, Urbana: University of Illinois Press, 1981); Chet Flippo, *Your Cheatin' Heart: A Biography of Hank Williams* (New York: Simon and Schuster, 1981); Colin Escott, with George Merritt and William MacEwen, *Hank Williams: The Biography* (Boston: Little, Brown, 1994); and Bill Koon, *Hank Williams, So Lonesome* (Jackson: University Press of Mississippi, 2002).

The evolution of the blues into an aggressive, electrified, urban art form came at the end of the 1930s and during the war years. The story of the emergence of rhythm and blues has generally been buried in music periodicals or in larger works devoted to the development of soul or rock 'n' roll. Too often, rhythm and blues is treated merely as the precursor of more modern forms of black music and is insufficiently valued for its own sake. Arnold Shaw's *The World of Soul* (New York: Paperback Library, 1971), however, provides a good discussion of rhythm and blues, though in the context of a larger historical discussion of black music. In *Honkers and Shouters: The Golden Years of Rhythm and Blues* (New York: Macmillan, 1978), Shaw concentrates more directly on the important decades of the 1940s and '50s. Both books are highly detailed accounts by a man who was a long-time producer of r&b records.

Tony Glover, a white musician who did much to introduce blues music to young white audiences, wrote a good short overview of rhythm and blues: "R & B," *Sing Out,* May 1965, 7–13. The most brilliant study of the modern blues, though, and one that should serve as a model for the study of other forms of music, is Charles Keil, *Urban Blues* (Chicago: University of Chicago Press, 1966). Keil contributes an appendix designed to help the reader/ listener distinguish among the varied styles of the blues and discusses some of the major blues singers such as Bobby Blue Bland and B.B. King.

Other good discussions of B.B. King can be found in Arnold Shaw's two books and especially in a two-part article by Pete Welding, "B.B. King: The Mississippi Giant," *Downbeat,* 5 October 1978 and 19 October 1978. The second installment contains material on T-Bone Walker who, despite his pathbreaking importance, had little of substance devoted to him until the publication of Helen Oakley Dance, *Stormy Monday: The T-Bone Walker Story* (Baton Rouge: Louisiana State University Press, 1987). Muddy Waters, one of the prime forces behind the transition of the Delta blues into urban blues, is the subject of several excellent studies, including Jim Rooney, *Bossmen: Bill Monroe and Muddy Waters* (New York: Dial Press, 1971); Robert Palmer, "Muddy Waters: The Delta Son Never Sets," *Rolling Stone,* 5 October 1978, 53–56; Sandra B. Tooze, *Muddy Waters: The Mojo Man* (Toronto, Ontario: ECW Press, 1997); and Robert Gordon, *Can't Be Satisfied: The Life and Times of Muddy Waters* (New York: Little, Brown, 2002). Charles Shaar Murray evaluates the most important recent apostle of the blues in *Boogie Man: The Adventures of John Lee Hooker in the American Twentieth Century* (New York: St. Martin's Press, 2000), while Ruth Brown, with Andrew Yule, tells her own story in *Miss Rhythm: An Autobiography of Ruth Brown, Rhythm and Blues Legend* (New York: Da Capo Press, 1999). John Collis, *The Story of Chess Records* (New York: Bloomsbury, 1998), traces the connections between blues and rock 'n' roll. Among Les Blank's many fine documentary films treating southern culture and music, *The Blues Accordin' to Lightin' Hopkins* is especially telling.

All of the general histories of rock 'n' roll include information on Elvis Presley and the other southern rockabillies. The most complete histories are Carl Belz, *The Story of Rock* (New York: Oxford University Press, 1969), and Charles Gillett, *The Sound of the City: The Rise of Rock 'n' Roll* (New York: Dell, 1972). The most entertaining book on the subject is the coffee table-style volume produced by *Rolling Stone* magazine: Jim Miller, ed., *The Rolling Stone Illustrated History of Rock and Roll* (New York: Random House, 1976). The important contributions made by New Orleans musicians, mostly black, to rock 'n' roll are discussed in John Broven, *Walking to New Orleans: The Story of New Orleans Rhythm and Blues* (Sussex, England: Blues Unlimited, 1974). Shane K. Bernard tells the story of other Louisiana musicians in *Swamp Pop: Cajun and Creole Rhythm and Blues* (Jackson: University Press of Mississippi, 1996).

Numerous scattered articles and a few books comment on individual rockabillies. Among the best are Chet Flippo, "The Buddy Holly Story," *Rolling Stone,* 21 September 1978, 49–51; Dennis E. Hensley's interview with Carl Perkins in *Guitar Player,* March 1975, 18, 39–40; and Nick Tosches's biography of Jerry Lee Lewis, *Hellfire: The Jerry Lee Lewis Story* (New York: Delacorte, 1982). Lewis is one of the artists considered in an interesting comparative study by Stephen R. Tucker, "Pentecostalism and Popular Culture in the South: A Study of Four Musicians," *Journal of Popular Culture* 16 (Winter 1982): 68–80. Collectively, many of the rockabillies are discussed by Colin Escott and Martin Hawkins, *Good Rockin' Tonight: Sun Records and the Birth of Rock 'n' Roll* (New York: St. Martin's Press, 1991); Nick Tosches, "Rockabilly," in *The Illustrated History of Country Music,* ed. Patrick Carr (New York: Country Music Magazine Press, 1979); and John Pugh, "The Rise and Fall of Sun Records," *Country Music,* November 1973, 26–32. But the best general surveys are Craig Morrison, *Go Cat Go! Rockabilly Music and Its Makers* (Urbana: University of Illinois Press, 1996), and Michael T. Bertrand, *Race, Rock, and Elvis* (Urbana: University of Illinois Press, 2000).

The literature on Elvis Presley is vast and proliferating. Peter Guralnick's two-volume biography of Presley is one of the best studies ever written about any popular musician: *Last Train to Memphis: The Rise of Elvis Presley* (Boston: Little, Brown, 1994) and *Careless Love: The Unmaking of Elvis Presley* (Boston: Little, Brown, 2000). Jerry Hopkins, *Elvis: A Biography* (New York: Warner Books, 1972), is still worth consulting. A shorter interpretation makes up part of Greil Marcus, *Mystery Train: Images of America in Rock 'n' Roll* (1975; reprint, New York: Penguin, 1997), a brilliant and critically acclaimed attempt to say something about the flawed American promise through the lives and careers of a few blues and rock 'n' roll entertainers. A side of Elvis that was generally kept hidden from the public is presented in Red and Sonny West and Dave Hebler, as told to Steve Dunleavy, *Elvis, What Happened?* (New York: Ballantine Books, 1977). For a review of this and other Elvis-inspired material, see Mark Crispin Miller, "The King," *New York Review of Books,* 8 December 1977, 38–42.

Chapter 7. The 1960s and 1970s: Rock, Gospel, Soul

Aside from listening to the music, one can best comprehend modern rock culture by reading the magazines devoted to the phenomenon. As Richard Robinson and Andy Zwerling note in *The Rock Scene* (New York: Pyramid Books, 1971), where a long list of English and American rock periodicals appears, rock music has been a graveyard for magazines. Of those that endured for any length of time, *Creem, Crawdaddy,* and *Rolling Stone* presented the widest coverage of music. *Rolling Stone* has also had pretensions of being a journal of politics and ideas, and its lengthy essays and interviews are not solely concerned with music. Many of its best articles have been anthologized in *The Rolling Stone Record Review* and *The Rolling Stone Rock 'n' Roll Reader.* Another excellent anthology of articles taken from a wide variety of publications is Jonathan Eisen, ed., *The Age of Rock: Sounds of the American Cultural Revolution* (New York: Random House, 1969).

Among the general histories or interpretations of rock, each of the three mentioned earlier by Belz, Gillett, and Marcus has information that helps to illuminate rock 'n' roll's evolution to rock, as do Robert Palmer, *Rock & Roll: An Unruly History* (New York: Harmony Books, 1995); Richard Meltzer, *The Aesthetics of Rock* (New York: Something Else Press, 1970); Stephanie Spinner, *Rock is Beautiful: An Anthology of American Lyrics, 1953–1968* (New York: Dell, 1970); and Stewart Goldstein and Alan Jacobson, *Oldies But Goodies: The Rock 'n' Roll Years* (New York: Mason/Charter, 1977). None of these books has much to say about the Macon Sound or the southern rockers of the 1970s. Janis Joplin, however, has inspired at least three or four books, the best being Myra Friedman's *Buried Alive* (New York: Morrow, 1973).

Tony Heilbut, *The Gospel Sound,* is the best general reference for postwar black gospel music, but Alan Young contributed a wealth of information about other singers who sang outside the national limelight: *Woke Me Up This Morning: Black Gospel Singers and the Gospel Life* (Jackson: University Press of Mississippi, 1997). James Goff presents the best survey of the white gospel scene, but no one should overlook William C. Martin's witty and provocative assessment of white gospel music in the early 1970s: "At the Corner of Glory Avenue and Hallelujah Street," *Harper's,* January 1972, 95–99. Biographies and autobiographies of any gospel singers are scarce, but something can be learned about Mahalia Jackson in Jules Schwerin, *Got To Tell It: Mahalia Jackson, Queen of Gospel* (New York: Oxford University Press, 1992); Laurraine Goreau, *Just Mahalia Baby* (Waco, Tex.: Word Books, 1975); or in Mahalia's autobiography, *Movin' On Up* (New York: Hawthorn Books, 1966). James Blackwood has told his own story, with the assistance of Dan Martin, in *The James Blackwood Story* (Monroeville, Pa.: Whitaker House, 1975), and has been the subject of a biography by Kree Jack Racine: *Above All: The Blackwood Brothers Quartet* (Memphis: Jarodoce Publications, 1967). Another useful autobiography is John Daniel Sumner, *Gospel Music Is My Life* (Nashville: Impact Books, 1971).

The commercial burgeoning of soul music in the mid-1960s, along with the emergence of the Black Power movement, provoked extensive media coverage and popular writing. Along with the material carried in such major music publications as *Billboard, Cashbox, Melody Maker,* and *Rolling Stone,* one can find an extensive number of articles and a few biographies such as Michael Lydon, *Ray Charles: Man and Music* (New York: Riverhead Books, 1998), on soul entertainers in the popular press. James Brown, for example, received lengthy treatment in *Time,* 1 April 1966; *Newsweek,* 1 July 1968; and *Look,* 18 February 1969.

Books discussing soul music exclusively or in part include Ian Hoare, *The Soul Book* (New York: Dell, 1975); David Morse, *Motown and the Arrival of Black Music* (London: Studio Vista, 1971); Phyl Garland, *The Sound of Soul* (Chicago: Regnery, 1969); Arnold Shaw's two books, *The World of Soul* and *Honkers and Shouters;* and Peter Guralnick, *Sweet Soul Music: Rhythm and Blues and the Southern Dream of Freedom* (New York: Harper Perennial, 1986).

Chapter 8. The National Resurgence of Country Music

Country music's commercial resurgence in the 1960s and '70s was the context for a rash of publications, both scholarly and popular. The joint role played by the Grand

Ole Opry and its owner, the National Life and Accident Insurance Company, in promoting Nashville's growth as a music center is discussed by Richard A. Peterson in "Single-Industry Firm to Conglomerate Synergistics: Alternative Strategies for Selling Insurance and Country Music," in James Blumstein and Benjamin Walter, eds., *Growing Metropolis: Aspects of Development in Nashville* (Nashville: Vanderbilt University Press, 1975), 341–57.

Country music's identification with conservative politics was another factor that promoted media, journalistic, and scholarly interest. Florence King, in "Red Necks, White Socks, and Blue Ribbon Fear," *Harper's,* July 1974, 30–34, and Richard Goldstein, "My Country Music Problem—and Yours," *Mademoiselle,* June 1973, 114–15, 185, saw only ominous implications in country music's burgeoning popularity. On the other hand, Paul DiMaggio, Richard A. Peterson, and Jack Esco Jr. presented a more balanced picture of the music's political stance in "Country Music: Ballad of the Silent Majority," in R. Serge Denisoff and Richard A. Peterson, eds., *The Sounds of Social Change* (Chicago: Rand McNally, 1972), 38–55.

In the multitude of magazine articles that accompanied country music's success, writers generally treated the art form seriously and with little of the sarcasm or condescension it had formerly received. Seldom does one encounter a title such as "Thar's Gold in Them Thar Hillbillies." Among the better magazine issues dealing with country music are *Newsweek,* 18 June 1973; *Time,* 5 May 1974; and *Newsweek,* 14 August 1978.

Such country entertainers as Chet Atkins, Johnny Cash, Eddy Arnold, Glen Campbell, and Dolly Parton have received book-length treatment, but the best is Loretta Lynn's autobiography, written with the aid of George Vecsey, *Coal Miner's Daughter* (New York: Warner Books, 1976). A movie based on the book and starring Cissy Spacek was released in 1980 to generally favorable reviews.

Several good general histories or interpretations of country music have appeared since the 1970s. Inspired by the rising political conservatism of that decade, Paul Hemphill wrote a widely known book that stressed the music's working-folks' image in *The Nashville Sound: Bright Lights and Country Music* (New York: Simon and Schuster, 1970). The wide-ranging cultural critic Nick Tosches contributed a book at the end of that decade that has stood the test of time: *Country: The Biggest Music in America* (New York: Stein and Day, 1977). Jack Hurst, *Nashville's Grand Ole Opry* (New York: Abrams, 1975), is a lavishly illustrated, coffee table treatment of that institution. Dorothy Horstman, *Sing Your Heart Out, Country Boy,* 3d ed. (Nashville: Country Music Foundation Press, 1996), is the most unusual, and in many ways one of the best books on country music. It is a collection of songs arranged by category—songs of home, prison songs, cowboy songs, etc.—and introduced by commentary, often by the composers themselves, about why each song was written.

A few short articles and reviews in the rock journals assessed the careers of Gram Parsons and the Flying Burrito Brothers, but the only extended essay is that by Judson Klinger and Greg Mitchell: "Gram Finale," *Crawdaddy,* October 1976, 43–58. Ben Fong-Torres, however, has written a good biography of the star-crossed country rock pioneer, *Hickory Wind: The Life and Times of Gram Parsons,* rev. ed. (New

York: Pocket Books, 1998). The fullest discussion of Austin music is Jan Reid, *The Improbable Rise of Redneck Rock* (Austin: Heidelberg Publishers, 1974). Michael Bane also discusses some of the Austin country singers in *The Outlaws* (New York: Country Music Magazine Press, 1978).

The urban folk revival is documented in the various magazines that promoted the phenomenon, most notably *Sing Out, Broadside,* and *Little Sandy Review,* and in the liner notes that accompanied the recordings. Oscar Brand, *The Ballad Mongers: Rise of the Modern Folk Song* (New York: Funk and Wagnalls, 1962), is a good overview of the subject, while R. Serge Denisoff provides analyses of the movement's left-wing origins and contemporary significance in *Great Day Coming: Folk Music and the American Left* (Urbana: University of Illinois Press, 1971). The best history and interpretation of the revival is Robert Cantwell's excellent cultural study, *When We Were Good: The Folk Revival* (Cambridge, Mass: Harvard University Press, 1996). Neil Rosenberg reminds readers that folk revivals have been recurrent in the United States, in *Transforming Tradition: Folk Music Revivals Examined* (Urbana: University of Illinois Press, 1993). Peter D. Goldsmith examines the role played by one enterprising folk music entrepreneur: *Making People's Music: Moe Asch and Folkways Records* (Washington: Smithsonian Institution Press, 1998).

Bluegrass has inspired several good articles and books. Alan Lomax did much to make the music intellectually respectable with "Bluegrass Background: Folk Music with Overdrive," *Esquire,* October 1959, 103–9. But L. Mayne Smith, "An Introduction to Bluegrass," *Journal of American Folklore* 78 (July-September 1965): 245–56; and Neil V. Rosenberg, "From Sound to Style: The Emergence of Bluegrass," *Journal of American Folklore* 80 (April-June 1967): 143–50, were the first scholarly accounts. Bob Artis wrote a good but now outdated history, *Bluegrass* (New York: Hawthorn Books, 1975), that has been surpassed by Robert Cantwell's interpretive study, *Bluegrass Breakdown: The Making of the Old Southern Sound* (Urbana: University of Illinois Press, 1984); Tom Piazza, *True Adventures with the King of Bluegrass: Jimmy Martin* (Nashville: Vanderbilt University Press, 1999); Neil Rosenberg's comprehensive survey, *Bluegrass: A History* (Urbana: University of Illinois Press); Richard D. Smith's balanced biography, *Can't You Hear Me Callin': The Life of Bill Monroe, Father of Bluegrass* (Boston: Little, Brown, 2000); John Wright, *Traveling the High Way Home: Ralph Stanley and the World of Traditional Bluegrass Music* (Urbana: University of Illinois Press, 1993); and Tom Ewing, *The Bill Monroe Reader* (Urbana: University of Illinois Press, 2001).

Chapter 9. A Future in the Past

To understand the enduring American fascination with the South, and the ways in which the region continues to affect the tone and quality of national life, the reader might begin with John Egerton, *The Americanization of Dixie: The Southernization of America* (New York: Harper's Magazine Press, 1974); Dan T. Carter, *The Politics of Rage: George Wallace, The Origins of the New Conservatism, and the Transformation of American Politics* (New York: Simon and Schuster, 1995); Jack Temple Kirby, *The*

Countercultural South (Athens: University of Georgia Press, 1995); and Peter Applebome, *Dixie Rising: How the South is Shaping American Values, Politics, and Culture* (New York: Times Books, 1996).

The Internet has enhanced the availability of information on current southern-born and southern-oriented musicians. Virtually every musician has an "official" website or one that is maintained by dedicated fans. Such journals as *Rolling Stone, Downbeat, Blues Unlimited, Country Music* magazine, *Old-Time Herald, Journal of Country Music, Bluegrass Unlimited,* and *No Depression* chronicle the activities of most musicians and singers who have any kind of relationship to southern culture, either real or imagined.

Students and fans of Cajun music should consult anything written by Barry Jean Ancelet, especially *Musiciens cadiens et Creoles/The Makers of Cajun Music* (Austin: University of Texas Press, 1984). The music made by French-speaking "Creoles" in Louisiana has been competently described by Ben Sandmel, with photographs by Rick Olivier, *Zydeco* (Jackson: University Press of Mississippi, 1999), and by Michael Tisserand, *The Kingdom of Zydeco* (New York: Arcade Publishing, 1998).

The best general account of the contemporary New Orleans musical scene is Jason Berry, Jonathan Foose, and Tad Jones, *Up From the Cradle of Jazz: New Orleans Music Since World War II* (Athens: University of Georgia Press, 1986). Much can also be learned from Jeff Hannusch, *I Hear You Knockin': The Sound of New Orleans Rhythm and Blues* (Ville Platte, La.: 1985). The biweekly magazine, *Wavelength,* published in New Orleans, has surveyed local music events and people since 1980. The city's best-known recent musical product, Wynton Marsalis, has written two books, *Sweet Swing Blues on the Road* (New York: Thunder's Mouth Press, 1998) and *Jazz in the Bittersweet Blues of Life* (Cambridge, Mass.: Da Capo Press, 2001). He was also featured prominently in Ken Burns's television documentary about jazz, and in the book that accompanied the series, Geoffrey C. Ward and Ken Burns, *Jazz: A History of America's Music* (New York: Alfred A. Knopf, 2000).

The entire realm of African-American music in the contemporary United States is described and evaluated by Craig Werner, *A Change is Gonna Come: Music, Race and the Soul of America* (New York: Plume, 1999). Kevin K. Gaines, *Uplifting the Race: Black Leadership, Politics, and Culture in the Twentieth Century* (Chapel Hill: University of North Carolina Press, 1996), focuses on the role of music, among other art forms, in the evolution of racial politics in the U.S.

Tejano and other varieties of music produced by Spanish-speaking southerners are discussed by Ramiro Burr, *The Billboard Guide to Tejano and Regional Mexican Music* (New York: Billboard Books, 1999). Manuel Peña, however, is the leading scholar of Tex-Mex styles. His books include *Texas-Mexican Conjunto: History of a Working-Class Music* (Austin: University of Texas Press, 1985); *Mexican American Orquesta: Music, Culture, and the Dialectic of Conflict* (Austin: University of Texas Press, 1999); and *Musica Tejana: The Cultural Economy of Artistic Transformation* (College Station: Texas A&M University Press, 1999). Much can be learned about the early recording of Tejano performers in Chris Strachwitz with James Nicolopulos, *Lydia Mendoza: A Family Autobiography* (Houston: Arte Publico Press, 1993), and Yolonda Broyles-Gonzalez, *Lydia Mendoza's Life in Music/La Historia de Lydia Mendoza* (New York:

Oxford University Press, 2001). The burgeoning of this musical industry can be discerned in the life story of its first superstar by Joe Nick Patoski, *Selena: Como La Flor* (New York: Little, Brown, 1996). See also Guadalupe San Miguel Jr., *Tex-Mex Music in the Twentieth Century* (College Station: Texas A&M University Press, 2002).

The best guides to contemporary country music include Paul Kingsbury, ed., *The Encyclopedia of Country Music* (New York: Oxford University Press, 1998); Nicholas Dawidoff, *In the Country of Country: People and Places in American Life* (New York: Pantheon Books, 1997); Bruce Feiler, *Dreaming Out Loud: Garth Brooks, Wynonna Judd, Wade Hayes and the Changing Face of Nashville* (New York: Avon Books, 1998); Curtis W. Ellison, *Country Music Culture: From Hard Times to Heaven* (Jackson: University Press of Mississippi, 1995); Mary A. Bufwack and Robert K. Oermann, *Finding Her Voice: The Saga of Women in Country Music* (New York: Crown, 1993); Laurence Leamer, *Three Chords and the Truth: Hope, Heartbreak, and Changing Fortunes in Nashville* (New York: HarperCollins, 1997); Melton A. McLaurin and Richard A. Peterson, eds., *You Wrote My Life: Themes in Country Music* (Philadelphia: Gordon and Breach, 1992); Cecelia Tichi, *High Lonesome: The American Culture of Country Music* (Chapel Hill: University of North Carolina Press, 1994); and James C. Cobb, "Rednecks, White Socks, and Pina Coladas? Country Music Ain't What It Used to Be. . .And It Really Never Was," *Southern Cultures,* Winter 1999, 41–48.

The broad and largely undefinable world of "alternative country" music is the subject of David Goodman, *Modern Twang: An Alternative Country Music Guide and Directory* (Nashville: Dowling Press, 1999), and the wonderful and all-inclusive journal, *No Depression,* edited by Grant Alden and Peter Blackstock and published in Seattle. The best of the alternative musicians, along with a wide array of other stylists, can be seen and heard on the widely syndicated television show *Austin City Limits.* Its story has been told by Clifford Endres, *Austin City Limits* (Austin: University of Texas Press, 1987), and John T. Davis, *Austin City Limits: 25 Years of American Music* (New York: Billboard Books, 2000). A story that needs to be told is that of the rise and transformation of what began in 1983 as The Nashville Network. Its popularity as a cable TV purveyor of mainstream country music, some mild variants of it, and general programming intended to appeal to southern audiences, its acquisition by MTV and move to New York in 2000, and reorientation as The National Network reflect in many ways the themes of this book.

SUGGESTED LISTENING

The following list of suggested recordings is confined to anthologies of original re-cordings. A listing of recordings by individual artists would get out of hand very quickly, as would a list of revival albums and boxed sets, though a few bear mention. The soundtrack from the film *O Brother, Where Art Thou?* helped bring southern music—especially bluegrass, blues, and gospel—to a wide audience. Director Joel Coen called the film a "valentine" to southern music. Produced by T-Bone Burnett, the soundtrack was released by Mercury Records/UMG Recordings. Another inter-esting companion soundtrack—which some reviewers have nicknamed "O Sister, Where Art Thou?"—is *Songcatcher,* based on the loose film portrayal of Olive Dame Campbell's and Cecil Sharp's forays into the collecting of Appalachian music, musical direction by David Mansfield, CD issued by Vanguard. A number of record labels associated with southern or southern-derived music have produced or inspired their own boxed sets, such as *Chess Blues, Atlantic Rhythm & Blues 1947–1974* (Uni/Chess Records), the *Complete Stax-Volt Singles 1959–1968* (Wea/Atlantic), and the *Sun Records Collection* (Wea/Rhino). Many southern musicians and genres, even labels, have been honored with tribute albums featuring covers of original songs. Many of these are interesting reinterpretations of southern music. We hope, however, that interested listeners will be moved to search out the groups and solo acts that appear on the anthologies listed below.

Notices and reviews of CDs made by individual performers can be found on Amazon.com and other internet websites or in *Billboard* magazine, *Downbeat, Old Time Herald, No Depression,* and other music journals. One of the most interesting, and often quirky, sources of vintage and recent recorded southern music is the annual *Southern Sampler* CD made available by the *Oxford American* magazine from Oxford, Mississippi. The best outlets for old-time music of varying descriptions are County Sales in Floyd, Virginia, Old Homestead Records in Brighton, Michigan, and Down Home Records in El Cerrito, California, each of which has a website. Additionally, the Library of Congress Recorded Sound Reference Center sells individual recordings to the public from its collection that began with a donation of four hundred discs by Victor Records in 1926.

Our intention has been to list only those collections that are on CD and still in print, but given the evanescence of contemporary recordings, we cannot guarantee that the material will still be available when the revised edition of this book appears. We wish to thank Ben Sandmel, Ramiro Burr, Charles Chamberlain, and Gene Hyde for their suggestions.

1. *Sounds of the South: A Musical Journey from the Georgia Sea Islands to the Mississippi Delta.* Four compact discs featuring 105 performances found originally on seven LPs. Recorded in the field in 1959 and 1960 by Alan Lomax. Forty-page booklet.

2. *Anthology of American Folk Music.* Smithsonian Folkways. Edited by Harry Smith. Eighty-four selections on six compact discs. Originally recorded on LPs in 1952.

3. *Crossroads: Southern Routes, Music of the American South.* Smithsonian Folkways. A CD-ROM with sixteen songs sampling music from the blues, southern rock, New Orleans brass band, Cajun, gospel, R&B, Tex-Mex, and country traditions, maps, interview excerpts, and other features about southern music and culture.

4. *Classic Country Music.* Smithsonian Recordings. Four CDs of music extending from the 1920s through the 1980s, organized and edited by Bill Malone.

5. *Roots 'n' Blues: The Retrospective, 1925–1950.* Columbia/Legacy. 107 blues, hillbilly, gospel, and western swing songs.

6. *Appalachian Stomp: Bluegrass Classics.* Rhino. An anthology of most of the leading bluegrass bands.

7. *Appalachian Stomp: More Bluegrass Favorites.* Rhino. Similar to the above.

8. *White Country Blues, 1926–1938: A Lighter Shade of Blue.* Columbia/Legacy. Forty-eight songs on two CDs.

9. *Back in the Saddle Again: American Cowboy Songs.* New World Records. Twenty-eight songs on two CDs.

10. *OKeh Western Swing.* CBS Records. Twenty-eight songs on one CD, featuring the Texas Playboys as well as some of the influential but less well-known bands.

11. *Altamont: Black Stringband Music from the Library of Congress.* Rounder. A reminder of how much African Americans contributed to a style usually thought to be the province only of southern whites.

12. *From Where I Stand: The Black Experience in Country Music.* Warner Brothers. Three CDs produced through the auspices of the Country Music Foundation. Also a surprise, especially for listeners who previously thought that the only African-American forays into country music were made by Charlie Pride and, occasionally, by Ray Charles.

13. *Testify: The Gospel Box.* Rhino. Fifty songs recorded by assorted African-American gospel singers from about 1935 to the 1990s.

14. *How Can I Keep From Singing: Early American Rural Religious Music from the 1920s and 1930s.* Vols. 1 and 2. Yazoo.

15. *The Half Ain't Never Been Told: Early American Rural Religious Music.* Vols. 1 and 2. Yazoo.

16. *Wade in the Water.* Folkways. Four-CD set of African American religious music. Edited by Bernice Johnson Reagon as a companion to the NPR television series.

17. *Jubilation! Great Gospel Performances.* Vol. 1, Black Gospel. Rhino.

18. *Jubilation! Great Gospel Performances.* Vol. 3, Country Gospel. Rhino.

19. *Yonder Comes the Blues.* Document. African-American blues anthology.

20. *Country Blues.* Document. Two discs.

21. *Sony Music 100 Years: Soundtrack for a Century.* Twenty-six CDs of songs recorded during the twentieth century, mostly on Columbia and subsidiaries. Jazz, pop, rock 'n' roll, country, blues. Accompanied by a huge book written by various experts. Obviously, not all of the included performers are southerners.

22. *A Treasury of Library of Congress Field Recordings.* Rounder. Thirty songs recorded between 1934 and 1946.

23. *The Alan Lomax Collection Sampler.* Rounder. Thirty-eight recordings from around the world, along with a Seventy-two-page booklet.

24. Rounder has also issued several CDs, collectively called *Southern Journey,* which sample Lomax's enormous cache of field recordings.

25. *Tejano Picante: Tex-Mex Classics.* Rhino. Eighteen-song sampler of such performers as Flaco Jimenez, Steve Jordan, Little Joe, Mazz, La Mafia, and Ruben Ramos.

26. *Tex-Mex Fiesta.* Ace. Anthology from Arhoolie vaults. Twenty-two songs by Flaco Jimenez, Lydia Mendoza, Santiago Jimenez, Narciso Martinez, and others.

27. *Taquachito Nights: Conjunto Music from South Texas.* Smithsonian/Folkways.

28. *Conjunto: Tex-Mexican Border Music.* Vol. 3. Rounder.

29. *Cajun Classics: The Kings of Cajun.* Ace. Twenty-four songs by Dewey Balfa, Nathan Abshire, Belton Richard, Doc Guidry, Vin Bruce, and others.

30. *Cajun: Abbeville Breakdown, 1929–39.* Sony/Columbia.

31. *Cajun and Creole Music: The Lomax Recordings.* Vols. 1 and 2. Rounder.

32. *J'ai Ete Au Bal (I Went to the Dance).* Vols. 1 and 2. Arhoolie. Cajun and Zydeco.

33. *Le Gran Mamou: A Cajun Music Anthology,* Vol. 1; *Raise Your Window: A Cajun Music Anthology,* vol. 2; *Gran Prairie: A Cajun Music Anthology,* vol. 3. Country Music Foundation.

34. *Music from the Zydeco Kingdom.* Rounder. Companion CD to the book *Kingdom of Zydeco,* recorded in 2000.

35. *15 Louisiana Zydeco Classics.* Arhoolie.

36. *Crescent City Soul.* EMI. Four CDs. Rhythm and blues from New Orleans.

37. *From Spirituals to Swing.* 3 vols. Vanguard. Produced by John Hammond.

38. *Creole Kings of New Orleans.* Specialty. Rhythm and Blues.

39. *New Orleans Jazz.* Arhoolie.

40. *Jazz the World Forgot.* Vols. 1 and 2. Yazoo.

41. *Jazz: The Story of America's Music.* Sony/Columbia. Ninety-four songs on five CDs. Companion to the Ken Burns film.

42. *Visions of Jazz: A Musical Journey.* Blue Note. Thirty-eight songs on two CDs. Selected and annotated by jazz scholar Gary Giddins.

43. *From Swing to Bebop.* Jazz History. 762 songs on ten CDs.

44. *Vocalists and Jazz.* Jazz History. Ten CDs.

45. *Swing Time! 1925–1955.* Legacy. Sixty-six songs on three CDs.

46. *Columbia Jazz Masterpieces.* Series depicting the music by decades.

Index